AGAINST ALL ODDS

MY JOURNEY TO BECOMING A FLIGHT ATTENDANT: A MEMOIR

LANDO SUCCESS

Edited by
TUMIKA CAIN

Book Cover by
ANNE BERKELEY

Copyright © 2018 Lando Success. All rights reserved. Except for use in any review, the reproduction or utilization of this work in whole or in part in any form by any electronic, mechanical, or other means, now known or hereinafter invented, including xerography, photocopying and recording, or in any information storage or retrieval system is forbidden without the written permission of the publisher.

ISBN: 978-1-7323614-0-9

eISBN: 978-1-7323614-1-6

THIS BOOK IS DEDICATED TO MY GRANDMA ALETHA.

"If you think you are beaten, you are,
    If you think you dare not, you don't.
    If you like to win, but you think you can't,
    It is almost certain you won't.

If you think you'll lose, you're lost,
    For out in the world we find,
    Success begins with a fellow's will-
    It's all in the state of MIND.

If you think you're outclassed, you are,
    You've got to think high to rise,
    You've got to be sure of yourself before
    You can ever win a prize.

Life's battles, don't always go
    To the stronger or faster man
    But soon or later the man who wins
    Is the man WHO THINKS HE CAN!"

By Walter D. Wintle

AUTHOR'S NOTE

First, I would thank you for reading my story. This is a memoir based on true events in my life. Everybody born into this world will have a journey of their own. This is my journey, and I want to reveal my story to the world. I sincerely apologize, in advance, if you're part of this story without me giving you prior knowledge. I will use fictitious names and will alter minor details, where possible, to keep your personal life private. I hope everyone enjoys the journey.

PART I

From the basement...

PROLOGUE

I'm here! My adrenaline is pumping and I can't stop reciting my pitch over and over in my head. *Lando, baby, it's your time. These motherfuckers don't work as hard as you. Damn sure don't dress and look as good as you. You think you flew all the way down here to be rejected? Nope.* I gave myself a pep talk, trying to keep my head right and energy high, so as not to succumb to the jitters I felt just beneath the surface.

Since I was one of the last people chosen to speak, I was forced to listen to multiple horrible sixty second rants of why the others wanted to become the newest flight attendant with Circle Airlines. Finally, I heard it!

"Orlando, it's your turn."

As soon as she said my name all of the nervousness left. Time seemed to slow down. This was my moment. I became confident and relaxed. Sporting a gold and navy blue Rolex on my left wrist, matching the navy blue suit tailored to my 5'6, 160-pound frame, paired with a pink shirt, perfectly matching tie and a pink handkerchief that complemented my suit. Finishing off the look, I wore shiny all-black Stacey Adam shoes, making me resemble a navy recruiter. Yup, I was ready. Walking to the front of the room with the confidence of the President of the United States, getting ready to give the State of the Union address. Everybody was chanting, "Lando! Lando!"

Just as I was beginning to truly bask in the moment...

1

"*L*ando, get yo' ass up here, and shovel this damn snow!"

I heard the voice of my mom, yelling at me at five in the morning about some goddamn snow. No, I wasn't at an interview in Jokerville, Washington for Circle Airlines. I was back home with Renae Lewis. The journey to my dream place was quite a colorful and winding one. Here's where it starts.

"Okay!" I yelled back to my mother, wishing at that moment I was anywhere but there and able to drift back to sleep. Ten minutes later she was back.

"Lando! I'm not going to tell you no more to get up here, and shovel this shit!"

"Mom, it's 5 a.m. I will do it when I get up." I pulled the cover over my head, hoping that she'd be reasonable and I could get more sleep.

Her sharp reply let me know that clearly I'd made the wrong move. "Listen here, motherfucker, you're going to get up here and do it now. You know the longer you wait, the heavier the snow gets!"

I finally got out the bed. As I was getting ready, she told me how I was never going to be any good.

"I don't know how you expect to get a wife being this damn lazy. Just like your daddy!"

I allowed my mind to go blank as she tore me down. That was not my first time hearing her bash my father. When she first started comparing my shortcomings to my father, I was deeply hurt and offended. He couldn't have been that bad, after all she married him and had multiple kids by him. Over time, I learned to just go blank when she started in. Hell, after twenty-one years I'd kinda gotten immune to it.

Mom rarely went downstairs. All she'd do was go to the door at the top of the stairs and yell down. Seeing her do that always gave me a mental picture of her being Moses standing on the top of the mountain shouting out commandments. Growing up, I loved it, because I could sneak as many honeys as I wanted over and keep them downstairs, knowing that mom would not come to investigate unless I didn't respond to her rants. But I knew not to test her, because there was that one time she shocked us all, especially my brother, OC Lee the third.

My friend Alvin and I walked into the house and headed downstairs. I had known Alvin since we were in the second grade. He was that one kid in school who was treated like the cute little brother. Growing up, dudes liked him, but didn't respect him, and the girls loved him in the cute-little-brother type of way. Once we graduated, things definitely changed. He became the little brother that would steal your woman if you didn't respect him.

At the time, my brother and I were living at my mom's, and as soon as Alvin and I walked into the room, we saw pounds of weed, marijuana, Mary Jane, pot, whatever you want to call it. Now, I wasn't shocked that my brother had weed because of his background. But the thing that shocked my friend and I was that he was bagging and weighing it in Mom's basement. To make matters worse, the guy was steaming the shit. Now, any fool would know if you steam anything, the smell would intensify.

"OC! Dude, mom is here, fool! What the fuck are you doing?" As I said this my friend, Alvin, is dying laughing, amazed by such stupidity.

OC replied, sarcasm dripping from his tone, "Well, little brother, what the fuck it look like I'm doing?" He gave me a dirty look, as if I was the stupid one. "I'm weighing my medicine, steaming it, and bagging it to get shipped."

"Um, so tell me what are you going to do if mom comes down here?" This fool is crazy as hell, I thought.

"She won't come down here, she never comes down here," he insisted. Not even 30 seconds after those words left his mouth, mom walked into the room.

"OC Lee! What the hell is this?" she screamed. It was clear that she and I shared the same confusion. The funniest part of the whole situation: I was just thinking, if she were to come down now, how would he hide his 'medicine?' There was so much of it scattered everywhere.' My thoughts were answered as I watched him take this little, brown grocery store bag and try to cover all that weed. All I could do was shake my head. Clearly, he hadn't thought that plan out.

IT WAS hours after I had shoveled the snow when my phone rang.

"Hello."

"Aye, man, I need you to help me with something, so come through." My boy, Sean, was on the line.

"You must have another STD," I joked.

Quick as a flash, he replied, "Yeah, from your mom! Now hurry up!"

A few minutes later, I stepped outside the back door. Following the trail I'd made earlier while shoveling, I jumped the gate. After knocking on the back door and being let in by one of his family members, I headed down the stairs into the basement where Sean usually went to chill.

The first thing I saw was Sean, standing in a wife beater tank holding a dark blue, button-up dress shirt in his left hand and a pink American Eagle collared shirt in his right. He already had on some nice dark jeans and all-white Rockports.

"Okay, if you were an extremely hot babe and was going on a date with me, which outfit would you prefer?" he asked while striking a pose.

"First, I wouldn't date you. Second, all I have to do is buy a Hot 'n Ready and a 6-pack to get some ass, so there is no need to waste the money. But to answer your question, the one in the left hand. Switch your shoes and lose the phone case. Where your black Stacey Adams at?"

"Upstairs, but I got to clean them. Why you say this one?" Sean's expression told me he didn't trust the advice I'd just given him.

"Because you'd look more grown and sexy in the dark business casual attire. The one to the right brings out the muscles. Also, pink implies you're too confident and a show off. So you wear that on the third date to lock the person in. Now, as for the phone case, that's just doing too much. It puts the perception out there that you're going to be answering your phone the whole date, and nobody calls you anyway." I gave him a smile and a nod after stating my case.

"So what's new with you, my turtle looking friend?" Sean said, while he was looking for something. I assumed it was his black shoes.

"To be honest, a whole lot of nothing. So why did mom wake me up at 5 a.m. to shovel some freaking snow?" I tried to say it with a serious face, but couldn't.

Imitating mom's voice, Sean yelled, "Lando! Lando! Get up here, and shovel this damn snow!"

Laughing, I said, "You sound just like her, as if you were there, bro."

"I told you she gave me a STD last night," he responded with a straight face. We'd been cracking jokes like that since we were kids.

"Dude, whatever. But really, my life sucks right now. I had a business going well, a nice condo in Dearborn, and now I'm back in Inkster-freaking-Michigan in mom's basement. Wow, I'm a total loser." I was mostly talking to myself, expressing what was in my heart.

Sean said, "Well, you can always go to school." I could tell he was trying to be encouraging, but it surely wasn't working.

"Hell naw. What for? So I can get a degree in something I will never use and then be in debt my whole life. I want more in life than 30k a year. I'm going be a millionaire somehow, someway. I just don't know how. Do you know that most of the richest people in the world don't have degrees?" I sounded like a religious Muslim in jail, trying to convince Brother Sean to stop eating the swine.

"Well, look on the bright side. You're young with no kids. You will be okay."

"Yeah, you're right, but..." I paused and looked at him, saying very calmly, "probably not for too long. Your mom called me to say she was late. And I'm not talking about for dinner, bitch!" I walked out of the house laughing. "Yo, have fun on your date, and hit me up later. I'm about to go over grandma's."

Sean is one of my best friends. From early in our childhood, our parents lived directly behind each other. We would take turns hopping the gate. Sean was German with a crazy last name, Klopfenstein, and couldn't speak the language any better than me. Standing about 6 feet, he really looked like a regular white guy, 185 pounds, athletic body. His family was my German family. Having a white best friend came with many benefits. Now, neither of us were born broke, but we also weren't the richest kids on the block. Over Sean's house, his parents had one fridge upstairs, one downstairs, one outside, even one for the dog. I mean food, candy, snacks and all, were unlimited. They were your average white family: two kids, father working for General Motors, mom stayed at home. I don't think I'd ever seen her work.

What brought Sean and I together was Inkster, Michigan. Inktown. Murder City. The dirty glove was ranked one of the most dangerous cities in America. We were ranked so high because the city is small as shit. A person could go through the whole city in ten minutes. It had a population of only about 25,000 people. In 2010, there were eleven murders and 33 rape cases—the highest in over a decade. So what I'm trying to say is that we were raised in the damn 'hood.

Now growing up there, it's wasn't the worst city to live in, and I considered the side where we were raised the 'good side' of Inkster. With that being the case, Sean didn't act black or use the 'N' word, but *all* his friends are black. Since he was raised with us as best friends, he possessed a different cockiness about him than the average white guy. His parents raised him not to judge based on race, so Sean would date whites, blacks, Asians, whoever was crazy enough to open their legs. But that was my best friend. One of my many brothers from another mother, and I would do anything for him.

Driving over to grandma's in my 1997 all-black Taurus, I turned on the radio. "Joe, jobs are at an all-time low in Michigan. If you want to make real money you better move out." The announcer on 92.7 continued to ramble about how bad the market was for lawyers, teachers, and definitely the original Motor City in its entirety. This made me think back on the conversation Sean and I had just had about the state of my life. Sighing, I tried not to succumb to the heaviness I felt trying to weigh down on me.

I walked into grandma's house and greeted her with a kiss. I saw grandpa messing with the side door to the house and said, "Hey, grandpa! What you over there doing?"

"Oh, nothing too much. Just meddling with this door." Grandpa hailed from Georgia and had a deep southern accent.

When he spoke, he dragged out every word. Like instead of saying, "Lando," it was "Heeeyyy Ooorr...Laaannn...doooe." Yup, that's how he was. Hard worker, he worked at Ford for forty plus years. He made sure we were the first ones at church and the last ones leaving out every Sunday. He was the perfect male role model, a positive example any person would want in the village, raising their child.

After my casual greetings, I bolted downstairs to play pool, which was my routine. Ever since I could remember, we'd always had a pool table over my grandparent's house. With that being said, it was basically against our religion to be in the family and not know how to play pool. All my siblings, aunt, grandparents, we all knew how to play. Now, my dad was on another echelon when it came to playing pool, never even letting his opponent make one shot type of good. He was on the verge of going pro, won the men's championship in Michigan, and was able to compete in Vegas for money. I must have thought him up, because at that moment, he walked by the top of the stairs and waved at me.

"Hey, what's going on, dad?"

"Nothing much." He walked down the stairs to join me. "You're just down here shooting around, huh?"

"Yeah, trying to get on your level. You want to play?"

"No, not now, man. My eyes been hurting me lately."

Concerned, I asked, "What you mean by hurting? As if you got pepper in them?" It wasn't like my father to complain, so I was really curious.

"Well, it's been this way for a few weeks. Like I'm going blind. I can't see that well late at night. I'm not sure exactly what's going on. That's why I'm here now, because me and momma about to go to the doctor. With the stuff they put in my eyes, I might not be able to see and drive. So she's going to take me."

"Okay, I'm not doing anything. I will roll with y'all." As he walked away, I said, "Dad!" He turned around. "Man, if you're scared to get whooped on, just let me know. No need to be lying on your eyes."

He responded with a laugh. "Okay, if you say so."

Before leaving, they told me to go ahead and drive since there was no point in them driving if I was going to be in the car as well. Grandma stayed with one of the newest Cadillacs in her garage. Every two years she would renew her lease and get a new car. As kids, her new Cadillacs always gave us a sense of pride that my grandmother was "successful." So I was all game to whip her new Caddie.

Once we arrived at the doctor's office, we went through the process of filling out his paperwork. Grandma asked me how work had been and made small talk until the doctor told dad to come into his office. Just like a regular checkup with the eye doctor, he performed a routine examination. He was very down to earth, asking about my educational level and if I planned to go to college. Since he was a nice guy, I didn't want to give him my real perspective on college. So, I just nodded my head and agreed.

"Okay, Ocie. This is the situation," stated the doctor. "It looks like you have retina problems. I'm not sure what's causing this. Have you been in any recent accidents or had an injury to your head or anything?"

"Yes, I hit my head when I got into an accident not too long ago. So that's what can be causing this?"

"I'm not sure. But as of right now your sight is getting worse. What we need to start doing is LASIK in your eyes. It's about a thirty-minute session once a week for the next month. We'll see how your eyes react to the LASIK, and we can go from there."

"Okay, thank you, Doc. I greatly appreciate you. So what's the first day we can get started?"

"My assistant will set everything up for you guys right over there." He pointed towards some sexy, young white female about twenty-two, who was sitting behind the desk. She reminded me of a younger Alicia Silverstone. *I wouldn't be too mad having to come back here with dad a few times,* I thought.

"Are you his son?" she asked.

"Yes, I am. Are you my future wife?" I asked, looking her dead in the eye, flashing all of my charm.

She turned bloodshot red, smiled and said, "You're funny. You never know, maybe I am." She looked shocked, as if she were thinking *did this black guy just really say that in front of his dad and grandma?* Still, she couldn't resist responding flirtatiously.

2

On the drive home, dad was still in shock about the whole situation. We updated grandma on what the doctor informed us. Her response was positive, as always.

"Pray and follow the doctor's instructions and see how that works."

All of dad's different scenarios were extreme. Like wondering if the doctors could give him new eyes, and what would happen if the LASIK didn't work, and so on.

By the time we got home, the word must have spread like cockroaches in the ghetto. One thing about my family: it's hard to keep a secret. Once my sisters Kenyatta, who we always call Keke, and Kelly, or even mom found out, then the whole family would be on notice. When I finally made it back over mom's house, all of my siblings were there waiting with a thousand and one questions.

"What's wrong with, dad?"

"Is he going blind?"

"Does he need new eyes?"

"Man, it's probably all them years of eating all types of bad foods."

"No, it's probably him not taking his medicine regularly."

"Heck, it could be from all that sex his old self be having. Ha-ha!"

"Okay, all y'all calm down," I said with my hands up, as if I were the Pope about to address a congregation. "The doctor said his retinas, or something in the back of his eyes, are not right and it's not going to get any better. So starting next week he is going to get LASIK surgery done once or twice a week and see how his eyes go from there."

"Damn, man! That's one rude awakening, going from partying everyday doing your own thing to not being able to see. I guess we just have to pray for him," said my brother OC.

Mom walked into the room and said, "Okay, tell me what's going on with your daddy."

We all looked at each other and started laughing, because we'd just gone through the whole scenerio and now she wanted me to regurgitate my words. One good thing about my mother is even though she and dad were divorced, she was still genuinely concerned for him.

To get a better understanding of my mom, she raised five kids, mostly as a single parent. Good thing she married my dad, a retiree from the Ford Motor Company. So, once they divorced, she was able to receive child support. She also raised my nephews and nieces, providing for all of us. Mom would literally give someone the shirt off her back, even if they were a complete stranger. She is the person in our family that tries to help everybody. Sometimes to a fault. Standing about 5'6, 190 pounds, she wasn't a skinny lady. She had dark caramel skin and usually wore some type of scarf or female garment over her head. Mom definitely knew how to stretch the little income she did have coming in. Growing up, we always shopped in thrift stores, and garage sales were her second home. She could smell a garage sale from miles away.

Our relationship was hard to understand. Growing up and

living together completely sucked. I think she treated me, OC, and Keke differently, because she and my father were separated. To make matters worse, I guess we looked like him so that didn't make our living situation any better.

At age eighteen, I got the hell out of the house and moved with my godbrother, who was also dealing with similar house drama. We had many parties and business adventures within our four years of living together. But once he had a kid and our lease was up, we decided to go our separate ways. That forced me to move back with mom until I got back on my feet. The best thing I can say is, as soon as I moved out the house, my mom and I basically became best friends. She would come over, bring me and my roommates food, and we never had any disputes.

The next morning Mary, my youngest sibling, came into my so-called room. Since I'd come back home unannounced, mom kinda made me a random space with a curtain to provide some privacy.

"Hey, what's up, Mary?"

We gave her the nickname Gizmo when she was young, because she reminded us of the movie *The Gremlins*. Mary was calm, like Gizmo, and she was always trying to do the right thing, but still got tricked by us evil siblings.

"You don't work today?" she asked.

"Nope, I'm off for a few days. I might pick something up, but I doubt it." I noticed her glance at a book on my dresser. It was *Rich Dad, Poor Dad* by Robert Kiyosaki.

"So, big-head, you think you're going to be rich?" she asked with a smirk on her face.

I looked her in the eyes. Since she needed some convincing, I said, "I *know* I'm going to be rich, little sis. Come here," I tapped the bed for her to sit next to me. "Aye, grab that notepad and pen on the desk, please. Now when I was in the 12th grade, this book right here changed my life."

"*Rich Dad, Poor Dad*, what's it about?" she asked. Her intrigue reminded me of a young ten-year-old wanting to know how babies are made.

I stood tall, as if I was a professor getting ready to explain how to attack an assignment. "I can show you better than I can tell you. Now, make a big cross on the paper. On the top left make an E and on the bottom make an S, top right an I, and bottom a B. The E is for Employee, write that down. The S is for Self-Employed, Mary. On the right hand side, we have I and that is for the Investor, and on the bottom we have B and the B stands for Big *Biznass*."

"Ummm, Lando, I think it's business not *biznass*."

"No, ninja. You heard me correctly. It's Biznass. Ha-ha. Okay, listen. Give me an example of an employee."

"You!" she said quickly and with a smart-ass tone.

"Okay, okay, that's how it's going to be, huh?" I replied sarcastically, before getting back into Professor Lando mode. "Yes, I'm an employee. You're 100% correct. Now, what's a self-employee? Give me an example."

"Um," she paused for a while and replied, "a business owner, right? Or like somebody who cuts grass and like to have their own lawn mower."

"Perfect!" I yelled, pointing to her, as if she was the only person in class who answered the question correctly. Never mind the fact she was the only one under the tutelage of Professor Lando. I could feel a surge of power course through me as I spoke to her. I wanted her to understand what I was saying so badly. I'd seen far too many people exchanging time for money only to end up tired, frustrated, and usually broke. If I could help my sister learn what I had, I knew it could change her life. "Now, Mary, you're working at Taco Bell, saved your money, and brought your very own lawn mower so you can hustle and make money for yourself right now. Guess what the employee and self employee has in common?"

"I don't know...they both make money," she said.

"What they both have in common is that if they *go to work*, they make money. But if they don't then guess what?" I paused to point at her expecting her to complete my sentence, which she did.

"They don't make money."

"Now, nothing is wrong with these two, but our goals are to make it to the right side of the road. Okay? Examples of big business are Taco Bell, Walmart, Prepaid Legal."

"Whoa, whoa," she said, stopping me. "Lando, I don't think Prepaid Legal is a big business."

I smiled and grabbed my phone, not saying a word at first. I pulled up my commission statement and said, "How much money did I make today?"

"$55.95," she responded.

"What the hell have you seen me do all day?" I looked at her with a smirk, indicating I hadn't done shit all day.

"So you're telling me you made $55 and did nothing?"

"Don't forget my 95 cents, my lovely dear. On the right side, Mary, if you go to work you get paid, but if you don't you still get paid. That's what we call leverage."

After that Professor Lando session, we turned on the TV in my room, and the first thing we saw was a couple kissing. I paused, got lost in my thoughts, and said, "I miss Amanda." Not realizing that I said that aloud.

Mary said, "Well, why don't you just hook back up with her?"

"It's not that easy, Mary, it's not that easy."

Mary's my youngest sister, and we are seven years apart. Just three of the five kids have the same father: OC, Keke and myself. Mary and Kelly were on the Lewis side. Mary's dad is Charles, a Chrysler worker who'd been around for as long as I could remember. For some reason, Mary and I were always the closest. I love all my siblings, but since she was the youngest, she always looked up to me. That made her my favorite. Go to school, get good grades, no sex until you turn forty-two, and you will be successful. That is what I advocated. I knew she wouldn't wait until forty-two, but hell, at least I had tried.

The back door opened and my friend Percy walked in the house. He stopped by to recruit me for another get rich quick idea he had. We were always looking for a way to make some money. After we'd finished razzing each other and discussing his plan, which surprisingly was a good one that involved flipping used computers, the phone rang. It was my sister Keke, saying dad was in the hospital, because he'd fallen down the stairs. I immediately rushed over to the hospital to check on him, praying he'd be okay.

3

The room was full of family members when I walked in. I started asking questions concerning his health right away.

"Well, physically he is doing okay, but his eyes are a lot worse than we expected. They are going to keep him here overnight and run some test," my aunt said.

Looking at my father lying on the bed just gave me a nasty taste in my mouth. I never was a hospital person, they all smelled like old people, pee, and cleaning materials.

"Hey dad. How are you feeling?"

"Hey son, I'm hanging in there. This is just crazy not being able to see where I'm going." His tone told me that he was having a difficult time dealing with the recent changes going on with his health. "Do you work today?"

"No, I go back tomorrow, so if you need something just let me know."

He nodded.

My aunt instructed us to let him get some rest and meet up over grandma's later. I asked her why grandma wasn't at the hospital with us. It was very unusual for her not to be present when something important was going on in the lives of her children or grandchildren.

"Grandma's not feeling the best today, so she is resting at home," my aunt told me.

Driving home, I decided to make a pit stop to my favorite place, 7-Eleven. Admittedly, I am a Slurpee addict. If I'm having a bad day just buy me a Slurpee. If you don't have enough money to buy me something for Christmas, then buy Lando a Slurpee.

Check it out. Here's the deal about me. Even more than I love Slurpees, I love the ladies. Since I was very young, I was always outgoing and loved to talk to people. Once I lost my virginity at age fourteen, I wanted to hump any and everything I could find. So I was always on the prowl looking for my newest conquest.

Finishing up my purchase, I saw this gorgeous light-skinned chick walking into the store. She was about 5'3, 130 pounds, and wore aviator sunglasses. By the way she was dressed, I could tell she was a female that liked the better things in life. I decided to make another Slurpee. So when I walked outside, I ran to her car, saying, "Excuse me."

She was sitting in the car with the windows down.

"Yes?"

"Here you go. I thought you would be needing this."

With a confused expression, she asked, "And why is that?" As she lowered her glasses to get a better look at me.

"Because you're just too damn hot for your own good." She laughed and gave me a smile.

"I'm Lando and you are?" I put my hand out, expecting her to shake it.

"Nicole."

"Well, nice to meet you. Nicole, do you or your boyfriend mind if I hit you up sometimes?"

"Who said I had a boyfriend?"

"I can tell by the way you carry yourself." Oh yes, I was confident.

"So if I have a boyfriend, why would you talk to me, Mr. Lando?" she responded, once again smiling.

"Because I can tell you're not happy!"

"Oh, how you figure?" she asked, clearly amused with our conversation.

"Because you just met me, duh!" A big Kool-aid smile on my face. *Bam take that, bitch! Royal Flush!*

"You're good, Lando, here is my number. Give me a call sometime and I might respond."

"Okay, sweetie, all I needed was a chance."

She turned up her music, put her glasses back on, and drove off. That was just the pick-me-up I needed to take my mind off what was going on with dad and grandma.

4

I wanted to check on grandma and go watch some TV over there since grandma's house was magical. She always kept French vanilla or vanilla bean ice cream in the fridge, my favorite. The house was always clean, no matter who came over and for what reason. I got the best sleep ever over grandma's. She had cable for as long as I could remember, and along with that pool table, she had an unlimited supply of canned Sprite.

"Heeey!" I yelled, as I walked into the side door, which they usually kept open.

Over grandma's, we had an undisclosed rule. Whenever anyone walked into grandma's house, we needed to announce ourselves or we would have an immediate problem.

"Where is grandma?" I asked, as I saw about four family members discussing arrangements for dad.

"She's upstairs and not been feeling good lately," Keke told me. I went upstairs to check on her.

"Hey, grandma!"

"Hey, Lando."

"Grandma, what's wrong?" Concern showed on my face, since I rarely saw her down.

"I don't know, Lando. The last few days I have been feeling really tired," she replied, her voice sounding lethargic.

"Do you want me to bring up some tea for you?"

"Yeah, that would be great." Grandma *loved* her tea. Everyday, religiously, she and my aunt would have tea and talk about everything—church, sports, politics or how my aunt's day at work went. As kids, we couldn't wait until we turned around thirteen and were old enough to make Grandma's tea for her. If we stopped pouring before she said thanks, she would give that motherfucker-did-I-say-stop look. It seemed like an art, because she always wanted it poured all the way to the top with her spoon and sugar on the side.

I stopped my sisters in the kitchen and asked, "Hey, what's going on with grandma?"

"I don't know. She's been upstairs, not talking to anybody today. She didn't even want any tea." I smiled, since I knew grandma wanted tea from me. Keke always had the real scoop, so I went to her with my concerns. As I was fixing grandma's tea, my whole family seemed to be in the kitchen, and I could overhear their conversation.

"Well, I can take care of him on Tuesdays thru Thursdays after work," my aunt stated.

Keke then said, "Since I'm back from Minnesota, I can help out."

"Well, somebody just needs to move in with him!" When my grandpa said that, they all looked at me.

"I guess I can go help out a little bit by going back and forth over," I offered.

Aunt Chris looked at me, her eyes sharp and piercing. Inside my heart thudded making me feel like the mallet was being slammed sentencing me to probation with dad. And then, my aunt said, "Well, it's set! I got these days. Lake can be over there in the mornings, and Keke got the weekends." Lake…short for Land 'O Lake, the name my dad and aunt always called me.

Damn, I thought. *I guess I'm moving in with dad.*

5

My brother and I walked into a Detroit local bar on 7 Mile and Greenfield. This was an area I was not familiar with, since I didn't have too many comrades in that part of Detroit.

"Do you have your pistol on you?" I asked.

"Nigga, what you think?" he responded sarcastically.

"That will be $10 each, and I also need to see IDs," said the 6'5 and over 250-pound security guard.

"Hey! Let them in! They're Ocie's kids," said one of my dad's friends.

"Oh wow, you guys. I didn't even know," he replied, his expression apologetic.

The music wasn't loud, but the place was live with tons of energy. Older women dressed to impress. Everybody was ordering drinks at the bar. One of my dad's friends stumbled over towards us, realizing who we were. "Is that Ocie's kids? Hey, follow me. Here he is!"

He guided us towards the back of the bar and there sat my dad at a table wearing a brown mink coat, matching mink hat, both the coat and the hat matching the table. He had a ton of gold jewelry piled on, looking like the Jerome character from the *Martin* show. On this night his hair was in finger waves and a long ponytail.

"Hey, what's going on, dad?" My brother, OC, spoke first.

"Aww man. Hey sons," he yelled, while standing up greeting us. He seemed genuinely surprised to see us.

"Happy birthday, dad! You know we had to come and check on you," I said.

Looking around, dad was surrounded by gorgeous women. Dad had always been *the man* since I could remember. He and mom were married for eight years. It was amusing how my parents are total opposites. Dad had a very young soul and loved to date younger women.

It was his 50th birthday. That birthday was one that I would never forget, because of one thing. After being at the bar for a while, I started to feel bad because my brother was buying him drinks. Everybody was ordering him food, and my broke ass didn't even have a dollar to my name to buy my own dad a beer. Till this day, I don't know why I felt so horrible about it, but I really wished I was doing better in life at the time. So, I sat there, listening to every one of his friends tell story after story.

"Li'l OC, man, me and your daddy..." "Boy, one time..."

All his friends took turns, sharing some of their adventurous times with my dad. The ladies talked about how they remembered me when I was around six. Dad would throw poker parties over the weekends. They would take care of me, bring me candy, and talk about how much I adored them. My dad was just a lovable type of person. He had friends and a lot were gorgeous women. Whenever dad threw a party, it was *a party*.

Once we were ready to leave, I notified dad, and as always, he preferred to walk us out. Grabbing his belt, an indication that he was checking to make sure he had his pistol on him, he came along. It was then that I told him exactly how dissatisfied I was with life.

I'm pretty sure he had multiple drinks that night. If so, I'm happy he had them, because he stopped at the door, looked at me in my eyes, and said, "Lake, listen to me! I don't care what anybody tells you. If you want to be a millionaire, you can! If you want to be successful, you can! I see it in you. One day, you will be successful. You just have to find your niche."

Since I'd never heard my dad telling me that I could do whatever in life I wanted, that was a day I will never forget.

6

I walked into the coffee shop and saw my coworker Ali.
"My brother from another," I said, as we greeted each other with our ritual handshake. I established handshakes with all my coworkers, as if we were a family in the fraternity of the underpaid and underappreciated workers.

"Yo Lando! Let me talk to you real quick in the office," said Jim the manager. "Lando, I'm getting the fuck out. I have been here all day and I'm leaving. Make sure you go upstairs and give Derrick a break. He has been calling for the last hour, bitching and complaining about a break. Oh yeah, and stay out of Jean's sight today." He pointed up towards the camera in the corner of the coffee shop.

"He has been calling all day today, bitching and moaning about nothing. So, I'm done with all the bullshit for the day. Good luck, Lando."

"Okay, Jim, see you later."

"Oh yeah, Lando, take out the trash, too. I meant to do it earlier, but been busy as all hell."

As I was helping Ali out with customers by making coffee, I heard Ali yell, "A-ta-a-lay-ya" which means *look at her* in Arabic. I turned around and saw a good-looking young lady around twenty-four, white, slim build, and he whispered, "Hey, do you want her?"

"Yeah," I responded.

Ali waited about a minute and yelled, "Hey, Boss. Can I borrow your Porsche tonight? I got a date."

"Yeah, I don't care." I pulled out my keys and threw them towards him, and the chick's eyes lit up. Yup, I ended up giving her my number. This was a regular routine with me and Ali. We would take turns, giving each other the assist to hit on women. We had lots of fun at work.

After walking all around the airport, making my rounds, messing with friends, I went and said a quick hello to my girl, Brown. She was the one that got me hired by the company. For whatever reason, she had been transferred to a different department. I finally went to relieve Derrick.

"What's good, my brotha."

"Man, I have been calling downstairs for hours. I have to freaking piss like a race horse!"

"Okay, okay. My bad. All you want to do is take a long break to go play with your little dick," I said, while doing our ritual handshake greeting each other.

Each coworker had their own handshake depending on what they did best in the coffee shop. Like Derrick, he was good at making shakes, so we'd slap hands twice, I'd mimic the gesture of pouring milk into a cup, shake it up, and throw it out. I liked Derrick a lot, because he was a young kid from Africa. He was around seventeen, but he was a genius. He'd graduated early, and in a few months, he would be on his way to the University of Michigan. He goofed around a lot and got on people's nerves, only because he was young-minded. He would listen to me, whenever I talked, so I mentored him.

I was cleaning up the coffee shop, since the rush had died down. There were no customers at the moment this gorgeous black model-looking woman walked in and started towards me. I'd swear she was moving in slow motion and "Who's That Lady" from the Isley Brothers blared in the background.

She walked up, and in a voice that made every nerve ending in my body come alive, said, "Hello, how are you?"

I was already in love and mesmerized. I went into macking mode. "Well, I'm doing fantastic now, since I just met my future wife."

She laughed and said, "Oh really, huh."

Taking her order, I took my precious time, so I could converse with her as long as possible. "You have to be a model," I said to her.

"I used to model, but I don't anymore," she said with a genuinely, thankful expression.

"Where are you originally from?"

"I live in Florida, but travel a lot. I'm everywhere. I actually just got back from China."

"China?" I asked. That was the last response I expected. There must have been a shocked expression on my face, because she giggled. "What type of work do you do, if you don't mind me asking?"

"I'm a wrestler."

"Ha-ha, okay. And I don't manage this coffee shop. No, seriously, what do you do?"

She rolled her eyes playfully. "Have you ever heard of the WWE?"

"Hell yeah, who hasn't."

"I'm on Monday Night Raw. My wrestling name is Alicia Fox," she said.

As soon as she said that, my heart dropped and I wanted to take advantage of her body right then and there. She was drop dead gorgeous, and to top it off, she was cool as hell. She stayed and talked to me for over twenty minutes. She even took a picture of me on her phone to send to her boss, since I used to wrestle and said she would love to give me a recommendation. Yup, I got that number. By the time Derrick came back, I was ecstatic, telling him word for word what happened and texted all of my friends that were wrestling fans that I'd gotten Alicia Fox's number. But first, I did have to use good old Google to confirm that she was who she claimed to be, since I met a lot of people were just crazy and would lie for no reason.

I walked into the coffee shop the next day and saw Jamie sitting down eating.

"Jamie, what the fuck? This is what you do when I'm gone?"

"No, no, no, Lando. I don't want to hear it. I been working all day and haven't had a break. So, I'm tired, Lando," she replied in her thick Cameroonian accent.

"Hey, Boo. Did you miss me?" I said, walking to greet her with a hug. "Jamie, let me have some of your sandwich." Every day she would mix and make her own specialty sandwich. This was one we definitely didn't have on the menu. I would always try to find a way to sneak a bite.

"No, Lando! You always eat my food. This is for me, and I need a break," she responded, demanding her break. The phone suddenly started ringing,

"Go answer the phone, Jamie! Jean has been calling all day, acting crazy," I pleaded, encouraging her to hurry and pick it up so I could steal a bite of her food. That's exactly what I did!

Running out the shop I heard, "Lando! I'm going to kill you! And hey! Where is my break?"

I finally made it back to the bar. Soon as Jennifer saw me, she was asking for her break. Since she was a bartender I prayed to not get left alone too much by myself, because once people asked for anything other than a beer, it was over for me.

"Lando, please, I will be right back, I promise, and the bar is dead. That guy is my only customer and he is drinking a screw driver."

Ahhh hell! What the heck is a screw driver? It seemed like she was gone for no longer than twenty seconds and a group of around eight people walked, in loud and having a good time. *Fuck me.*

"Hey brother, I would like to have a..."

I cut him off and said, "Beer!"

"Um, yeah I'll take a Miller Draft."

I asked the next guy, "Would you like the same thing?" Trying to convince him to keep it simple.

"I'll take a Bloody Mary." I turned around and slowly grabbed the hot sauce.

Another guy yelled, "I'll take a Guinness." In my head, I remember seeing Jennifer making a Bloody Mary with hot sauce, and a Guinness, I had no idea how to make one of those. He looked at me with a weird face, probably noticing that I was kinda confused and said, "It's a beer!"

I started laughing like I was just playing. "Man, here you go." One older white lady asked me what I would recommend.

"An amaretto sour," I replied, since I liked the taste of them.

"So that's what I will have," she responded, as I grabbed the cheat sheet we had in the back and started to make the drink all wrong. But eventually I figured it out. After a while I started to get the hang of it and the customers were having a ball.

Jennifer walked back in and she saw me pouring a lady some wine and said, "Lando, you're not supposed to give them that much wine."

"You don't have to, but I am," I responded snarkily just to get a rise out of her. The lady gave me a high five and a $20 bill. "See, I told you," I said as I walked away, "Oh yeah, he needs a Bloody Mary," pointing towards the man whose drink I never poured, since I'd gotten confused.

That was my job, the coffee shop. The coworkers were amazing, but the job and management sucked. We were all underpaid and overworked. I had to be a coffee maker, a chef, bartender, and a manager all in one day, and had to train people here and there.

Most of my friends/coworkers were pissed off because they were all making one or two dollars per hour less than me, but they were the ones who trained me when I first got started. To make matters worse, just about all of them had college degrees, settling in life for $8.50 an hour. I used to tell them all the time "don't get mad at me, get mad at yourself, you're still working here." I was just smart enough to tell them whatever they wanted to hear at the interview and had the confidence that I was going to be a manager, but the good thing about having that job was that it looked great on my resume.

7

I convinced my godbrother Carl to bring over his truck and to help me move my bed and a few items over dad's.

"What your girl been talking about lately?" I asked to strike a good conversation, since their drama was equivalent to a reality TV show.

"Aww man, your boy got caught up the other day," he said, while shaking his head and laughing.

"What the fuck you do?" I swear my friends were ranked top ten in the nation when it came to cheating and getting caught. It might be because of my dad, but I knew how to hide things. None of them had the slightest idea what they were doing.

"Li'l Carl hated on me."

"What! How?" I replied, confused because his son was so young.

"So, I'm talking to this bad chick named Sherry. The three of us and her nephew went to go see the movie *Cars*. I told Carlos's little ass to shut up and don't tell Megan that we went. The father-son secret, right. Followed with a don't tell mom. But guess him and Megan was driving and drove past the damn theater over near…you know Wayne Road and he was like 'I went to the movies over there, momma.' And she was like 'no you didn't.' His ass was like 'I did. I went with Daddy, Sherry and Gerald.'"

"Haha. Hell naw he didn't, bro."

"She started going off! 'You had bitches around my son' and all that."

"You're so damn nasty." I laugh and joke as we pulled up to the house and started unloading my stuff.

Mrs. James, my dad's neighbor, walked outside and said, "Oh hell naw, now what's going on over here?" she yelled as she walked over with her nappy gray hair, while wearing pajamas.

"I'm moving in for a little bit to help out my dad, since his sight is going bad."

"Well, let me tell you something here, little man. I know how y'all young men do with sex, weed, blasting that loud ass hipity hop music, rumble jungle, and shit in my yard."

"Okay, Mrs. James, you don't have to worry about that."

"Well, where is yo daddy, little boy?"

"I'm not sure, but he should be here soon."

Now Mrs. James was about 70 or 80 years old and used to be the elementary school teacher for what seemed like everybody in the hood. She reminded me of a mixture of a character off of the *Boondocks* and Mrs. Shirley from the movie *Friday After Next*. About 5 feet tall, gray hair and wore some of the biggest bifocal glasses ever, that was Mrs. James.

"Man bro, that old lady is crazy as hell," I said as we were cleaning up.

"Ain't that his landlord?" Carl asked. "Ocie, you don't have to pay rent this month if I can *suck yo dick!*" Carl yelled as he demonstrated pulling out his teeth, imitating her funny voice, because it was high pitched and squeaky. Right after saying that dad walked into the house with my Aunt Chris.

"Pump dawg in the house!" Carl yelled, joking with my dad.

"Hey son."

"You alright, pops? We were just talking about you," Carl said, while reaching to shake his hand, noticing dad didn't laugh or respond like he usually would.

"Hey, who is this?"

"Man, pump, your eyes are getting that bad. This ya boy, Carlton."

"Oh hey, Carl, how's everything going?"

"Everything good. We were just talking about your girlfriend."

"Who?"

"The one next door you been dating to get your rent lower." We all laughed.

"Y'all some funny people."

"Alright, see y'all good people later. I actually have to do some work today," my aunt said as she was leaving the house.

"Ocie, I know you don't just have a pool table soon as you walk in the house, man?" Carl stated.

"I might have to get rid of it now, since I'm not going to be able to use it. I might sell it on Craigslist."

Dad didn't live in a house; it was more like a weird apartment that was shaped like a motor home, but with a basement. His place was 100% bachelor set up. Walking into the house this man had a nine-foot-long pool table in the living room, instead of having seating, accompanied with a TV. In the kitchen, directly to the left three steps away, was a poker table with chairs. I guess he used this as his dinner table. One bathroom in the back and one bedroom next to it. I assumed I was sleeping in the dungeon, also known as the basement, just like always. Now the basement was huge, lots of space, nice and cool, so I had no problem with setting up shop down here.

Carl left while dad and I were cleaning up and we started talking about our future plans for the house.

"Well, son, I might need you to go and get your CNA license so I can put you on payroll, then we both can make some money.

Since my eyes are going bad, I'm going to need care, so I might as well pay you instead of somebody else, you know."

"Yeah, that's what I'm talking about. The more trades I got the better, and you know how many bad women are in that field? I can only imagine how lovely that class would turn out."

"I know that's right. What's been going on with you since you and Amanda broke up?" he asked.

"Well, I just been single really, just working on my business and knocking off a few chicks here and there, whenever I can. I got this bad one I'm going out with later on today."

"Oh really, who is she?"

"It's the younger sister of a girl I went to school with. She's white and Asian, and she bad as hell, dude."

"Oh, white and Asian, huh?" he said out loud, giving her a new nickname.

"What's been up with you and Diamond?" I asked since that was dad's most serious relationship I knew of and remembered.

"She still crazy as heck. Calling me all the time talking about cheating on me was one of the worst things she's ever done, and how hard it is to get a good man like me. Ha-ha, but I still have my regulars that usually come through and knock me off once in a while."

After finally setting up my bed, I get a text message from my date giving me the directions to her house. Playing Kanye West's *The Good Life* as I was getting dressed in the bathroom and feeling great, I walked into dad's room and asked him which shoes should I wear? Basically doing the same thing Sean had done to me.

"Those," he said, pointing to the loafers I had in my hands. "What car are you driving?"

"The biscuit!" I yelled out smiling.

He laughed. "Son, since I'm not going to be doing too much driving anyway, just take the truck."

"Okay thanks, dad," I said as I walked outside and saw the

forest green Ranger sitting pretty and clean, looking all good and sexy. I ran and did a heel click in joy of excitement since I didn't have to drive my Taurus.

Mrs. James, out of nowhere, said, "You better watch that young man." That old lady scared the shit out of me.

"Okay, Mrs. James." I shook my head and laughed.

I pulled up to my date's house and she called saying, "Park on the other side of the street, my baby daddy actin' crazy."

"What the fuck did she just say? Damn, I wish I had my gun license. This chick got me in the hood at night with a crazy baby daddy," I said out loud to myself.

I see her running to the truck, she jumped in, and said, "Drive!" As if she'd just robbed a bank and I was the getaway driver.

"What the fuck was that about?"

"Well, my son's father just got out of jail and he is acting crazy. But I need to smoke. Do you have some weed?"

"No, I don't smoke," I responded. Shaking my head, I wondered what I just got myself into.

"So, where are we going?" she asked, since we didn't make any date-like plans.

"We can go see a movie, bowling, out to eat, or whatever you feel like really."

"Do you have some movies at the crib? We could get some food and go there," she said smiling.

At that moment, I realized how fucking sexy she was looking, I remember it like this happened today. She had on this perfect body fitting blue dress with some sexy black heels, hair curly, long, and sandy brown. Makeup perfect - not too much, not too little. Basically, she was looking like she was ready to go to the most expensive restaurant in Michigan and all this fucking chick wanted to do was come back to my house. Ha-ha. *Yes!*

So I ordered us some Chinese food and went home. Since I

wanted her to be comfortable, we did make an extra stop in the hood to get her some "medicine" from our local pharmacist.

"Why the hell you look so damn sexy?"

"You're about to make me blush," she replied as I looked in amazement.

We get to the house. Now when I'm trying to get laid I stick to a routine. Show her the house, grab a drink, pop in a movie, find out a way to get her in my room, and by the grace of the vagina gods, I can get laid. Now with this chick, things were different because she didn't want to watch a movie nor drink.

Confused with how to respond, I scratched my head.

"Well, um... Let's go downstairs."

I have to say at that very moment I just knew I wasn't going to get laid, but I might as well try something. I surely underestimated her and myself. To this day I still get excited at how amazing she was in bed. To make matters even better, she had a new birth control where they put something inside of her and she couldn't get pregnant for like three years and she had two more years to go. At first I didn't believe her, since I'd never heard of that type of birth control.

"See, Lando, feel right here on my arm. This is where they planted it in me. Since I had my son at such a young age I wasn't ready for another one, so I have been on this for about a year." I can't lie, the first time we had sex I definitely used a condom, but knew it would become more difficult as time went on. Don't judge me y'all but... Um, yeah... Don't try this at home.

The next day I was at the airport taking coffee orders and a flight attendant named Heather from Continental walked up. We conversed back and forth about how I'd wanted to become a flight attendant when I was younger and missed having my flying benefits. Years ago when I was about eighteen I worked for the airlines before as a bag handler. I'd interviewed to be a flight attendant, but was turned down due to my age. The other workers always said once flying for free is in your blood you can't get rid of it.

"Lando, go to this site soon as you get home. It's a site that shows all the airlines that's hiring. Keep me updated if you get a job. I'll help you out."

"Okay, I will. Thanks, Heather," I said as we exchanged numbers.

As I was dancing in the shop, since I was in a good mood, the phone rang. "Hello, Lando, this is Jean, stop dancing in my damn store and clean up."

"Oh, um, you seen that? Yeah okay, my bad, Jean. Hope you're having a good day. Goodbye."

It was crazy how that man owned like thirty of those stores and all he did was watch that one all day and fuck with us. Rumor had it that he had a camera app on his phone. So we would make jokes saying he would be on vacation still watching us from his yacht.

Later on that day after we had closed and I was in back counting money, Ali sneaked up on me and in his deep Middle eastern voice said, "Lando! This is Jean!" I jumped, as he started laughing at me.

"Yo, you better tell yo' uncle to leave me the hell alone, Ali."

He grabbed a muffin, took a bite out of it, and sat it on the counter.

I replied laughing, "Clean the front and stop eating those damn muffins before I call your uncle."

A few weeks later, I decided to get up early and make it a point to search for some airline jobs. I always thought about the time I worked for Meme Airlines. The other employees would talk for hours about all of the crazy destinations they'd traveled to and how many women they slept with every time they visited various places. I would think, if I could just get my flying benefits back, I would be able to travel the world. The benefit of working for most airlines, was being able to fly for free.

Dad walked into the room, and I said, "Remember when I use to work for the airlines a few years ago? I'm starting to miss all those good benefits, so I'm gonna see if I can find a job as a gate agent or something. I see they have an opening for a flight attendant to be based out here, but the interview is in Minnesota."

"Since you been helping me out, see if you can find a cheap ticket. I might be able to help you cover the airfare. Just let me know."

"Okay, pops, I appreciate it."

∽

WHENEVER I WENT to Sean's house, nine times out of ten, I entered through the back door, since it was usually unlocked. Soon as I walked in, the dog started barking, and Sean's dad yelled, "Is that Lamont?"

"Who is Lamont?" I said. "It's ya boy, Lando!"

"Lamont is the big dummy that sneaks in my house through the back door. Jamie, did you leave the door open?" he yelled. "A big dummy done broke in." He laughed.

I walked downstairs, and Sean was sitting on the couch with a cigarette in his mouth, wearing a wife beater, looking like he'd just had sex.

"Whoa, big fella! Is somebody over there smackin' his own meat? And take that crap out your mouth! It's been two years! So stop playing!"

He replied, "Actually, me and my dog, Dingo, was about to have sexual intercourse, but you rudely interrupted."

"Dude, isn't that animal bestiality or something? But why do I think your dad just called me Lamont from *Sanford and Son*?" I said and we both started laughing. Sean started humming the theme song. "I might be going to an interview in Minnesota."

"For what?" he said, finally putting down his cancer stick.

"To be a flight attendant."

"Whoa. Okay Lando!" he said, sitting up.

"Oh Lord, here you go," I replied, trying to stop him before he even got started.

"Nope, hear me out!" he said, standing. "First, you go and become a Certified Nursing Assistant. Next, you want to be a stewardess. Do you want to hand over your man card now or later?"

"Umm. Later. Because when I'm traveling all over the world *for free*, banging anything and everything that walks, I don't wanna hear it! 'Dude, can you give me a buddy pass?' 'I wanna fly to Vegas, Bro.' 'Lando, hook me up, I wanna go to Cancun.'"

"Okay, until then, you're still suspect, Lamont."

Yeah, I don't know how this dude or any of the other motherfuckers became my friends.

LIVING WITH DAD, hanging out and getting to know each other, was amazing. It's funny how we never knew how similar we were until that time. I remember when I moved in with him the first time. Growing up, he was always around or at least a phone call away, but we were primarily raised by mom during the weekdays, and grandma and grandpa on the weekends. We would stay with dad on occasions, but preferred grandma's because dad never had food or kid entertainment over his house. It was strictly a bachelor pad.

We all had our fair share of moving in over dad's during our years in school, because sooner or later mom would run us out. My turn came around my junior year. As I was getting older wanting to do my own thing, mom would just start random arguments.

"You need to just go move with your damn daddy."

One day I followed up on her offer, especially when I found

out how much child support she was receiving, but I was only getting a hundred dollars or so a month.

"Man, I have been trying to tell you to come move over here and I'll give you all your check. I don't need it."

When I was younger, I never understood why dad would get so mad when we would ask for some money.

"Get it from your momma, she's the one that's getting all the money." After complaining and whining he would give in and approve our requests. Once I realized how much she had been making from four different kids at a time from two plant workers, I thought, *oooohhh wow now I understand why he was pissed ha-ha.* To her credit she was taking care of us, feeding us, and still giving us money, so knowing what I know now I was lucky to get what I was getting. But I didn't care at the time, I just wanted my forty acres and a mule.

Once I moved in with pops, everything worked out in my favor when my first day over I woke him up at 6 a.m. demanding a ride to school, since I no longer lived near the bus stops or close to friends. Even though I knew he'd just come home from partying, he got up with no complaints and drove me there. I asked if I could drive his 1997 XJ6 Jaguar to school and he said, *"hell no!"*

The very next day he walked in at 3 a.m. again from partying. I woke him up at 6 a.m. and he said, "Grab the keys, son, they're in the drawer."

Ha-ha Yes! I knew he wasn't going to be able to continue our 6 a.m. routine. I was seventeen years old with a clean Jaguar in high school, so I was the man. Everything was perfect except for when I lived with mom all of my friends lived literally around the corner from me, which is where I spent most of my time. Now I lived on the other side of Inkster and that Jag only took premium gas at $2 a gallon. It was killing me. Especially since over dad's house the only thing to do was play pool on his mini pool table. Read one of his pool books which taught the tricks of the trade. Do homework, since we didn't have any television, or lastly watch some of the porn collection he had scattered around the house. After doing all the above hundreds of times, I decided to move back with mom.

But this time around we would stay up until anytime in the morning talking nonstop sports, women, and religion. The show on ESPN, *First Take,* we would watch it religiously at 10 a.m., let them debate a sports subject, then it would be our turn, as if we were the special guests on the show.

I decided to take dad up on his offer and was able to find a cheap flight that would get me in and out of Minnesota, and with a nice hotel across from the Mall of America. I was excited! I was one step closer towards my dreams come true with the help of my new right hand man. My dad...Ocie the Second.

8

I thought again about becoming a flight attendant. I knew I would have to interview, convince the recruiters to hire me, which wouldn't be a problem, because I'd had so many different jobs by the age of twenty-four, no one would believe it. I worked fast food, the cemetery, cars, UPS, the airport, sales. I had just about any job you could think of, because my philosophy was if I could just get to the face-to-face interview I could convince anybody to hire me. 100% of the time I was correct until now.

"Do you have a suit?" dad yelled from his bedroom.

"Yeah, I think so!"

"Well, wear that and I got some cuff links, if you need them. I have an appointment on Monday at U of M to get me ready for the surgery."

"Okay, I'm about to go into work a little bit today, so they can give me the day off on Tuesday. I'll be back in a few. Just let me know if you want me to bring anything back."

The plan was to arrive early in the morning and take the shuttle bus to whatever hotel the open house was held. I was only going to Minnesota for a day. I didn't want to stay overnight since dad was paying for everything. I wanted to save him as much money as possible. I flew on Spirit Airlines since they had the cheapest flights. I was checking every two minutes to make sure I had my folder with my resume and documents I was required to bring. It felt good walking through the airport and not working for a change. I would imagine myself walking with my crew joking and laughing, planning where we were going to eat during our 20-hour layover in Miami.

"Ladies and Gentlemen, welcome to Spirit Airlines en route to Minnesota. The flight is approximately one hour and fifteen minutes." As she continued with her announcements, I watched how professional and nice she was, thinking I could do the same thing.

I was born in St. Paul, Minnesota, but it had been years since I'd been here. By the time I was three-years-old, we'd relocated back to Michigan.

The flight was nice and quick and the interview started at 9 a.m., so I had time to make sure my paperwork and other things were in order. The interview was held at a hotel not too far from the Mall of America.

I had a dingy black Sean Jean suit I'd gotten from mom. I assumed she brought it from a garage sale or one of her off-price, retail stores.

As I sat down, waiting with about twenty people, I saw this black woman walk pass, and oh my God she was sexy. She looked like Foxy Brown in her prime and was completely stacked with legs, thighs and ass for days. Next, I saw a good-looking foreign woman who was maybe in her late 20s, early 30s walk pass greeting people and asking where everyone was from. The recruiters opened the door and spoke loudly saying, "Make sure everyone signs in over here before you walk in."

As I walked in the door, she said, "There is a height and reach test. I need you to put your back against the wall and stretch your arms out as far as you can." I did as directed, not knowing they were going to make us do this. I was wondering what would happen if my arms weren't long enough. My question was answered immediately. A short, thick, sexy, black chick walked in and did the same process and got turned away.

"Please, I have flown here all the way from Texas to be here!" she pleaded.

"Ma'am, I'm sorry. We have certain requirements that must be met in case you get hired. It's for your safety."

Damn! You're telling me this chick flew here from Texas and they just turned her ass all the way down. Yeah, I would have been pissed the hell off, but that wasn't my problem because my short arms made the cut.

The foreign girl sat next to me. "Wow. I would have been pissed if I made it this far for no reason you know," she said, talking to me.

"Hell yeah, that's crazy. I saw it written on their website, but didn't know they were for real. By the way, I'm Lando."

"Welcome ladies!" the recruiter said, as she walked in front of the class.

I cleared my throat, so she would notice I was the only male there.

"Oh I'm sorry, ladies and *one* gentlemen," she said and everyone laughed.

"The way we are going to do this is, first I'll give you an overview of the company, and then everyone will stand up individually, giving your name and also answering the questions on the piece of paper we gave you. There are two scenarios of a time when you went over and beyond to help a dissatisfied customer or when you were in a bad situation and how you were able to overcome it. After that, we will take a quick break and give one-on-one interviews."

There were two recruiters that came to the open house. Both were average white women. They showed us an overview of the company and how long it had been in business, breaking down the pay and how their reserve system worked. As a rule of thumb, new airline employees start on reserve, meaning the person is on call and essentially becomes the company bitch, having no idea where they're going or who they're going with. The person knows to just be packed and ready when the call comes. The pay sucked, but I was so intrigued by the flying benefits I didn't care. Hell, I was already making crap at the airport anyway. We all took turns standing up introducing ourselves, I'm not sure what I said, but I was confident, mainly because I was the only guy and I was black. So if they didn't pick me then it would be obvious they were racist. That's what I thought anyway.

First to go up front was Annie, telling us her story of why she wanted to become a flight attendant. Next up was Foxy Brown who was from Texas. I could tell by the way she carried herself, she was a hood chick, but also knew how to be very professional and carried herself as a successful young woman searching to become America's next top flight attendant, with a big ass. I wish I had a picture because *oh my god* she had a body.

Next was a lady that I will never forget. She was the type of person who appeared perfect, said all the right shit, and pretty much made everyone else look like a dumbass. She was a cute, older, skinny white lady in her 50s. I could tell she had been gorgeous when she was younger. So she calmly walked up, wearing a very warm, wholesome smile, and with a cool voice said, "I'm Sandy Smith and I had the great pleasure of being an airline stewardess back in 1980 with Trans Am Airline. We chartered around military people and I was also a nurse for them."

I turned to look at the recruiters and they had their mouths open damn near drooling.

"I had kids and God blessed me with a great man that swept me off my feet, and I left the aviation field. Now my kids are grown and I'm ready to jump back in. One example of being put in a pressure situation is when I was working a flight going from San Fran to Jacksonville, Florida on a CRJ 700."

I thought, *This bitch would know the damn aircraft and the city.*

As she continued on, "On those planes, for those who do not know, there are two flight attendants required. I was FA1. At some point on the flight the captain buzzed to let me know our right engine was out, but we could still fly the plane. I said 'ok, just keep me updated.' So he rings me right back and said our left engine also just went out, so prepare the cabin for an emergency landing. We're going to try to land at the closest airport. So I hang up and tell the other flight attendant what's going on. She just started to cry and froze up. So after I saw she couldn't perform, nor was fit for duty, I grabbed her and said 'Ann, do you want to sit this one out?' She just nodded her head yes and she sat down as a regular passenger. I grabbed my FAM and followed the right procedures and before we landed the engines came back on and we had a perfect landing." Everybody, including the recruiters, started clapping and she sat down.

My name was called. "Orlando, you're next."

Fuck me!

I started walking slowly, my legs felt kinda heavy, I was nervous.

Once I reached the front I introduced myself, then went on with my spiel. "I work at the Detroit Metro airport. The example I'm going to use is when I used to work as a Family Service Counselor for a cemetery. When I first started working there, the company was run badly and a lot of the customers that prepaid for their loved ones headstones were never ordered. Once I had a guy threatened to fight me and to call Channel 4 News on me. When he came in, I personally told him I understood where he was coming from and if I were in his shoes I would be equally upset or worse, but the most I could do, since I'd just started, is get it reordered. He agreed and apologized and even sent me a thank you card."

"Okay, everybody! We will review your application and next

we will call each of you in individually and talk to you," said the recruiter.

I went outside in the waiting area and saw the woman from Texas I'd nicknamed Foxy Brown.

"Hey, how are you?" she said to me as we greeted each other.

"I'm great. I'm Lando."

"I'm Kerry."

"You are from Houston, right?"

"Yep, born and raised," she responded with a heavy southern accent.

"Where are you from?"

"Detroit," I replied, not as confidently.

"Shut up! I have a friend I'm talking to that live out there. I'm going to visit today."

"You know what flight?" I said with the biggest Kool Aid smile on my face.

"No, but I'm sure I can switch to whatever one you're on and we can ride together." *Sweet Lord Jesus Yes!*

"Kerry Smith," the recruiter said, as she opened up the door ready to interview the next person.

"Okay, that's me, let me see what they are going to say. I'll be back."

After I returned from the bathroom my turn was next. I walked in to see two recruiters sitting side by side. There was a lone seat opposite them that was for the interviewee to sit. We greet each other and the first thing one recruiter said was, "How did you like our presentation?"

"It was great! I love the aviation world and how you can meet so many people."

"Well Orlando, we see on your resume you used to work for Northwest Airlines. What happened with them?"

"What?! I mean, excuse me," I responded.

"You use to work at Northwest, right?"

"Yes ma'am," I responded with a shocked voice, because that question caught me off guard.

"Well, what happened?"

"Oh yeah, Northwest. It was a good company, but I couldn't get to work at the time because my car broke down."

Damn Lando, why did you tell the truth? I thought to myself.

"Oh okay. We will email you within the next few weeks with our decision."

I walked out and saw Kerry.

"Are you taking the 6 p.m. flight?" she asked.

"Yeah."

"I am too. First, I'm going to meet my friend at the Mall of America. You want to come?"

"Hell yeah, I don't have anything else to do for the next few hours."

We walked into the Mall of America and she called her friend to get the meeting spot. We walked upstairs and once I saw her friend I realized that she was the short girl that was kicked out of the open house at the beginning. She looked good all dressed up for the interview, but in her casual clothes she was just as stacked as Kerry. She was just shorter with longer hair.

"Hey, what's up? I'm Lando." I said, extending my hand out for a handshake.

"Hey, I'm Stacey."

"Yeah, I remember you from the open house."

"Yeah, I was pissed that I flew all the way out here and couldn't get in the room."

Kerry asked, "What was the problem? Were you too short?"

"No, they said I was tall enough, but my arms couldn't reach. But it's cool. I got another one to go to next week."

"Damn," I said, surprised that she was ready for another one already.

"Boy, we stay going to interviews all the time," Kerry responded with that southern drawl.

"I also work for Delta as a gate agent and fly for free."

"Oh okay, that's what's up." I was thinking, *these chicks are professional interviewers, but whta's bad is they're not even getting hired anywhere.*

"I waited for y'all to get here. I know you are hungry."

"Yeah, let's go to the food court."

As we were walking, I made sure that both of them were in front of me so I could appreciate and enjoy the situation I was blessed with. Stacey wanted details on the interview process.

I responded, "They were cool. Broke down everything and you had to stand up in front of everybody and tell them about yourself."

"I was nervous as hell," Kerry stated.

"Shit, I was too, until I got up there. But we will see how it goes."

Stacey said, "I love this mall. Have you ever been here?"

"Yeah, I was born here. Well in St Paul."

"Oh really?"

"Yeah. I don't come here that much, but I visit from time to time."

"Can you watch my stuff? I'm about to go in that store and see if I can find my son anything," Stacy said.

"How old is your son?" I asked.

"He is three months."

"You just had a kid and you're looking like that? Wow, that's what's up." I watched her sexy, caramel-skinned, five-foot-nothing self walk away. After she went shopping, paying no taxes, the three of us walked around getting to know each other. Kerry was getting kinda jealous that I was more into Stacey. Now both of them were sexy in their own way, and Kerry had the fatter ass, but she said she was going to see one of her boos anyway, so I wasn't about to give a girl with a man all my attention. Once we were about to leave, Stacey and I said at the same time, "Take down my number." I guess it showed that we were on the same page.

"It was a pleasure meeting you. I will text you so you can lock me into your phone."

On the shuttle to the airport, Kerry started talking about how she used to date a football player from the Vikings and blah blah blah. I noticed again that she was jealous of me and Stacey because she kept saying, "Detroit, it looks like you like Li'l ole Stacey. Y'all should get to know each other. That's my girl and she is down to earth."

On the flight there weren't enough seats for us to sit next to each other, but when we made it to Detroit. We also exchanged numbers and decided to keep in touch once we heard back from Miracle. As she walked away, I just shook my head with so much excitement, because all I could think was *I can't wait to tell dad about this one.*

∼

"WHAT'S UP, DAD?"

"Hey there, son, how did everything go?"

"Not too bad. The bases they have are Detroit, Minneapolis, and Milwaukee, but this one was in Minnesota and I would be able to transfer sooner or later."

"Oh, that would be great, because you got Keke's people out there and your fraternity brothers over there, right?"

"Yeah, I forgot about them. But let me tell you about the two bad chicks I met from Texas!" I yelled, excited to give up all the details.

"Oh man, they have some bodies out there in Texas," he stated.

"Dad, let me tell you, so I get there and they started turning people away left and right."

"Why?"

"Because online they said you have to reach a certain height, so the little midgets couldn't make the cut. Now there were about fifteen of us that made it and one girl named Kerry stood up to do her speech and I went crazy, pops. All that body, dad, I almost lost it. Now the kicker is her friend also came to the interview, but couldn't get in because her arms couldn't reach. She looks *even better* and her butt is just as fat!"

"No, it ain't, Lake." He nodded his head in approval, clearly amused by my antics.

"We went to Mall of America and kicked it for a while and exchanged numbers."

"Man, I have been trying to tell you that in this industry you are going to be meeting so many new females every day. You flew out there and met you Miss Big Booty and Miss Little Booty." I laughed because he gave them nicknames. Dad continued, "This is a big field that everybody wants to be in. I told you about my boy, right?"

"Naw, what boy?" I asked, confused.

"My boy I went to school with. When we graduated back in '73, they'd just started thinking about hiring niggas in the aviation field. So, this guy hits me up and told me to come to a thing. You know, one of those things you just went to."

"An open house, dad." I shook my head.

"Yeah. Yeah, but we both went. He wanted to go all the way with it. Right around that time I got offered to work for Ford. He did the flight attendant route and I did Ford. Man, he lives in North Carolina. Now I forgot what airline he works for, but he is doing good. Ole boy got a huge house and a wife that's a nurse."

"Is he black?"

"Yeah, he black! He's a nigga, I'm trying to tell you!"

"Oh yeah, I forgot. My bad, sir," I responded sarcastically since I was laughing at the way he said it. "Is he from Inkster?"

"Yes, sir! I went to Inkster High with him." Pausing for a moment, he asked, "You think you have a shot at this one?"

"I'm not sure. There were the people who went in front of the room that said everything perfect and the people that already had experience, but I did mess up on one part. They asked me why I quit Northwest and I kinda froze up a little. I just wasn't prepared for the question, so I was pissed off."

The phone rang and dad paused the conversation to answer it.

"Hello?" He followed with, "What! Aww man. Who was there with her? Okay, we're on our way. Come on, Lake, momma fell down the stairs."

Nothing more needed to be said. We raced over to grandma's house. My aunt speculated that grandma had been trying to walk down the stairs when her leg went out, causing the fall.

"Where is she now?"

"Upstairs," My aunt responded and before I could get the words out, dad said, "Why is she not in the hospital?"

"She didn't want to go to the hospital."

"Whew, good thing she isn't seriously hurt." Dad started walking up the stairs to check on her.

9

A few days passed, I was sitting in the chair watching ESPN when dad asked, "Did you hear from Miracle yet?"

"Nope gotta check my email." I pulled out my phone to check the email. "Nope I didn't get the job."

"Well, what did they say?"

THANK you for taking the time to attend the Information Session with Miracle Airlines for the Flight Attendant - MSP. We enjoyed meeting with you and learning about your background and experience.

We are fortunate to have many qualified candidates apply to each of our positions. We have reviewed the qualifications of each candidate and after careful consideration, we have determined that the credentials of other candidates may better fit our needs at this time.

Please accept our best wishes and thank you for your interest in Miracle Airlines.

SINCERELY,

Human Resources
Miracle Airlines

DAD STOOD UP, saying, "Well son, this is one of the hardest fields to get into. Nobody said this would be easy."

∼

DRIVING, I called Kerry and put her on speaker.

"Hey Lando. What's up, boo?" she said with her sexy southern voice. "Did you hear from Miracle yet?"

"Yep, they sent me the good ole thanks, but no thanks email," I said with sarcasm.

"Damn. I still haven't heard nothing. I hope that's a good thing."

"Yeah probably so, they seen that big ole booty and just knew they had to hire you."

"Shut up, you damn fool. Have you heard from your girl Stacey?"

"Naw. I thought that was your girl."

"Me too, but she acting all fake and not giving me any buddy passes to go see one of my friends out there. She just been hating."

"Ha-ha. Do you know of any other airlines that are hiring?"

"Yeah, I filled out some today. I will email them to you." I heard her sigh before saying, "Aye, Lando. These motherfuckers keep on calling me. I will call you back, baby."

"Okay, talk to you later."

Now, since dad has a degree in Womanology, he went on to give me a breakdown of what was going on. "So, son, Kerry wants you!"

"You think so?"

"The thing is she is jealous of you and Stacey. I heard it in her voice. How she gone ask you how her friend is doing? So be ready to hear both of their drama, because they will be calling."

We arrived at Bert's Furniture Store. Dad wanted to come here since he knew the owner.

"Hold on, it's dark. I can't see nothing in here," he stated, once we made it into the store.

"You're standing in front of a darn wall." Shaking my head, I laughed, grabbed his arm and guided him to the counter.

"Hey, what's up, Bert?"

"Hey, this is his son. What's up?"

"Oh your dad isn't here?" dad asked.

"No, he just stepped out. But I got you guys' back."

"Okay, this is what I'm looking for..."

Once he started talking, I just went into a deep daydream thinking, *Damn, Lando, what could you have done differently? Hell, I should have been prepared for some of the questions. I could of asked more questions and done a better speech to make myself more noticeable.*

"Lando! Lando!" I heard my pops yelling snapping me back into reality.

"Oh, what's up?"

"Dang, did ya fall asleep?" dad asked, obviously trying to get me to pay attention.

"Oh, no I just was thinking."

"Follow him and we're gonna pick some stuff out."

Now, my dad always had a pimpish type of style, so he would like loud outlandish colors. His ass could barely see, but he picked out a bad ass two-piece couch set. The base of the couch was cream with a hot red/pink trim and a black counter mounted into the couch. Believe me it was *baddd* with three Ds and they had the red pillows to match.

After we were done, I knew I needed to go over Alvin's house to fill out some more applications, since he had a computer and printer. Soon as I walked in his mother greeted me warmly. After I kissed her cheek, she asked, "How did your interview go?"

"It was okay, but I just got the email that I didn't get the job."

"Just keep trying and praying and you will get it one day, if you really want the job. Alvin Jr. is in the back room."

"Yo! I need your computer services, my friend. What's going on Mr. Dean, how are you?" I said to Alvin's pops.

"I'm doing good now that I get to meet Alicia Fox's new boyfriend," he replied.

"Aww man, every dog gets a bone every once in a while," I replied, laughing, since I assumed that Alvin told his father that I met the sexy wrestling chick.

"I was wondering what was on her mind lately, because she was getting beat up and down the ring yesterday," Mr. Dean said.

"Aww man, not my girl getting beat up like that."

Alvin walked in and cut into the conversation. "Man, she got power bombed and all. I was like I need to call Lando," he said while laughing.

Alvin's father was in his mid-60s. He was a southern boy with a deep Texan accent. The difference with him and the average Texan was he was very laid back and smooth when he talked. His words would drag out and he took his time before he would speak, so it was rare to catch him saying something that he hadn't intended to say.

As I logged into the computer, I was thinking about how Alvin's mom encouraged me to keep trying and being positive about the situation, and God willing, it would happen."

I was thinking as I applied to other airlines that it was my first time ever getting rejected for a job once I made it to the actual interview. I have always felt no matter what the qualifications were, if the recruiter just gave me one chance to sit down and talk to them, I could manipulate myself into whatever was needed to get the job. So it was weird to be rejected. I didn't like it.

After a few hours went by, I checked my email and I saw that Les Brown, a top motivational speaker, would be in Michigan to do a seminar. I reserved my ticket to attend. Alvin walked into the computer room to ask how long until I was done.

"I'm finishing up now. What you about to get into, sir?"

"Go over Southfield's and get some 'knowledge,' because I haven't been doing good in school." He was referring to getting some head.

"What happened to the lame young chipmunk I knew in high school that couldn't get no pussy?" I asked.

"Back in school, none of them wanted me. Now I'm hot they all on me." We both started rapping Mike Jones' song with the same lyrics.

"Alright, man. Come through tomorrow. I'm going to need a haircut."

I made it back home and once I walked into the house I notice that there was flour everywhere.

"Dad!" I yelled.

"Yeah," he responded from the back room.

"Man, what did you do in here?"

"I was trying to cook some chicken and dropped the bag, stuff got everywhere and I just gave up."

"Wow, you are one crazy old man trying to cook."

"Yeah, so I just decided to eat this salad and listen to my gospel tapes. It's hard trying to adjust to this crap, man."

I noticed it just wasn't a good day for him and he was frustrated about his situation. "We have to keep praying and stay positive, pump daaawg!" I yelled, jumping and grabbing him until he started laughing.

"How did it go over Alvin's?"

"It was great. I filled out about 10 applications."

"I'm sure you're learning there is no quit in you, son. That's the spirit you're suppose to have. We don't quit on anything."

"Yeah, you're right about that, dad."

"Hey, son, grab me the ranch please," he asked as he sat on his bed ready to eat his salad, which also looked like a bad idea. I assumed he would spill that all over his bed, but it is what it is.

Lying in my bed, I YouTubed Les Brown and started watching a few of his clips, since I decided to go to his seminar that was coming up. He seemed very inspiring with a great story of being raised by a single mother and all odds against him, but became rich and successful. I couldn't wait to hear what he had to say at his seminar.

The next morning, while I was walking into work, my business partner, Rico, called me.

"What's up, boss man?"

"It's a blessing in disguise that you called me, because I was just thinking about you. I got two tickets to go see Les Brown. He's a black guy that go hard, so if you're not busy today, soon as I get off work I will come and pick you up. Then we are in that bitch!"

We hung up and went into work.

"Jamie, hurry yo' slow ass up!" I yelled, joking with her as I walked into the shop. Time for me to clock in.

"Shut up, Lando, I can take my time!"

"Depatchtai damnit Depatchtai," I yelled to her in French, since that was her language.

Jim walked into the shop. "Hey Lando, let me talk to you."

"What's the deal, my good friend?"

"I have two things. First, Jean thinks somebody is stealing money, so he wants everybody to start doing blind drops only."

"Okay. And what's the second?"

"I got some extra money for you if you wanna stay until close tonight."

"Nope, you know I would, but I have to go to a seminar about money and have to get the hell out of here today."

"Thanks anyway."

"Denada."

Soon as work was done, I went to pick up Rico, because he didn't stay too far away. I was involved in a business called Prepaid Legal and Rico was my number one producer. We had been building a team for years and since we both read self-help books and motivated each other to do better, he was the perfect person to take.

"What's up, boss man? I looked up Les Brown and I can't wait to hear what he is about," Rico said as he got in the car.

"Yep, same here. He's supposed to be one of the best out there and we get to see him for free."

"I brought some CDs and a little bit of motivation to get us hyped." As I spoke Rico pulled out a blunt. "And that's what you call motivation?"

"Yep, for me." He shrugged like it was no big deal.

"Yo' dumb ass better not pass out while we there."

The event was held at the Novi Emagine theater. I introduced myself and Rico to the receptionist.

"Okay, do you guys have your business cards?"

"Yes, we do."

We walked into the theater and the place was 100% full. Since our asses were late, we ended up sitting on the steps. He was talking and telling the story about his life as we took copious notes. His story of how he was raised by a single mother with all odds against him was impeccable. Now he spoke all over the country and people paid him heftily to do it. He talked about the plans he had to help lots of kids in Chicago. One thing that caught my attention was when he broke down the percentage of how people pay more attention to what a person is saying depending on what color suit they wore. He wore an average navy blue suit, with a white shirt, and red tie, looking very presidential. As we were leaving I saw some of my PrePaid Legal family and started asking how each other been doing and talking about how good it was to be able to see Les Brown. I just loved going to seminars, because they were full of nothing but positive, confident people giving good energy and trying to move forward in life.

"Man, I really appreciate you taking me. The event was out cold," Rico said as we pulled up to his house.

"It's time to go hard. I'm tired of being broke and we got what it takes, so hit me up tomorrow and let's get it Young Gunz style."

"Okay, I'll hit you up."

Young Gunz was our team slogan.

My next stop was mom's house. Soon as I walked in, she demanded me to grab my mail. "I think something important came in for you. I think it's from the IRS. You need to read it as soon as possible."

"Okay, mom, I will."

"Have you been eating right? Because I know your darn daddy just go out to eat and never wants anything home cooked. How has he been doing? I hope he is doing okay. Losing your sight overnight it's a hard thing to swallow, you know."

"Yeah, he is hanging in there."

I went to my room, sat down, and started texting a few females, since I'd been busy lately. I'd gotten an email on my phone. Another thanks, but no thanks email from three different airlines.

"Fuck!" I said out loud in frustration.

My little sister Mary walked into the room saying, "What's wrong with you?"

"I keep on getting denied from these airlines."

"Oh, I was just going to ask you how was your interview," she said and laughed.

I just needed to grab some clothes from mom's. "Have you been doing okay?"

"Yeah, I have been cool. Are you staying over here tonight?"

"I doubt it. You know the longer I stay around, the more

chores mom can think of for me to do. So let me get my sleepy ass up and get out of here."

"Ha-ha. Whatever, brother, keep on trying and you will become America's next top flight attendant one day," she replied sarcastically.

Driving back, I put in a Les brown CD that I purchased from his seminar, trying to keep myself motivated. I walked in the house doing my routine "Hey dad" roar to see if he was home, but that time he wasn't. The phone rang as I got settled in.

"Where you at, Lando?" were Keke's first words as I answered her call.

"Just walking into dad's crib wondering where his ass is at."

"You know grandma in the hospital?"

"What?! How did she end up in the hospital? What happened?"

"Aunt Christ came in the house and she was on the floor again and wasn't trying to eat."

"Damn, is she okay?"

"Yeah, they have her at Annapolis now 'bout to switch her to somewhere else."

"What the hell! Ain't nobody telling me shit!" I screamed in frustration. What the hell was going on with my family? It troubled me immensely that two of the key people in my life were struggling with their health. In a way I felt helpless, wanting to do something, but not knowing how to help them. I let out a heavy sigh.

"I don't know. They acting crazy around here."

"Well, I'm 'bout to get some sleep, Keke. Just keep me updated."

∼

THE NEXT DAY as I walked in the airport, I started thinking about the seminar with Les Brown. *He always wears a blue suit, white shirt, and red tie,* I pondered on that and some of the other motivational points he gave us. I looked down the terminal and I saw a black man with a blue suit, white shirt, and red tie walking right towards me. I thought, *That looks just like Les Brown.*

That's when he walked straight up to me with the most genuine smile. "Hey, how are you?" he greeted me in his very distinguished, deep voice.

"Hey, Mr. Brown! I swear on everything, I was just thinking of you! I went to your seminar the other day!"

"I know you did. I saw you there. I see a lot of potential in you. When are you going to start working for yourself?" he asked me, looking me dead in the eyes.

"Mr. Brown, do you care if we walk and talk?" I asked. We were originally headed in opposite directions, but I wanted to pick his brain and wasn't about to let this opportunity of a lifetime pass me by.

"No problem, come on," he said as we started walking.

"So what do you do right now?" he asked.

"Well, I'm a manager of a few coffee shops and some bars in here. I've also been doing Prepaid Legal for a few years."

"Wow, I'm real familiar with Prepaid Legal. Do you know Katrina Ferguson?"

"Yeah! That's my girl! She is a six-figure ring earner and a millionaire club member, out of the Maryland area."

"Yeah, I trained her. And was down at one of her team events in February."

"Wow, that's awesome! What are the odds of that?"

"Lando, I'm going to be working with some youth in the near future, and you're a smart young man. I could use your help."

"Man, I would *love* to help you out."

"Okay, take down my email. Lando, it was a pleasure meeting you."

"Okay, talk to you soon, Mr. Brown."

I was stoked! I've read books on the power of the mind and

had been learning how to put that into practice. To see it in action was blowing my mind. *Are you kidding me?! Did the renowned Les Brown really just ask me to help him with a project?* I felt like the unpopular, nerdy girl in high school who had been asked to the prom by the popular football player. That was just the pick-me-up I needed. It was rare to meet someone whose presence alone can shift my mood for the better. That's the type of dude this man was.

I ran into the coffee shop. "Ali! I just met Les Brown!"

"Um, Lando, who the hell is that?" he said, taking a bite of something he'd probably gotten from the coffee shop.

"Well, motherfucker, only one of the utmost successful speakers in the world. Remember when I said the other day I had to leave early to go to a seminar?"

"Yeah."

"Well, that's who I went to see! I saw him walking in the airport."

"Did you talk to him?"

"Hell yeah! He told me he might need my help in Chicago in a few months, because he's setting up shop out there."

"Damn, bro! That's what's up!" he responded, half-way excited while he continued eating.

When I arrived home, dad and Aunt Chris had brand new furniture in the house and no pool table.

"Whoa, what happened here?"

"You like it, son?"

"I love it! This is the same one we picked out, isn't it?"

"Yep, it is! Hey Lake," my auntie said.

"Hey, auntie. How are you doing?"

"I'm doing okay. How you making it?"

"The other day I went to a seminar because one of the top motivational speakers was coming into town. Why am I at the airport today thinking about him and the man walks right up to me?"

"Shut the noise!" she yelled with the kind of excitement I had been looking for from Ali's ass.

"So who was he? What's his name?" she asked with a tone that said 'come on with the goods!'

"Les Brown."

"Yeah, I have a few of his books."

"You even know about him, Chris?" dad said with a look of surprise on his face.

"Yeah, he is big time. Well, I still got some running to do. Talk to y'all soon."

"Aye son, I was thinking since you keep on getting turned down for the airlines, there must be some information you don't have. When I was working at Ford, and there were no blacks in the tool and die section, me and my boy Jimmy started hanging with all the white people, because we were wondering how they kept on getting hired and no blacks weren't. Come to find out they all had a cheat sheet going around for $60 and a guy let us get in on it. Man, we were the first black people in that division making crazy money. So what I'm trying to tell you is that this is like the fraternity thing you're in. It's like a secret society. You need a cheat sheet to get in."

That had never crossed my mind. Amazed with disbelief, I replied, "You think so, dad?"

"Man, I know so. Get on your computer thing and you should be able to find something."

"Okay, I will check, but I doubt it will have anything." After he said that, I sat on our new pimped out red and cream couch and got on Google, going hard looking for every possible site and source about flight attendants. Eventually, I found a forum on Indeed.

When I typed in 'flight attendants' a listing of all the airlines showed up, along with a series of posts from people talking about the interview process and other airline topics pertaining to work. I stayed up all night reading the forums learning about each and every airline imaginable. In the morning I told dad about the site and had to give credit where it was due.

"See, son, I told you! Just keep looking, and you will find something."

Sitting down on the couch I got a call from Kerry, my friend I'd met in Minnesota, who was also on a journey to become a flight attendant. "Hey Lando, boo boo. How are you?"

"I'm doing good, babe. What's the deal?"

"I never heard back from Miracle's asses, but have you heard that Miracle is having an open house in Detroit coming up?"

"No, but I was on some site called Indeed and lots of people were on there talking about who is hiring and stuff. They were also talking about the steps they were taking during their interviews."

She cut me off, saying, "Lando, hold on." She clicked back over. "Yeah, I'm sorry. Wait. Oh my god, hold on again. Yeah, my daughter's father is calling me acting crazy, so I'm about to call you right back, go on their site, and put in an app."

"Okay, talk to you later." We hung up.

"Aye dad, I'm about to go to the library and put in an application. What you about to do?"

"Chris is about to pick me up and go run some errands. Just hit me up later."

"Okay."

I walked into the silent library, conversed with the front desk clerk, and started filling out the application for Miracle Airlines. Come to find out the interview would be tomorrow. Good thing she called me, because I had no idea Maybe it was some type of a sign. Putting in the applications, I had no idea what I was getting myself into, but I was ready for the adventure.

10

*I*n the world we live in today, just about whatever you need to know is in a book. Want to learn Spanish? Go to the library and get a free book that will teach you. Pipes busted? Then go to Home Depot and purchase Plumbing For Dummies. Because of this, I feel Americans are lazy as hell. We're one of the only countries that feels we should know English and that's about it. We are so used to living in the 'Land of Opportunity,' but never start any businesses or learn how to get grants. I appreciate people that take time out of their busy lives to write books like these, self-help or anything that's informative to the masses willing to teach people how to better themselves. Challenge yourself to start reading one positive, informative book a month and be blessed.

∼

I walked up to the door and they were very organized with two people at a table, both in uniform. Upon checking in, we were asked which base we preferred. The options were: ATL (Atlanta), DTW (Detroit), or MSY (New Orleans).

As I sat down, I met a guy named Eddie B from Chicago, and

he was really cool as we exchanged jokes. Miracle Airline's setup was basically the same as Miracle's with how they did the company overview. This open house just had a lot more people that showed up and this did not require an arm stretch drill to enter the kingdom of heaven. They explained the company, as well as the pros versus cons about being a FA. As I paid attention to the details, I noticed they surely knew how to eliminate the weak people as soon as possible.

"If you want time with your family, then this is not the job for you. If you want to become rich, then this is not the job for you."

They basically bashed the airline business, but they couldn't fool me. Because if it was so darn bad, then why the hell were they here? The recruiter instructed everybody to go up front and tell them something unique about themselves.

"Don't say you love to travel, and you're a people person, we already know that," said the recruiter. She called up Bella Smith first.

"Hey everybody, I'm Bella Smith, and I just want this job and opportunity so bad. I drove all the way from California to have this opportunity, so that tells you I love to travel."

The next person. "I love to travel."

Next person. "Yeah, I know you said don't say it, but it's true because I love to travel."

I was just sitting here, laughing at these dumb fools that had no idea that there is no way they were getting the job, if they couldn't even pay simple attention to what the recruiter had just told them.

"Next is Young!" Miss Young was a black chick in her early to mid twenties, decent slim body, with a nappy weave.

"Hey, everybody! I'm excited to be here. I feel I'm a very unique person, so I came up with five different things that makes me unique. 1. I never met a Juanika Young before, so that makes me one of a kind. 2. I can sing."

The recruiter quickly interrupted and yelled out, "please don't demonstrate," as we all laughed.

She continued. "3. I always wanted to pose for Playboy and do nudes."

"Juanika!" The male recruiter yelled, "Thank you. Thank you, expedite the process, thanks."

I looked at Eddie and whispered, "Did this bitch just say 'pose for Playboy?'"

Ed had a very deep voice that reminded me of the tall God from the movie 300 Xerxes. "Oh noooo...Naw, I know this heifer didn't."

I was up next. Everything slowed down. *Damn, I'm next.* I said to myself as I stood up. *Shit!!!! Something unique about myself, umm Lando, it would have been smart if you thought of something before you had to walk up here, fucking dumb ass. Just don't say porn or whatever ol' girl said.* I finally make it to the front.

"Hello, everybody I'm Orlando and I live a few minutes away from the airport. What is unique about me is that I'm a very outgoing person who loves to help people. Most of my friends say I'm an honest person, and also at my job I'm a hard worker and..."

"Thank you. Okay, ladies and gentlemen, what we are going to do is take an hour break and review all of your applications. Then around noon we will post a list of the people we want to talk with more. Thanks everybody for coming."

In the hall, Eddie B walked up. "Man, I hope I get it. I have to do this long drive all the way back home, either happy or mad."

"How long was the drive?"

"A little bit over 4 hours," he responded. "How far you stay from here?"

"About 10 minutes." I smiled.

Eddie was a black, bald headed, and very well dressed brother. At his previous place of employment, he ran a bank. So that's probably why he was in a nice suit. When I went to the bathroom and looked at my suit in the mirror, I realized how damn old and sad it looked. It was a nice black Sean Jean blazer with purple on the inside. My problem was the color had started to fade, as if it had been washed way too many times.

"They just posted the names!" A random white girl yelled, and everybody rushed over to the door. I saw Eddie with his head down as I walked up and assumed he didn't get it.

"Nope, I didn't get it," he said as he stared at the paper.

"Damn. I don't see mine either," I told him. I had a flashback of me trying out for the basketball team in my freshmen and sophomore years of high school. "Wow, we both didn't get it, huh?" I said in disappointment.

"Nope, but I'm about to head back to Chicago. I will see you around," Eddie said as we exchange our goodbyes.

I went home, pissed this time, thinking to myself *Lando, you are better than that. There is a way to get hired. There is a way, just figure it out.*

11

"Master P, what's good brother?" I said, answering Percy's phone call.

"What's the deal, boy?"

"Just at the crib thinking, I don't know why it's so hard to become a flight attendant. Wonder if it's because I'm straight! I don't know even one straight male flight attendant," I said answering myself. Not that I'm a homophobe, but it did make me wonder if there was some sort of bias operating I wasn't aware of. "How many do you know?" I asked in a rhetorical way, already knowing the answer.

"Well, brother, together we done achieved way harder stuff than this. Remember when Carlton and Jimmy wouldn't give us the connection to get clothes overseas and you went harder than ever to find us a supplier? Once you had that done, we took the game over and was selling more clothes than retail stores."

"You're right man."

"Nigga, I know I'm right!" he replied, yelling through the phone. "We gone be rich if you keep going hard, and then invest in the stuff with me."

"Oh boy! Thank you, sir, my signal is fading," I yelled, trying to rush him off the phone. Percy always had something up his sleeve, but I just wasn't in the mood for it. I hung up and started looking for more airlines that were hiring. The bulk of my search was really trying to find a way to get hired.

I wrote on the forum venting, *Why is it so hard for me to get hired for any airlines? I'm a young, black, heterosexual male and it just seems like nobody wants to hire me since I'm not gay or white.*

A guy responded, 'Lando, it's not that you're black or straight that you won't get the job. But the thing I can help you with is a book that taught me every reason why I got denied at my first four interviews. After I got this information, I was hired at my next four. It's *that* good. *The Essential Guide to Becoming a Flight Attendant.*'

"Thanks, I'm going to look into getting it."

Another person replied and said, "I got the book and it did not help at all! I don't recommend it. I studied religiously and it still didn't help me. So just do what you gotta do."

"Aye, Lando!"

"What's up, dad?"

"Well, this what we need to do, since you want to really get this thing moving. We have to clean up your image by getting you a clean, new suit, and work on some things."

"I appreciate it. I was on the forums, and a guy told me about a book that I needed to get. It helped him a lot to start getting hired."

"*Man*, I have been trying to tell you! It's a cheat sheet you need! That stuff, it's like a fraternity. We can go to a bookstore tomorrow and check it out."

I went downstairs and put on some Jim Rohn and laid down so I could clear my mind. *"To become the best, you have to work harder than your competition. You have to wake up in the morning knowing you cannot be defeated, success is yours."*

"Hey, dad. Are you about ready?" I yelled up the stairs, so he could start getting dressed and we could go get the book.

"Let's go get something to eat first," he stated.

Walking out the door, we ran into Mrs. Jones getting her mail. "Hey, Ocie. How are you and those blind ass eyes of yours doing?"

We both start laughing. "I just got a date with Dr. Johnson at U of M, the one you referred me to."

"Oh, thank the Lord, I was able to help. So I'm going to pray for you."

Walking away, dad turned to me and said, "Yep, Dr. Johnson called and gave me a date to get the surgery done."

"Wow, that's great. What's the date?"

"The 26th."

"That's a blessing! We have to pray and get it done now."

"Yeah, I hope so. You get nervous when you got to do stuff like this, you know."

"Yeah, I feel you. But what other options do you have?" I responded, trying to give him confidence, since he didn't have many other choices.

We first went to a coney island, a local dine-in food chain that's big in Detroit. Many stay open 24 hours. They're known for their coney hot dogs. I guided dad into the restaurant, because I noticed his eyes had been getting worse lately. Dad was popular, it was hard to go anywhere without him being noticed. One of his friends greeted him, as we sat down,

"How you doing, old man?" Dad walked right past him.

"Aye dad, he is talking to you," I said, since I saw he didn't notice the guy reached out to shake his hand.

"Hey! Who is this?"

"What!" His friend said feeling disrespected, because he didn't know dad's eyes were bad.

"Man, my eyes done went bad with my retinas, so I can"t see as well."

"Oh man, Ocie! I'm sorry to hear that, this Wayne."

"Hey Wayne. How Dorothy been doing?"

"You know we got a divorce."

"No, I didn't know. I'm sorry to hear that."

He got closer to dad as if he was going to tell a secret. "I won't be doing too bad when you bring one of those bad woman you be having over."

"Aye, well I'd love to see how you feel when I bring *two*." They both started laughing.

"Alright, Ocie, it was good to see you."

We sat down and I said, "Dad, your eyes getting that bad?"

"Man, I'm telling you it's tough to have to deal with this. I have known him for years. Now the real deal is that his wife been cheating for years, and we all have been trying to tell his dumb self to leave her alone, but he didn't wanna listen to anybody. But, son, every man gotta learn from his own mistakes."

Dad grabbed a menu and asked, "Have you heard from Amanda? Or even Gina for that matter? She *is* the reason why you lost Amanda."

"Naw, not really. But the way I look at it, we broke up. And you know I wasn't the best boyfriend, but I sure wasn't nowhere close to the worst. Once you're not in a relationship with the person, you realize how good they were compared to everybody else. For example, we break up, right? Now it's gonna take her a few months to mourn and so on, but since she is good looking and have friends they're going to attempt to set her up on dates. On date number one, he is a cool guy, but since she is a church-going person she finds out he's atheist."

"You already know that's not going to work," he responded.

"I know right. Guy number two wants nothing but some ass and makes it too obvious by him trying all the time. And you know that's a turn off to most woman because he is thirsty. Then guy number three is verbally abusive and will sooner or later start whooping her ass right," we both laugh.

"Man, you're learning day by day. You just about right. Now

let me tell you something that my uncle told me. Women are like rabbits, if you look outside you will see the rabbit sitting by the tree, and if you go outside and chase it then it's going to run and you won't catch it. But after a little while you look outside again and it will be sitting right there back in the same spot. So what I'm trying to tell you, son, is that no matter what you do these women ain't going nowhere. Son, they will always end up back to you. I have been knocking off the same women for the past twenty years, and since you stay with me you see it's true."

"What about when they get married?" I asked.

"They disappear for a few months or years and they still come back. You know Kara is married?"

"She is?"

"Man, I knocked her off a few weeks ago. I'm trying to tell you these women aren't no good."

The waitress walked to the table, interrupting our conversation. "So we're not no good, huh sir?" she said as she puts her hands on her hips. I was dying with laughter.

After breakfast dad wanted to take me to a store called K&G Warehouse to get a suit and dress attire.

"Hey, how you guys doing?"

"I'm doing alright."

"Is Stephanie in today?" dad asked.

"Um, I think she works tomorrow."

"Okay, now what deals do you all have on suits? My son's about to be a flight attendant and if he is flying all over the country, then I need him to start looking as good as his dad does." Laughing, she pointed us in the right direction. As we looked around I saw a nice navy blue suit I liked. "Wow, dad, this is a nice one and it's my size."

"You should be around a 42. What one is that?"

"It's a 42. Now from doing your business on the side you should already have lots of shirts."

"We can go get this one tailored for you next door. Let's head to the front."

"So you're going to be a flight attendant?" the brown-skinned, tall clerk asked as her eyes sparkled, followed with a shy smile.

"Yeah." I responded.

"Oh my god, I always wanted to be one since I was younger. Do you know where you would be based at yet?"

"I'm not sure. I'm trying to go down south somewhere, like Atlanta."

"Yeah, you have to keep me updated so we can travel."

"Alright, I'm Lando."

"And I'm Ocie," dad said with his blind ass.

"Here take down my number and text me so you can have me locked in." She gave us a nice discount on our purchase.

"Well, I might have to pay you back," I said as I pulled out my phone.

"What's your number?"

"Are you going to call me?"

"Yeah, I will, nice meeting you."

Dad and I ran quite a few errands that day. It was fun hanging out with him. We accomplished everything that was on our agenda except getting the book that was the initial focus of our outing.

A few days later the mail came and I had a package. I ripped it open and the there it was. *The Essential Guide to Becoming a Flight Attendant* by Kiki Ward. I had to order the book online because none of the local stores had the correct book. Once I started reading the book, I could see clearly right away where I needed to make some adjustments in my approach. I really couldn't stop reading it. So I called Stacey in excitement wanting to fill her and Kerry in on the mix.

"Hey, what's going on girl?"

"Nothing much. Just came back from this date with a guy, and he is such a lame nigga."

"Why is that?"

"Because we went out to eat and had a little date. Since he lives in Dallas, we decided to meet up in the middle and got a hotel room together."

"Oh shoot! You must have given him some of that crumb cake."

"What the hell? Naw, that's why I'm mad, because we went on a date he thinks he's automatically entitled to some ass."

"Wait a minute, wait a minute! So you're telling me that y'all met up, went on a date, slept in the same bed, and he did not get any pussy?"

"Yep," she replied with confidence. "Well...he just went down on me."

I guess she thinks I was born yesterday, but okay. "If you say so, Booboo. I called you for something else. Have you ever heard of a book called *The Essential Guide to Becoming a Flight Attendant*?"

"Naw, what is it about?"

"It breaks down everything you need to know to get hired. I don't think I would ever get hired without knowing about any of this stuff I'm reading."

She responded with a negative tone. "Man, that stuff doesn't work, Lando! All you have to do is go to the interview and be on point. You will get the job. I have never seen somebody have to read a book to get a job." There was a baby that began to cry in the background. "Hey, let me hit you back. My own boo boo is crying."

"Okay, I'll talk to you later."

∼

"Hey dad, my book came in, and I've been reading this thing all day. The book said go to www.flightattendantcareers.com. That site lists every airline that is currently hiring, what dates, and more.

"I was wondering why you been so quiet today. So who is hiring?"

"A company called Samer Airlines. I'm 'bout to look them up, and see what they're talking about."

"That's crazy that you can go on that computer thing and just about find anything you want," dad said as he sat down on the couch. "You would never think that you could find a book on everything you need to get hired, huh. What are they saying in there?" He was curious about the process and was in an affable mood.

"About little stuff that you wouldn't know, unless you know somebody that's already in the game," I answered as I continued to read. "Like when you go on an interview make sure you wear exactly the airline colors, wear a watch, because it's a required item. It even goes so deep to show you how to update your resume the way they would want to see it. It's *on* now, dad! I been thinking the whole time that you had to be gay to get hired."

"Well, go ahead and keep on studying, Chris about to come pick me up, and we're going to go meet with my attorney and talk about everything we need to get paid."

"Okay, just hit me up."

Over the next few weeks I had completely turned into a ghost. I cracked down on studying everything there was to know about the industry. I learned about all the different airlines. I went and bought me a watch, found some announcements online, and even started to practice those. Every day I was in the library religiously, putting in resumes and when I was at work. I was studying all the flight attendants I came across in the airport.

One day I received a call from the girl I met at Krogers when dad and I were supposed to be out purchasing my book after leaving K&G Warehouse.

"Hey, can you talk?"

"Yeah, what's up?"

"Nothing much, just thinking about you."

"Oh really?"

"Yep, so what're you doing tonight?" she asked.

"I don't know. Nothing really, just chillin'. What about you?"

"Nothing, that's why I was calling you. I'm off and wanted to see if you wanted to do something."

"Yeah, we can go to Buffalo Wild Wings or something and watch the game."

"Okay, boo, that works just call me and let me know when."

It was time to come up for some air. It would be nice to go out for a while and have some fun. I figured I'd look into a few more job related sites online before getting ready for my date with Krogers. Checking on that airline's website, I saw that a company named Smith Air was hiring out of Willow Run. Now the difference with that company was they gave very little information and said something about charter flying, which I had no idea what that meant. I was off work the next day. So I applied to give it a go. Before my date with Krogers, I also looked up Samer Airlines and started reading the forums about the company.

Please!!! Do not come to work for this company it is horrible. They treat their workers like crap and the pay is terrible.

Next post. *I agree with Beth I been here for 4 years and regret every second of it. Blah blah blah.*

Damn. If I knew anything, I surely knew I didn't want to work for a company that the employees didn't even want to work for.

12

*J*got a text message from Keke. *Make sure you go see grandma in the hospital. She is down the street at the Jerry Manor.*

I responded. *Okay, I'll call you when I leave.* I hopped in the car and headed to check on her. On my way there I also stopped at the gas station to purchase grandma some flowers so I could give her something when I arrived.

"Hey, how are you?" asked the receptionist.

"I'm doing great, and you?"

"Not too bad. Who are you here to visit today?" I gave her grandma's name.

"Wow, she has been getting visitors all day," the older lady responded with a smile. "So just go to room 202. It's over to your right hand side before you get to the elevators." I thanked her and walked off in that direction.

"Hey grandma." I slowly opened the door and saw her lying in bed relaxing.

"Hey Lando, how are you?" She greeted me with the biggest smile. It was like a ray of sunshine to me. I love my grandma!

"Not bad. Will be doing better when we get you out of here."

"Boy oh boy, tell me about it." Her voice was weak as she spoke, while also trying to adjust herself in bed and straighten her hair. Grandma was always big about her personal appearance, as well as the appearance of her home. I could tell it was eating her inside to not have her hair done as she lay in the bed.

"How have they been treating you?"

"They have been great. I have a nice nurse, she's young and good-looking," she responded with a smile.

"Gone 'head, grandma." I shook my head, chuckling inside, hoping she wasn't getting ready to play matchmaker. "Have you been eating?"

"No, I just haven't been hungry lately."

"Knock-knock," said a voice I didn't recognize. I turned around to see my future wife dressed in greenish color scrubs. Light-skinned with natural hair and a great smile. *Maybe grandma playing matchmaker wouldn't be so bad!*

"Hey, how are you doing?" she asked.

I looked at her and said, "A lot better since you walked in."

Blushing, she said, "I'm not talking about you, silly. I'm talking about my girl, Mrs. A."

"I'm hanging in there."

"Is this your grandson, Mrs. A.?"

"Yes, it is my handsome grandson." We all laughed.

"Well, handsome grandson, try to get her to eat, because she hasn't been lately."

"Okay, thanks. I will and your name is?"

"Tasha."

"Okay thanks, Tasha."

Right after she left, dad and Aunt Chris walked in. "Hey y'all. How you feel, mama?"

"I'm hanging in there."

Dad came up to me and said, "Man, I think she got a bad nurse, around your age."

"Yeah, I already know. She just came in here, looking all sexy."

"Have you heard back from Krogers?"

"Yes, sir, we are going out tonight to Bdubs."

"You're in there, but watch out. That one seems like the aggressive type."

"I think you're right, because she's the one who got my number and basically *told me* I'm taking *her* out." We laughed.

"Yeah, we will talk later. Alright y'all. See you later, grandma. I'm heading out. See if y'all can get her to eat. The nurse said she hasn't been having a big appetite."

Once I stepped out of the room, I called my brother OC. "What's popping, black man?"

"Making some money. How is grandma doing?" I heard a lot of noise in the background.

"She is doing good, just saying she 'bout ready to get out of there. Go see her when you get some time."

"Okay, what you got up for the day?"

"Going on a date with this chick I met at Krogers."

"Good luck, man. Well, I'll hit you back in a few. When is dad's surgery?"

"In about a week or so. I'll keep you updated," I said hanging up.

Driving home, Krogers called to ask if I was ready for our date.

"Yeah, I will be in a few. Just went to see my grandma and now heading to the crib to get dressed now."

"Okay, don't keep me waiting too long."

At home, I was getting ready in the bathroom. I was in a good mood. I was dancing and singing when Sean called my phone.

"Hello! What you doing besides dancing naked in the bathroom, señor?"

Dying laughing, I responded, "Aye, Papi. You don't know me, so watch yo' mouth. I'm about to go to Bdubs with Krogers."

"Dude, what is her real name?"

"Shit, I really don't know. I locked her in as *S. Krogers*. All I know is it starts with an S."

I heard him laughing through the phone. "So you're telling me you 'bout to go on a date with a chick that you don't even know her name?"

"You are 100% correct, señor."

"Well, excuse me motherfucker. Just hit me up later, turtle man."

I looked down at my phone, and I saw I was confirmed for my interview tomorrow. Good thing it was an afternoon interview, so I had more than enough time to get things situated.

Once I was fully ready I texted Krogers, and told her to meet me there in thirty minutes.

I arrived first, driving dad's truck. She pulled up in a blue 1996 Escort. We hugged and walked into the restaurant. Her hair was short and done nicely. She wore black stretch pants. I saw she had a little gut in the front popping out, but nothing too bad.

"Hey, where would you guys like to be seated?" asked the waiter.

"At a table over by that TV would be great," I said with a smile.

"Oh lord, you one of those sport fans," she said quickly, as if I was about to watch sports the whole date.

"Aye. Sometimes you have to let a man be a man," I responded. "You know right now Carmelo is officially playing with the New York Knicks, and they got Mr. Big shot. Don't get me started, woman. Did you eat today?" I asked, as I pick up the menu.

"Nope, I have been waiting for you. So I'm 'bout to order everything on the menu." She smirked.

"Aye, I'm a motherfucking boss! You can order this whole menu, and I got you, baby," I said, as I slapped down the menu. I couldn't stay serious longer than two seconds. Laughing, I said, "I almost sounded like a boss right there. Please don't, because I only brought $5 and we gotta make this stretch tonight."

"Just shut up, Lando!"

So as we were eating and talking, Carlton called me back to back. I decided to answer, just in case it was something serious.

"Hello!"

"It's ya boy! Where you at?"

"At Bdubs with this hot babe," I said loud enough for her to hear me.

"Which one?"

"The one on the Ave in Dearborn."

"Me and Carlos 'bout to stop up there," he said, as if they were right around the corner.

"Whoa, whoa. You don't know me like that, señor. Your boy working on a mission."

He laughed. "You so nasty!"

"You already know.

"Just hit me up when you finish. Later."

I hung up and said to Krogers, "So basically, I have been single for a while now. It kinda sucks that I'm the nucleus of all my friends. Whenever I'm on a date or trying to just be alone with my girl, I have a random friend popping up. So I sure as hell wasn't about to let Carlton come here and fuck something up."

"What you 'bout to do?" Krogers said with a concerned look on her face. I wasn't sure if she was inviting me over or not.

"You," I said quickly.

"Oh really." She smiled. "Do you want company?"

"Well, it depends on who it is."

"I'll follow you home, Lando."

Once I was in my car, I looked back and saw her in the Ford, checking her makeup in her visor's mirror. I snuck a call to dad to update him on the situation at hand. "Hey, pops. What's up?"

"Nothing much. How the date go?"

"Great. Just leaving BWild Wings with Krogers. She's about to come through. Are you at the crib?"

"Yeah, I'm here. I'll clean it up for you."

"Okay, see you in a minute, pops. Aye, dad?"

"Yeah, what's up?"

"Man, I still don't know her name since we keep calling her Krogers. Find out for me when we get there."

He agreed and laughed at me. Many parents don't talk to their kids like that, but me and dad were different, because we had no problem with talking about sex, money, cars, and hoes.

"Pump pump!" I yelled as I walked into the clean house.

"Hey," dad said, as he was closing the refrigerator.

"You already met my dad," I said as I walked her into our place.

"Hey, nice to see you again," she said, sticking out her hand.

"What's your name again?" he asked.

"Shamecia."

Yes! Now I know her name. Damn you my clutch, dad!

"I love this house! Wow, the furniture is just great!"

"He thinks the old man doesn't have taste anymore. But I still think I can do something." They laughed, and he walked away into his bedroom.

"Do you want something to drink?" I asked.

"Um, what do you have?"

"We have red wine, white wine, liquor, water, juice. It all depends on what you're in the mood for."

"Surprise me." As I poured her some wine, she yelled, "Don't be putting nothing in my drink!"

"Oh, never that!"

"Do you have any movies we can watch?"

"Yeah. Come on downstairs. Let me show you what I have."

The next morning, I walked her out and gave her a kiss on the cheek. "Call or text me when you make it home."

"Hey there, young man! How are you and your daddy doing?" I heard someone speaking in a distinctive, squeaky voice.

"We are doing great, Mrs. Jones."

"Okay, I'm watching you, young man," she replied as she craned her neck to look at Shamecia's car.

I walked back into the house and the first thing dad said, "Did ya girl stay the night?"

"Yes, she did."

"Oh, sounds like you mighta got *lucky*."

"And lucky is what I got, baby!"

"Good ole Krogers done gave you some play, huh," he replied, smiling.

"Yes, sir, but even better. I have an interview today in Willow Run later on. So let me get everything ready."

Now this interview was the most unique one by far, because it was to work for a charter airline. I completely fell in love with this company and here's why. Once I walked in there was a sign-in sheet. On the sheet it said 'Name to the left and do you have a passport to the right.' I didn't have a passport and ALL names in front of mine checked Yes. *Fuck Me!* I thought from the get go. I knew I didn't have a shot now, but hell might as well see what they had to offer, since I was already there.

Since I didn't get hired, I'm going to break down how everything went. A charter airline can transport sports teams, politicians, one recruiter even said they transported Bush before. Every year they chartered The Red Wings, the Michigan State basketball team and a few other colleges. Some even did military passengers only, but this airline didn't and I was happy they didn't, because I was not a fan of smelly, horny military guys on one plane.

Now with charters, they fly whoever hires them. The flight

attendants with this airline started off at about $40 an hour. It sounded like a lot, but the work was seasonal. Once I heard the full details, all I could think about was meeting all the athletes and having the right connections with the right people.

The recruiters were very firm and said, "I want everyone to come up and tell us something about themselves and why you would be great for this job. But if you don't have a passport then you might as well not even come up."

Damn. I just can't catch a fucking break, I thought to myself.

The guy asked who wanted to go first and hell since I was a dead man walking anyway…why not. I walked up there and did a sweet-ass presentation, since there was no pressure. Needless to say I didn't get hired, but one good thing about going here was that I knew I needed a passport ASAP, because that was embarrassing.

On a good note, I heard from AirStar Airline and they wanted me to come to an open house in Chicago the following Thursday. When I told dad he was excited, but wanted to know how was I going to get there.

"Yeah, I was thinking about driving Keke's car, but I'm not sure yet."

"Well, you got the outfit, now we have to see what you can do."

I updated my resume the correct way. Thanks to Kiki Ward, it was impressive, an obvious difference from the one I started with. I went over to grandma's. I was in the basement reviewing all the interview questions I could find when my sister Keke walked downstairs, ran over and pounced on me.

"Get yo' fat ass off me!"

"I heard you got an interview! Now tell me how their domestic partner benefits work."

"I haven't been yet, so I don't know."

"Hopefully, as soon as you get this job, we are going to be traveling all over the world."

"Yeah man, I can't wait," I responded, not really paying her crazy self any attention.

"So you need to use my car?"

"Yeah, I'm just going to make that long drive out there and make it happen."

"What day is it?"

"Thursday."

"Now I got to look up this AirStar and see if they're big time," she said excitedly.

"Okay, I'll hit you up and switch cars when I'm ready to head out."

Since my sister had gotten me hyped up and excited I went home and got back into study mode, so I could be ready for this interview. My phone rang and it was Stacey, telling me she had been invited to Chicago for an interview also.

"That's what's up. I got the same thing."

"Are you going to go?"

"Hell yeah. I'm going to drive. So are you going to fly in?"

"Yeah, if I can take that day off. Are you getting a hotel?"

"I'm not sure. I might just drive down and do everything that day and leave, but let me know if you want to share one."

"So you can try to hit on me at night?"

"Ha-ha. Nobody is thinking 'bout that, Little Booty."

"I don't have no little ass! So watch yo mouth!" she said as if she was offended that I called her ass little.

"I'll call you back. Bye."

Dad walked in from the back and said, "I haven't seen you go this hard since you and yo boy Slim was running track back in the day. Y'all hair was nappy and was looking like them boys from the movie Cool Running." He laughed at his own joke.

"You are crazy, but yeah, I'm working on getting my 'flight attendant' voice. Dad, after reading this book most of the interviews I have been to, I wouldn't have even hired myself, when I think about it. I wasn't prepared, was nervous, and had on that busted suit. It's rough out here," I said laughing at myself.

"Well, this what you need to do, I got a recorder and what you can start doing is recording your voice and practice your speech. Just keep on playing it and after a while you will have it down pat. Yeah, you're right about that. Have you heard from any of your girls tonight?" I asked.

"Yeah, Skinny mini says she wants to come through and get some loot."

"She needs some money?" I said curiously.

"No," he said, and paused for a second, showing he was ready to elaborate more.

"Well, she needs money, but she's got to work for it."

"Don't she have a man at home?"

"They all have a man at home. They ain't no good. I'm trying to tell you something!"

"Wow, I see now. You're a funny old man."

"Do you work tomorrow?"

"Yep, so I'm 'bout to get some sleep, because Jim wants me to do a double tomorrow."

"Alright, I'll let you know after she leaves."

I went downstairs to do a quick workout, then put on some Jim Rohn, and went to sleep.

I walked into work and do my routine hand shake with Ali. Derrick was standing there watching and said, "Hey, do you know what today is?"

"Yeah boy! Come over here and give me some love! Happy Birthday! What're your plans for the big day? You're eighteen now, player!"

"I need to see if Dawn will let me bum a cigarette off of her, so I can smoke for the first time."

"Lando, please tell him that it is stupid to be smoking," Jamie said.

"Well, yeah it's stupid, but it's his birthday so he can try it.

Why not, you only live once." To Derrick I said, "Okay, this is the deal. Promise me you will destroy Michigan when you get up there, give me your tickets to the football games, and I will get you a cigarette. Lunch is on me today."

I usually gave Derrick a hard time, since he was like an annoying younger brother, but I was proud of the young man he was and I knew he had a bright future.

After doing my daily routine of making sure the workers had the correct amount of money in the back, I got Kunta to help me grab some of the trash. On trash runs we went through 'the bat cave,' as we liked to call it. It was like a random underground route that most people didn't know about, so we kept that route a hush to most employees, so people wouldn't mess it up.

Kunta's real name was Jerry. He was an educated white guy in his 30s. A 100% hard worker, who wouldn't show up late, and could do it all. It seemed there was always that one worker that's been on the job forever, trained everybody, but never became a manager. Here that's Jerry. And to be honest, he settled, but that's another story. So his nickname was Kunta referring to Kunta Kinte because the job whooped his ass.

On our way to the dumpster listening to him complain about the married life and so on, Brown called me. "Brown, what's the deal?"

"Lando, are you here, at work?"

"Yep, I'm in the bat cave now, pissed off because I'm working for Jim and he has this place all messed up. I can tell the trash hasn't been taken out for days. He knows I'm the only one with a blue badge."

"Hold on, they gave you a blue badge?" she responded in shock. "See, that's that crap I'm talking about, but anyway I gotta talk to you. They're up here lying on me."

"I'm 'bout to go upstairs, so I'll be there in a few."

I walked into one of our shops upstairs and saw that Moe was working. "Aye, what's up, my brother?"

"Lando, guess what?"

"What?"

"Fuck this place!"

"Whoa there, sir. I'm going to need you to calm the hell down."

"Lando, I'm pissed. I been working my butt off so much today I think I done pissed on myself by now and the receipt paper's not working."

"I don't need you to quit until I quit first, and the receipt paper is down there." I grabbed the paper for him, since he was too lazy to look under the cash register.

"Where are you going to go if you leave?"

"It's not if but when, my friend. I been interviewing to become a flight attendant. I have an interview coming up, but don't say nothing to anybody."

"Man, good for you. I got one with Bank of America, but don't say nothing either, because it's not a for sure thing yet."

A gorgeous woman walked in the store. "Atalayaha," Moe said in Arabic. "Wow. Hey ma'am, how are you doing today?"

"I'm doing great, but feel old after somebody calls me a ma'am," she said responding to Moe as we all laughed.

"I wanted to say gorgeous, but that came out. I'm sorry," he replied with his chunky self.

"Thanks, you're sweet." After taking her order he told me he would be back since he hadn't been to the bathroom in forever. Now the difference between the main coffee shop downstairs and the two upstairs was usually only one person worked the two that were upstairs inside of the terminal, because they were so small most of the times the person working didn't need help. Now the con about being alone was there is no bathroom in the shop, so if the worker needed a break, another worker had to relieve them. I was working my butt off making a few drinks and after I swept the floor, he finally walked back in after the longest piss break I have ever seen in my life.

"Okay, Moe, I gotta run."

"Okay thanks, brother."

I walked over to the Caliente and saw Brown messing with the pizza.

"Hey Lando," she said as she waved.

"What's up, Brown? How you like being the pizza lady?"

"Man, I hate this shit. Ever since I got you in here they only let us work one week together. I need to get out of here like asap."

"Brown…you have a *degree* and doing the same job as me. If you don't start applying yourself you know they aren't going to ever pay you what you're worth," I said angrily, since I love her and she is a close friend. I had to tell her the truth. Jasmine walked over and asked if it was cool for her to go on break.

"Hey, baby, where you been hiding at all my life," I said to Brown's sexy, caramel-skinned co-worker Jasmine.

"Shut up, Lando," she replied, smiling.

"So, Lando, they're trying to fire my ass!" Brown yelled with a worried expression.

"How you figure?"

"Because Nick's girly self called me yesterday and said somebody sent him a picture of my food and it was old and not safe. Now how the hell is it old and not safe if we change it every five damn minutes? But Lando, I'm hungry. Do you want something?" she said as she looked at their food.

"Naw, I don't want no old and not safe food," I responded jokingly. "But I have another interview coming up to be a flight attendant."

"What! Another one, you never told me how the one you flew to went. You seriously would leave?" she asked as if I was joking.

"Hell yeah, this job has been just a temporary stepping stone to get me to the next level. But I gotta get back before everybody starts going crazy in this bitch and Jean sends the dogs on me."

I made it downstairs and Jennifer said, "Jean's been calling for you."

"Well, what did he want?"

"I'm not sure, but he sounded mad that you were not here."

I walked in the office and the phone started ringing.

"Lando! You were gone for the last thirty minutes. I don't pay you to just walk around and do nothing," Jean yelled into the phone.

"Man, I have been down here counting drawers, taking out trash, giving people breaks. I been working hard man."

"I hear you, but I prefer to see it and you have been off the cameras, probably over there with Brittany, so I'm watching. Stay working hard, Lando."

Jennifer walked in. "Lando, since you love me so much can you massage my back, please?"

"Okay, I got you once I get finished." I walked in the bar and rubbed her back as we watch the Red Wings play.

"I want to be a flight attendant," I blurted out of the blue.

"What? That's random," she responded, shocked.

"I don't know if I have ever seen a straight flight attendant before. I just guess it's very rare."

An older white gentleman walked into the bar.

"Hey, how you doing, sir?" I greeted.

"I'm doing well and would be doing better if I could get a massage like that." He pointed towards us as we all started laughing. "But all I need is some nachos. Do you have crew member discounts?"

"Yes, sir, are you a pilot?"

"No, I'm a flight attendant."

"What? I have been trying to become a flight attendant for a while. I actually have an interview in two days."

The gentlemen was bald and was wearing regular clothes, but he didn't seem gay. Jennifer looked and said, "We were just talking about how he wants to become one, two seconds ago."

"My name is Dan," he said as he stuck out his hand.

"I'm Lando. It's a pleasure, Dan. Do you have time to talk?"

"Yeah, I'm waiting for my wife to pick me up." *Did he say wife? What?!*

"So this is the deal, I have been working on getting hired left and right, and it seems like being a young, heterosexual male, it's impossible to become one."

In a perfectly soothing voice he said, "It's not an easy job, Lando, but what I can tell you is that depending on how hard you work, shows up in your interview. If you go to that interview looking sharp from head to toe, and know your stuff, then they can't touch you. Just keep trying and sooner or later somebody will hire you. It took me three times before I got hired by United, and with this job I found my wife and we travel the world everywhere together."

So Dan and I sat and talked for about an hour straight. I could care less about Jean, since I was getting hired somewhere else in two days anyway. He was very inspirational, and his last words were, "Lando, you and I will probably never meet again, but with me sitting here and talking with you I know you will make it. Good luck and see you in the friendly skies." As he reached for his wallet, I stopped him saying, "This meal is on me, Dan, I appreciate it." He smiled, gave Jennifer a tip, and walked away.

Jennifer looked at me and said, "Wow, what are the odds of that? He is like your angel. He sat here and talked with you and answered all your questions. I'm amazed."

The thing I loved about Jennifer, besides her attractiveness, and that amazing ass she has, especially for a white girl, was her positive, optimistic personality.

As I drove home I thought about everything that just happened. I thanked God and gave myself a pep talk. My phone vibrated and it was a text from Krogers. "Hey, I need a favor!"

"What's up?"

"I need to borrow $300 'til Friday, because I'm 'bout to buy a new car."

I laughed out loud and said, "Woman, I don't have $300 for you to borrow."

DAD and my cousin Cain were watching a basketball game, conversing while Cain was having a beer. "What's up, Lando Lake!" dad yelled.

"Finally getting off work. How y'all making it?"

"You got it, because I heard you trying to get in that air," Cain replied.

"Yeah man, it was a blessing today at work." I filled them in on the miracle I'd gotten.

"Wow, thank God. Man, that was right on time, huh?" Cain responded.

"You know that Cain's ex-wife is a flight attendant?" dad stated.

"What! She is?" I responded, shocked.

"Yeah, she has been with... I'm not sure which airline, but I know it's one of the big dogs."

"Yeah, so it's probably United, Delta or American, I think. I'll find out so you can hit her up. I remember when she was going to the interview, and they flew her out to somewhere like Houston and her class started with over fifty of them and she lasted to the end, they only graduated with about fifteen to twenty of them."

"Wow," dad said, "So you're tell me you have to first put in your application, then they have to like it enough to give you an interview. If they like you they send you to training and it's possible you won't even pass that? Now that's a competitive career."

"I'm going to get her number or email and tell her you are going to contact her."

"I would appreciate it, cuz. I'm 'bout to watch this game and go to sleep."

I went downstairs and started watching flight attendant

Youtube videos of trainings and how hard it is to get hired, so I could learn more. I was so intrigued about how competitive the job was and why.

In the morning I woke up hearing OC and dad talking, so I joined them upstairs.

"Duck man done quacked up the stairs," my brother said as he walked over to the couch and pulled out a huge stack of cash and started counting it. "Come help me count this." I sat down and started counting. "How the ladies been treating you?"

"Not too bad. I had an okay one come through the other night. We went to Bdubs then she came back through and I knocked her off."

"Was it that easy?" he replied, as if he was surprised.

"Yep."

"You know it's never that easy."

"Why you say that?"

"Well, little brother, they are always going to want some money or something of value sooner or later. You will see."

"Damn." I said out loud. "Why did she text me last night saying she needs to borrow $300 for her car. Damn, you're right," I said as I laughed. "Here is $3,000 right here, my friend." I slid the money on the table.

"You can count that good without paying attention?" dad asked as he sat down.

"I hope so. That's my job, isn't it?"

Then OC gave me $300 and said, "Here's your money for the month. Good looking out, I appreciate you." I gave him a nod. "Alright dad, I'm 'bout to head out. Good luck on the interview, little brother."

"When you work hard enough, you don't need luck," I responded with a smile.

Keke walked in after as he left. "Hey dad, Hey Lando, you ready to fly them friendly skies?" she yelled out with enthusiasm.

"I researched AirStar and they do let you have a domestic

partner or a enroll a friend. They give us flying benefits on Delta and some other airline."

"I can't wait!"

"It looks like she should be the one going to be a flight attendant with all that info you know," dad said.

"Her fat butt won't be able to fit in that jump seat," I responded laughing.

"Here are my keys. I cleaned the car up for you."

"Okay, here goes the keys to the truck."

"See you later, dad. I'm about to go pick up Kristian," Keke said as she left, heading out to pick up her son.

"One more day, son, and you out of here."

"Yep, I have been thinking about my speech, because when I go to the interviews they usually make you stand up in front of everybody and say why you want to be a flight attendant. The people that usually get picked are the ones who nail this part, they make everybody laugh, and that's a borderline thing to do, because if you say a bad joke then you're screwed."

"So Mr. Lando, why do you want to be a flight attendant?" dad said, putting me on the spot.

"Give me a minute. I know I'm going to give them my past experiences with my jobs and how they would help me with being a FA."

"Let me know when you finish, *baby!*" He yelled as he walked away all hyped up.

It was very sad seeing dad lose his sight, but he always stayed positive. I didn't know how he was doing it, can't say if I was in his shoes if I could stay so optimistic. Soon as I was thinking that he tripped over my shoes walking back to his room. "Man, if you don't move your stuff. It's a death trap living with you."

"My bad!"

I was sitting on the couch with a pad and pen thinking of what to write. 'Speech' is what I wrote at the top of the paper and start writing. I was getting calls, Facebook messages, and texts, but kept on writing.

"Aye you know the trash go out today," dad yelled from his room.

"Okay, I'll take it out." I got up, walked outside, and saw a rabbit standing on a stomp looking at me. Once I started to chase it, as if I were an eight-year-old kid again, it ran away. When I walked back in the house I saw a missed call from Stacey and had a voicemail saying call her back. I called her to ask is she was coming to the event tomorrow. She gave me lots of excuses, like she couldn't get off work, or she just was too tired to fly out here, so whatever. "But Lando, good luck. I hope you get it."

"Okay, I will let you know how it goes. I'm practicing my speech now."

"What the hell you doing a speech for? You suppose to just go up there and knock it down."

Yeah that's easy to say, but it's better when you're prepared. I'm thinking, *Yeah Lando, take advice from the chick who has never been hired.*

"Hit me up tomorrow," I told her.

After long hours of studying, I finally got it. Well, most of it, because I needed a joke if I wanted to stand out from everybody. I needed to say something that would get everybody laughing.

"Pass the ball, man!" dad screamed from the other room.

"Who is playing, dad?" I asked as I walked into his room to check on him and to give him some eye drops.

"Michigan playing some bums and 'bout to get blown out. I don't know why this coach let them shoot all those threes." We talked basketball for a few minutes before dad asked, "So have you heard from anybody today?"

"Stacey just hit me up and said she wasn't coming."

"I could've told you that. She ain't trying to do nothing. How you coming along with your speech?"

"I got my speech down pat, but with my personality I have to do a joke. I was thinking, dad, since I have to drive down there 4:55 minutes and 32 seconds I wanna put that in there at the beginning. So dad, go through a few different scenarios and I'll figure it out."

It finally hit me later on that night while I was taking a shower.

"Yes! I got it!" I was too excited to even get dressed, wearing only a towel I went to dad's room and said, "First off, I would like to thank Rachael and Karen for allowing me to interview here today. Ladies and gentlemen, my name is Orlando, and I have had the pleasure of driving 4:55 minutes and 32 seconds to be here today and I'm still excited. The reason I want to be a flight attendant with AirStar Airlines is because I did my research on the company, took copious notes, and I saw how successful and team oriented the company is as a whole and I could see myself being a part of it.

The reason I know I would be a great, qualified flight attendant is from my previous work experiences. I first started my career off in the cemetery business as a family service counselor and that job taught me how to help people during very emotional times. Next, I went into the health care industry as a CNA and I helped families on a sixteen hour basis with daily needs. Last, and most recently, is my current job. I'm a manager at Detroit Metro Airport of a few coffee shops and bars. That job really...really I just teach people how to get drunk. But overall, I know I will be a great flight attendant. Thank you all for your time. God Bless."

Dad looked at me and said, "Wow! You're gonna knock it out of the ball park. But this is what I would do. When you say the time in the beginning pause and say 4 hours 55 minutes and 32 seconds and at the end you can throw that back in there. And say even though I have to drive 4 hours 55 minutes and 32 seconds to go back home, I will still be excited."

"So just drop the mic and walk off like Jay Z, dad?" I said being goofy, imitating what Jay Z the rapper had done.

"Don't drop no darn mic."

"I'm just playing around. I'm gonna switch it up a little and get some rest." I laughed.

As I was walking away, dad said, "Aye, son, what watch you gonna wear?"

"I have a little cheap one mom got me." I wasn't enthused about it, but I'd learned to be grateful and to work with what I had available. When I can do better, I do.

"Naw, this is your future career. You have to dress like it. Go in my closet and grab that Rolex you bought me for Christmas."

"You still got that?"

"Yeah, you got it for me, didn't you?" he said as if I was dumb as shit for asking such a crazy question.

I walked in the bedroom and opened his jewelry box and saw all types of stuff. "Dang man, you still have all this stuff?"

"I probably got blind for having all of that bling," he said joking around as I shook my head laughing.

"Thanks, dad."

I woke up around 2 a.m. to get all my stuff together. Resume, folders, and so on while thinking I wish I had my passport. As I walked towards the door, I saw the tape recorder on the table, grabbed it, and walked out.

Driving straight down 94 heading west, looking at the directions on my phone, I pulled out the recorder and started. No music, no nothing, just me, the recorder, and the road.

"Ladies and gentlemen, I would like to first thank you Sally Mae and can't forget about Gay Gary. I know I would be a great flight attendant with the company, because... Fuck!"

End and start recording again. "The reason I would be a great flight attendant is because I took copious notes and did my due diligence regarding the company and..."

Stop the tape again. "Why are you trying to use all these big words. Just one, Lando, just one," I said out loud to myself.

For the next two hours I kept going over it and finally got it fully recorded without any mess ups. I was so excited I blasted the radio. Ludacris' *Shake Ya Money Maker* came on as I danced my way to Chicago.

Once I saw the hotel I decided to pull into a gas station, that was also a 7/11, to get a French vanilla coffee, since I had been driving for a few hours straight. The Clarion Hotel, where I was staying, was across the street. I pulled into the parking lot and called dad.

"Hey, what's up, dad?"

"Where you at?" he responded, sounding as if he was sleeping.

"I'm just pulling into the parking lot, grabbed some coffee, shaking off these nerves, getting ready."

"What time does it start?"

"I think in about an hour. Oh my bad, I forgot you know the time goes back an hour in Chicago. Oh man, it is only 7 something. I'm extra early," I said, shaking my head, because I was rushing to get here. "I'm 'bout to pull out my book and study. I'll let you know how it goes."

"Okay, good luck, son."

I pulled out *The Essential Guide to Becoming a Flight Attendant* and started studying. Stacey called me. "Hey Lando, are you there yet?"

"Yep."

"Good luck. I'm just making sure. Let me know how everything goes, okay?"

This chick is literally up early as hell stalking me. Why didn't she just come to the damn event herself?

Now the good thing about the book was it had a lot of scenario questions and stuff they would ask at the interview. Also, it gave the correct responses, so I studied a few of those just so I could be extra prepared. I wore travel clothes while on the road, so when I walked into the hotel I had my suit in hand to change clothes in the bathroom. I saw cars everywhere, people in their cars on the phone, some studying, and the rest walking towards the hotel with their folders and briefcases. There was an 'AirStar this way' sign pointing towards a conference room just inside the lobby. I walked over to the bathroom and was happy that no one was in there. My suit was a perfect navy blue. Deciding to go hard, I wore a pink dress shirt with a stylish pink tie to match. The gold cuff links I wore matched the Rolex I was also wearing, and finished off the look with brand new shiny patent leather shoes. I was sharp! I looked in the mirror and took a picture so I could send it to Stacey.

"Damn! That's one fine brotha right there," I said to myself as I popped my collar and walked back towards my car. The first time I walked into the hotel I don't even think anybody even noticed me because I was in regular clothes, but now everybody was staring and looking. I was having one of those moments where I knew I was the shit! I smiled as if I was doing one of my Prepaid Legal presentations. Hello. Hey. Hello, how you doing? Wave there. A smile here.

There was a check-in line in the lobby, but I think I was feeling myself so much I probably just walked right up to the front.

"Wow, I'm loving the pink," said the person who was working behind the desk.

"Aw, thanks I appreciate that. I love those earrings."

"Thanks. Do you have your invitation letter?" she asked as she couldn't stop smiling.

"Yes." I handed her the paper.

"Once you're done stand over here so we can do your height test." I stood against the wall to be measured. "Good. We didn't expect this big of a turnout of people, so we are going to divide into three groups. You can go to room 4."

She handed me a piece of paper. There was a handsome, bald, black guy standing at the door to greet me and he didn't look gay, so that got me even more excited. I was in one group of fifty we'd been divided into. I hurried to the front row thinking, *Brian Carruthers at a seminar says all the big money is made in the front row.* He was one of my mentors in PrePaid Legal, who was making crazy money. His tips were always effective. I sat down next to this foreign girl and introduce myself. "Hey, how are you?"

"I'm great. I'm Janika."

"Okay, I'm Lando. It is a pleasure to meet you. Are you from Chicago?"

Shaking her head no, she informed me, "I flew here from Saudi Arabia." I looked at her like she was crazy as hell.

"Are you serious!"

"Yeah," she answered with a goofy smile.

"Hold on, *hold on.*" I repeated in amusement. "So you're telling me you flew out here just for this? You have to have some friends or something out here."

"Nope, but I'm going to stay here for a few days and go downtown and stuff."

"So how much was your ticket, if you don't mind me asking?"

"$1600."

"Well, I'm rooting for you, dear."

I grabbed my notepad and pen and wrote 'AirStar' at the top of my paper and put the date on the side and started the writing. So far all of their employees looked very presentable and were very nice. There was even a black guy present I thought was straight.

"Welcome, ladies and gentlemen. I want to be the first to thank every one of you that drove, walked, flew and more to get here. My name is Karen and I'm the in-flight manager with AirStar. I have been with the company for six years. I started off in Chicago, switched to LA, and now live in Utah, ever since I took the in-flight position two years ago. Now what we are going to do is introduce a few people that will be helping me out and I want them to tell just a little bit about themselves."

Karen was a white lady in her mid 30s. Out of a scale from 1 to 10 she was a 8.8. Karen was fine!

"To my right we have Daryl." She pointed to the black, bald gentlemen who'd been at the door when I came in.

"Hey everybody. I'm Daryl. I have been with AirStar for two years and I'm from Chicago. I was first a ramp agent and worked my way up to a flight attendant after years of wasting money on college, just to realize I really just wanted to travel."

"Last, but not least, is the famous Karly."

We all started clapping I guess because she said it with so much energy. I guess Karly was a big deal or something and yes I was right about it. Now Karly was a 8.9 with boobs the size of floating devices. Oh my god!

"Well, everybody, my name is Karly. I love this job and been with AirStar for eight years. I was able to work myself up in the management chain. I'm going to tell everybody right now..." She pointed her fingers. "This is the airline you want to be with, because we work harder than every airline, we have service better than every airline, and hell, we look better than every other airline." She shouted out and people stood up clapping.

The next thing I knew this one random black hood chick stood up and yelled, "Yes! Yes! You gone girl!"

I just laughed and shook my head. Right there I knew that was my airline. They were confident, cocky, and everybody wanted to be with them.

They started going over the pay and how they had been able to become a successful regional airline for 30 years. As I was taking notes, one recruiter said, "I'm going to say truthfully this job is not for everybody. At first it's hard and you have to get used to being away from your family, because it's no promise that you will get the base you want or how long you will be on reserve. So what we are going to do is to give everybody a quick ten minute break to decide if this is what you would like to do. Now if you leave, you have the opportunity to come back to any upcoming open house, but if you come back and don't get hired you have to wait six months to reapply. But before we break, we want to give everybody the opportunity to ask some questions one at a time."

So I raised my hand immediately so I could stand out, but had no idea what I was even going to say.

"Yes, sir, you're first," she said, pointed, and waited for my question.

"I'm wondering how long and what was the process to become a recruiter? It seems like you can move up quickly with this company." *Bam! Take that motherfucker!*

"That is a great question. I actually moved up after my first year. I saw an opening and applied. But the rule of thumb is that you have to be with the company for over six months and in good standing, meaning no write-ups. I hope that answered your question."

"Yes, it did, thanks." A few hands went up of people asking dumb ass questions.

"So the time is now 9:55, come back at 10:10."

I walked out in the hall and started mingling with people making small talk. I heard this cute black girl say "No, I can't do this. I have a young son. I need to be based in Chicago" and walked out.

I heard a deep slow voice behind me. I turned around and it was Ed from the Miracle interview.

"Man, you must be stalking me or something," he said as we both laughed.

"What are you doing here?" I asked, confused, since this was all the way in Chicago.

"I actually live in Chicago."

"Did Miracle call you back?"

"Yeah, I heard from them, but they denied me."

"Yeah, me too. I got the good ole thanks, but no thanks letter.

They probably hired the porn star," I said as we both laughed some more. "Man, I wish I had her freaky butt on my flight. I can see her doing the demos now. But this would be good if you get this and you live in Chicago."

"Yeah, I know there is a lot of competition here and I'm loving the pink, sir," Ed said as he checked out my outfit.

"And I'm loving those gators, Chicago pimp style," I said as I looked at his dapper outfit.

"Let me introduce you to my friend. Hey John, this is Lando, he's been stalking me at all my interviews."

John was in the background looking kind of jealous, so it would have been too awkward or rude for Ed not to say something.

"Hey, nice to meet you."

"Well, good luck and see you in training when we all get hired right!" I walked away, looked at my phone and had five text messages from Stacey. "How is it? What are they doing? Did you get it? Text me back, I want to know what's going on? Good luck!"

I smiled and walked back into the room. I didn't have time to deal with that chick and she had a chance to be here. As I returned to my seat, I looked at Janika and said, "Man, there are a lot of people that left."

"I know, I was just thinking the same thing, but I wonder why do so many people come here like they don't know what to expect. We all know we're applying to be a flight attendant and we have to fly." Her sexy middle eastern voice almost made me melt.

"Okay, everyone we have the final survivors. Give yourself a hand."

We all clapped as we listened to Karen. "Now, since we told you guys all of the bads, low pay, time away from your families, and being on reserve, now let's talk about the flight benefits."

Everybody clapped with excitement, since that's what most of us only cared about.

"I want to bring back up Karly, because she uses the benefits the most, so this department is her specialty."

"Where is everybody who really just wants this job for the benefits?"

Most of us raised our hands, but some like myself were very skeptical, because at most open houses they tell you to not talk about the benefits.

"I was the same way. I always wanted to be a flight attendant, but just the thought of being able to travel around the world for free, I loved the idea. Now myself and a few other flight attendants, we go to Hawaii once a month. I have been to 46 different counties and wouldn't be able to do any of that without this job. So if you get hired make sure you use the benefits. But what we are going to do is ask everybody, starting with the order of when you came in, to come in front of the class. Say your name, give us your background, what you're currently doing right now, and why you want to work with AirStar. So we are going to start with Anrae Smith." *Damn, I would hate to be Anrae.*

"Hey everybody, I'm Anrae and currently work as a manager at Sears in the shoe department. So if y'all need shoes just let me know. I would be a great flight attendant with AirStar, because I'm a hardworking, love helping people, and it just seems fun. I hope I get hired."

The longer I waited to go, the more I started talking silently to myself. *Come on, Lando, you didn't drive all the way out here to get sent home, you better be ready.*

"Hey ladies and gentlemen, I want to thank Karly, Daryl, Karen and the rest of the AirStar family." *Okay, Lando, you're ready, let's make sure you have all the primary names correct.*

"Next up is Johnny."

Damn, I wish I was next. I'm ready. I was looking at Johnny and he completely froze and told everybody he was sorry, the kid got so nervous and walked off. I hoped I wouldn't do that. I was thinking to myself after seeing him choke and now was praying they didn't call me next because I went blank! *Lando, how the hell did you forget what you were going to say? Don't call me, don't call me, don't call me I repeated silently.*

"Ireland is up next!"

Whew, thank you, Jesus! *Lando, come on, baby, no more thinking about it, just do it.* So my heart started beating slower as a few more people went up and then she called my name. Everything went in slow motion as I walked up to the front thinking *It's game time.* I seriously got into a zone. *I'm doing this for dad.* With 100% confidence I walked up to the front and smiled.

"Hey, ladies and gentlemen. I would like to first thank Karen, Karly, Daryl and the AirStar recruiting team for allowing me to be here today. I have had the pleasure of driving 4 hours 55 minutes and 32 seconds to be here today, but I'm excited that I did. I did my research and due diligence on AirStar and just loved how the company is successful and family oriented. With my multiple years of customer service experience I know I would fit well with the company.

"I first started my career in the cemetery business as a family service counselor and that job taught me how to deal with families in their time of need. Next, I went to the healthcare field as a certified nursing assistant and I worked helping people meet their activities of daily living sixteen hours a day. At my current employer I'm a manager of a few bars and coffee shops at Detroit Metro Airport. That mainly teaches me just how to... Well, really I just get people drunk." Everybody laughed. "But on a serious note, I have to deal with international customers from all around the world, and helping all my co-workers stay working as a team. So I hope I have the opportunity to become a part of the AirStar family. Thanks." Everybody started clapping. Even the recruiters joined as I noticed them in the back taking notes and smiling. Once I walked towards my seat people were congratulation me on my speech.

"Thanks, I appreciate it. Yours was fantastic also."

Karen walked in front of everybody and said, "Well, what we are going to do is take an hour break and really just go over every application. Once we decide, we will post names outside of the door. We would like to personally thank everyone for coming out. It really means a lot to us. We never thought we would have a turn out like this. So the time is 1 p.m. Come back and see if we are ready by 2 p.m."

As I walked outside more people congratulated me, saying how good I did. Even a chick or two wanted to exchange numbers. I felt like a superstar, but I just wanted to hurry up and get into the car. I had more texts from good ole Stacey. Hell, she even left a voicemail, saying "Oh my god! This is taking forever. Hurry up and let me know how it went. Damn." First person I called was dad.

"What's up, Lake, do we have the newest AirStar flight attendant?" was the first thing he said.

"Dad, I'm the man…"

"What happen?"

"Man, it's over two hundred people here. I walked in looking like a million bucks, I had the recruiters going crazy, and these women here are so bad two already gave me the number."

"What! No, they didn't!" he said is disbelief. I could hear the pride in his voice. "Me and Chris are leaving Ann Arbor, getting everything right for the surgery. Hold on, let me put you on speaker."

"Hey, Lake!"

"Hey Aunt Chris!"

"Hey, how is it going at your interview?"

"It's great so far. They did the intros and talked about how hard the job is and how we're going to miss our families and all of that. Basically trying vet out the bums."

"Yeah, they gotta get rid of the weak first," she responded.

"They said everybody had to come up to the front, say their

name, background, and why they want to be with AirStar and I went up there like a Pro Baby!"

"So that tape recorder helped you?" dad asked.

"Did it help me?!" I yelled repeating his question rhetorically. "I used that thing the whole ride here. When I get back you will hear the thirty mess ups I made."

"So what's the next step?"

"You know how at basketball try outs they post the sheet on the wall of who all made the team? So that's what they're doing and going over all the applications, then going to let us know."

"We are keeping our fingers crossed. Hit us up when you hear something."

"Okay talk to y'all later." I immediately started praying once I got off the phone.

Thank you, Lord, I appreciate you helping me to have the strength to do this. Thank you. Then I opened my eyes, replied to everyone's text messages, and started walking back to the hotel.

I walked in, sat down by myself, and saw a good looking chick walking up to me. She looked like a celebrity she was so fine. "Hey you're Lando, right?"

"Um, yeah," I replied as I admired her beauty.

"Well, I know you don't know my name, but I'm Brittany."

"How do you figure?" I said.

"Because I did okay and you were up there working it." She laughed.

"Where are you from?"

"I'm from Chicago on the south side."

"Okay, that's what's up. You need to take down my number and let me know if you made it, Brittany."

"Well, I know I didn't make it, but when you get based out here you can call me and we can do something."

"I'll text you so you can have my number."

A random chick yelled, "Oh my god! I made it!"

My first thought was to run over to check and see if my name was also there, but since I had been *the man* I had to keep it calm. As I casually walked towards the door, I scanned the list and didn't see my name. I didn't panic, because it had to be a mistake. So I scanned it again and still didn't see my name. My heart stopped.

"I knew Lando would make it," I heard a random girl say in passing.

I looked at her shocked and looked again at the list. There it was, my name right there in black and white. *Yes! Thank you, Lord!*

There were woman crying, hugging each other, people saying 'I missed my flight for this, just to not get hired, I don't know what to tell my mom.'

A recruiter opened the door and said, "If you have been selected, come in the room."

I grabbed my stuff and walked in and saw Janika, the girl I'd sat next to earlier, smiling inviting me to sit next to her.

"Oh my god, we made it!"

"Yes, I'm so happy," I replied in excitement as I looked back to see who else made it. Mostly were the people I assumed did better with their speech. I looked at the door and Eddie B was walking in. "Ed, you made it boy!"

"Okay everybody take your seats. I have something you all need to sign. Everything we talk about must be kept confidential."

Due to the disclosure agreements we signed, I can't share more of what happened or what we talked about. The gist is that we'd all made it and had the paperwork in hand to prove it!

I walked out so happy, just thanking God and needing a place to eat, drink, and celebrate. Not far from the hotel was a Hooters. That was perfect. Good-looking woman, good food and big breasts – a combination that couldn't be beat!

Keke called as I pulled up. "Bro! Did you make it?"

"Yep!"

"Aye dad, he made it!" she yelled in the background.

"So tell me all that happened."

"I'm not fully hired yet, but they picked about forty of us to sign some papers, said they liked us and would email us in a week."

"So what they do with the other hundred people?"

"Shoot they sent their asses home," I replied, laughing. "I'm at Hooters now getting something to eat. Then I'm gonna change and do this drive back. I'll be back there in a few hours. *Thank you, Kiki Ward*!

13

*G*etting accepted with AirStar was such an adrenaline rush. I was flying so high nothing could bring me down. All of my hard work had finally paid off. I felt accomplished and happy. But all of my excitement, this was only the beginning of the process. I needed to make it all the way to the end and still be standing strong.

∽

"Hey, Lake. You see that chili in there?" dad asked.

"Yeah, I'm looking at it now. You cooked it last night?"

"Yeah, and it's good. I need your help real quick."

I walked into his room and looked at the outfit he was sitting on the bed and yelled, "Man, what are you doing?!" I wondered why he had this ugly outfit out and what he planned to do with it!

"Trying to get what I want to wear to see Johnson tomorrow, but can't see nothing, so I hope this works. Does it match?" he asked, with frustration on his face.

"Heck no, you have a black hat, greenish outfit, brown socks. Ha-ha, you're a funny man."

"I'm not funny, I'm blind!" Dad shook his head, frustrated. He was not in a playing mood.

"Okay. This is what we can do." I went into his closet, pulled out a nice tan outfit for him to wear and put it on the bed.

"I think I have some shoes that go with that," he said. "Go grab the gold ones with the gator skin on the side from downstairs."

As I was looking in the basement through the thousand pairs of every gator and snakeskin shoes you can think of, I finally grabbed the shoes I thought he wanted.

"Dad! You have like fifty pairs of gators down there."

"Aye son, don't worry 'bout what I'm doing. You got the right pair?"

"Yeah, here." I placed the shoes in his hands.

"These aren't it!" he yelled, shaking his head as he sat down. "Whew, it's hard, Lord. It's hard."

"They look good. Okay, okay. I know what you're talking about. It's not my fault you own over twenty pairs of the same darn shoes," I responded and ran to grab another pair.

"Okay thanks, son. Now grab my jewelry box out the closet. You know where that's at?" he said sarcastically. So I stuck my middle finger up at him. *Hell he can't see it anyway.*

"You think I'm dumb until I grab my gun and shoot it off. Then we will see how much I can see." *Guess that wasn't such a great idea. Ha ha.*

As I was sitting on the couch watching Sports Center, he walked in and tripped on my shoe I had in the corner.

"Okay, Imma throw all this stuff away if I trip one more time, I'm telling you. Just keep on thinking I'm playing with you. We have to be at the University of Michigan at 7 a.m., so we have to be up early."

"What time do we have to be there?"

"I said seven," he responded quickly.

"Man, you're lying. I don't remember him saying that," I

responded back, because I knew it wasn't that early. Dad was just trying to get me.

"If you paid any attention to anything and stayed off that phone, you would've known the correct time is posted on the fridge."

I went and looked at the paper and saw it read 7:45.

"Aye dad, on this paper, it says be there at 7:45."

"Oh, so now you can read, huh? But we have to get up early to switch cars with grandpa so we can just drive his down there."

"Okay, that works. I'll call him in a little bit to tell him the deal." I grabbed some of dad's chili and just relaxed the whole day.

I woke up the next morning to the sound of my cell phone ringing. It was dad giving me a wake up call.

"We got to be out of here by 6:30. Lets go."

We stopped by my grandparent's house to trade cars for the day. Grandpa had lost the keys. I'd noticed him getting more forgetful the older he got. After a short delay to our schedule, we eventually found the keys inside the car's ignition. I guess he was trying to make things easier for us, but forgot what he'd planned. The three of us got on the road.

Arriving at U of M, we made it to the preparation room where the process of dilating dad's eyes began.

"Dr. Johnson should be in soon. I just have some paperwork for you to fill out, and we need to get your eyes ready."

"Hey, Ocie! How you feel?" Dr. Johnson said, as he walked into the room.

"I'm doing okay, Doc. I would be doing better if I could see something."

"Well, that's the overall plan we're working towards. Let me check your eyes. Sit back for me."

The doctor did his regular flashlight routine to see how well the eyes were dilated. "We are going to take you in a prep room, and I will see you in a little bit for surgery."

Grandpa and I sat in the waiting room. I could tell he was bored because he kept asking me for coffee and if I'd been to see grandma lately.

I pulled out my Napoleon Hill book, *Think and Grow Rich*.

"What book is that?" grandpa asked.

"*Think and Grow Rich*. It's a book where a guy... well, basically it's a book that teaches you how to be successful and a millionaire."

"A millionaire!" He repeated to me, looking at me as if I was crazy. "Don't you have a job?"

"Yeah."

"You just work on not getting fired and moving up in the company. Keep working hard. Nobody needs to be no millionaire."

"I'm not a regular person. I have big goals and need a lot of money to achieve them. My main goal is not to be working for somebody, but to be working for myself."

"You can be what you want, as long as you go get me some food," he responded.

"Okay, let's go, grandpa."

Now grandpa worked for Ford Motor Company for over forty years, so hard work was all he knew. 'Wake up early and get something done.' He was of a different mindset, but oh well, to each his own. They say the reason most people are not successful is because they listen to their friends and family. Not me. I never let anyone deter me from my dreams.

After we ordered our food we took a seat in the cafeteria. Grandpa asked, "How long do you think he will be in there?"

"I'm not sure. They said for a long time."

We talked about life and what all had been going on. I'm blessed to have been raised by such a man. My grandparents had been married for almost 60 years. With a strong church background, every weekend we had the option to go over their house and go to church or stay home with mom and do chores. We didn't really want to go to church, but grandma was so smart. She gave us an allowance and that was all I needed to convince me. All kids love money. She increased the amount as we grew with age.

Once I got my driver's permit, grandpa would let me drive to church. He really taught me most of what I know. How to treat a lady and to be a godfearing man, since at home I wasn't fully raised in that atmosphere.

Sooner or later I figured grandpa would pass out after eating and waiting for hours. Dad was finally rolled out in a wheelchair.

The doctor walked up and said, "In my twenty-one years of doing this, I've never seen eyes like his. It was hard at first to see the back of his eyes, because the more we did, it got a little foggy, but overall it went great. Now he is going to be a little tired for a while. Samantha was there to help me. She will be going over all of his eye drops he will need to start taking, so I'm going to need to see you tomorrow."

"Tomorrow?" I replied, shocked.

"Yes, we will take off his patch and see how everything clears up."

"Okay, see you tomorrow. Karen, up front, will set a time for you guys."

"You're the son, correct?" Samantha says.

"Yes, I am."

"What we will need to do starting tomorrow, he has four different drops he will need to start taking. The ones with the yellow top is four times a day and red top twice and everything else just once daily."

"Okay, can you write it down for me?"

"Yes, I already have it written down. It's in the box I'm giving you guys. See you back here tomorrow."

"Hey, how you feel, dad?"

"I'm okay. Just feel a little woozy."

I helped dad put on his clothes and we took him home. He was really quiet all day. He mostly stayed in his room and slept.

"Hey, dad, how you feeling?" I checked on him some time later.

"Way better. I have been so woozy all day. Can you bring me some water? I'm finally starting to get some energy."

He finally had an appetite and was willing to eat a little something. I made him a salad, because he really didn't like eating what I cooked. I took him his salad and we chatted for a while.

"Turn on my gospel tape for me before you leave out. Do you know what time we have to be there tomorrow?"

"Hell, you're going to need more than those gospel tapes with your crazy self. We have to be there at 7 a.m. and I don't think grandpa is rolling with us tomorrow."

"Grandpa did his job. He was a trooper for seven hours I wouldn't think he would have survived that. What was he saying while y'all were out there?"

"Just complaining about coffee and kept on asking about grandma. You know how he does. Repeating the same questions over and over."

The next day at U of M, dad was sitting in the chair while the doctor removed the patch. "Ocie, can you read the letters on the wall?"

Dr. Johnson said, "Wow!" to himself as he examined dad's eyes.

"What's up, doc?" I asked.

"His recovery is fast and great. I'm really optimistic to see how everything turns out."

"So how long will it be until I can see again?" dad responded in frustration as he concentrated on looking at the letters on the wall.

"Well, Ocie, the surgery is not a 100% guarantee that you will fully see again. We have to accept that, but we are trying to improve your vision the best we can, because you were on the route to becoming completely blind."

The doctor had a very sincere look on his face as he spoke. I appreciated his bedside manner. Even though he was a very busy doctor, he never rushed us and was fully present and patient when he met with us.

"We just have to be optimistic about the situation and see how it goes from here. I'm going to give you a month, then come back in and we will see how it goes, okay?"

"Okay thanks, Dr. Johnson."

On the car ride home, I noticed dad kept closing his right eye and opening his left to see how well he could see. In the middle of the drive he said, "Man, we are going to have to go somewhere else to get checked up on."

"Why you say that?"

"We spent all this money and my sight is the exact same."

"This is just day one. Give it some time. They reattached your retina, it's going to take some time to heal, you know."

"Yeah, I hope you're right, man, I hope you're right." He sounded frustrated.

Kerry called me. "Hey, sexy lady, how are you?"

"I'm good. I heard you went to the AirStar open house."

"Yeah not too long ago."

"Did you hear anything back yet?"

"Naw. I can't stop checking my phone, but I think I did good."

"Guess what?"

"What, Kerry!"

"Guess!"

"You are going to move to Michigan and marry me?"

"No, fool, I got hired with Onar."

"What! Congrats! I saw they were hiring. When did you go to an open house?"

"About two weeks ago and they called me yesterday. I'm going to be based in Houston, so I'm good. But the thing is, they don't know when I'm going to start our training, so they are going to send out the training packet soon and have it prepared."

"Okay, where all do they fly?"

"They only kinda do charters and military flights."

"That's lame, but at least you can find you an army man."

"Have you talked to your girl Stacey lately?"

"Yeah, not as much as y'all been talking. I saw she been hitting you up, so I backed off a little."

"Ha-ha. Whatever, man, you're usually too busy with your hotline ova there anyway."

The phone clicked and she says, "Hold on one second, Lando."

She came back. "Yeah, my bad, but yeah, Stacey is hating lately, because I told her I got the job. I didn't get a congrats. It was more of a 'you know they only do military and you know their flight benefits are not as good as Delta's and talking shit. Hold on," she said, but right before she could click over I interrupted her.

"Aye! Just call me back."

"Okay, I'll call you right back."

"Them women are crazy, aren't they?" dad said. "Man, you got both of them girls fighting over you."

"Ha-ha! You think so?" I said, smiling, as I drove onto the expressway.

"Yeah. You see she even said she had to back off of you, because her girl wanted to get on. Stacey is going to make her move to come to Detroit to give you some in a minute. Watch it happen." Dad smiled.

"Well, I'm going to head to the hospital to see grandma and let her know how the interview went. You want to roll up there with me?"

"I'm down."

As we pulled up, dad said, "Tell her how everything went at

the doctors. I'm just going to sit out here. I don't want to get this eye infected or nothing, going into the hospital."

"Okay, I'll be right back."

I signed the book at the front desk and went to her room. I saw the sexy nurse's assistant I met the first time I was there to visit.

I knocked on the wall to get her attention as she was cleaning up, "Hello."

"Oh hey, how are you?"

"I'm okay. What can I do for you?"

"Well, my grandma was in this room last time I checked. Did they transfer her to another one?"

"Oh... She left out this morning, because she was having bad bed sores. We transferred her to the hospital."

"Wow, I wish somebody would've told me, okay thanks."

As walked out, she stopped me. "Do you want to know which hospital she is in?"

"Yeah." I'm sure the sadness I felt showed on my face.

"Okay, follow me."

As we were walking, I started thinking *should I go for the kill and ask for her number? Since grandma's not here any longer, this could be my only shot.*

"How long have you been working here?"

"For about six months."

"How you like it?"

"It's not bad. It's a job, but it doesn't feel like it when I have great people like your grandma around."

"I know, I love her. Hopefully, she gets better soon so we can get her back where she needs to be."

"And where is that? Here!" She smiled. "She is at St. Mary's hospital." *Lando, get her, get her.*

"Well...I will hopefully see you soon." *Damn, Lando, you choked,* I thought to myself because I didn't pull the trigger and get her number.

"Dad! She's not even here."

"What do you mean by that?"

"She got transferred earlier today."

"What! Nobody has told me anything. Isn't this a blow? Call Chris for me." I called as soon as he said that.

"Hey, what y'all got going on?"

"We at the place on Venoy where momma supposed to be at, but they're saying they transferred her."

"Yeah, they did it this morning."

"What's wrong? Why you haven't called anybody?"

"Because y'all had your appointment. I was waiting until you got out. I didn't want you worrying about her and your eyes at the same time. She is having bad bed sores from sitting in the bed too long and not moving around and the place she was at don't treat her for stuff like that, so they transferred her to St. Mary's."

"Okay, how is she doing?"

"Not talking too much and kinda grouchy."

"Okay, well, we're about to head to the house. Just hit me up when you are heading this way," dad responded, sounding more relieved.

The next day as I was clocking into the coffee shop Jon said, "Hey Lando, come here. I want to talk you."

"What's up?"

He looked both ways suspiciously, and said, "Don't tell anybody, but I think they're trying to fire you."

"What, why? They just fired Brittany and Saha. They've been here forever."

"Yeah man, I'm just telling you to watch out, because people are hating and telling Jean shit."

Jim walked in. "Hey Lando, can I talk to you in the office?" he said, not giving me a chance to respond, and walked back towards the office.

Jon gave me an 'I told you so' look as I walked to the back. We went into the office and he told me he thought someone had been stealing money out of the registers, because there was a shortage upstairs. "So, it's only upstairs?" I responded.

"Yep, so from now on until we get things right, I want you to train people how to do a blind drop. Get the two shops upstairs to wait for you to close. Help them close the drawers and count the safes at night."

"Okay, I got you."

I went upstairs and Linda was making a coffee. "Hey, Miss Linda, how you doing?"

"I'm truly blessed. See, Lando, whenever Jesus wakes me up in the morning, I know I'm doing good. Here you go, sir," she responded and handed her customer his drink with a smile. "How you been doing lately?"

"I am good. Working on becoming a flight attendant, so I've been going to different interviews."

"You will leave this job?" she asked with a shocked expression.

"Yep, it's not like I work for the president. It's an okay job and I'm happy they hired me, but it's just a stepping stone to my next level of what I want to do in life."

"That's good to hear, Lando. Mark 9:23 says 'Everything is possible for one who believes.'"

"Yep, you are right about that. How long were you married, Linda?"

"Twenty long years."

"Wow, so how do you get a divorce after being married that long?"

"To tell you the truth, I knew it wasn't going to work right after year five, but at the time I was young and already had kids with him so I stayed until they got grown."

"That's what all women say...that they stayed for the kids," I respond sarcastically. "Do you still talk to him?"

"No, he worked for Ford for over twenty years. He don't gotta talk to me. His check talks every month," she said, laughing.

"Wait, so you're still getting a check? And how long y'all been divorced?"

"Over ten years. The law in Michigan is if you're married to somebody for over ten years you get half or a pension check every month. This little job is not enough. Do you know how far I have to drive to get here everyday? I live in New Boston, but hopefully the Lord has a plan for me with a job somewhere closer. Can you take over so I can go and use the bathroom, please?"

I went behind the counter and started cleaning stuff and stocking. Brown called me on my cell phone, but I told her to call the work phone so I wouldn't get in trouble for talking on the phone while working. "Lando, why did they fire me off of some bullshit. I'm pissed off."

"What happened?"

"Our new manager, Adrian, works at the Caliente now and I really think it was a set up to fire me. I don't know what to do now."

"Man, it's good you got fired," I said laughing.

"Why you say that?"

"Because you have a *college degree!*" I yelled and looked up. A gorgeous woman walked into the coffee shop. "Aye Brown, let me call you back. My wife just walked in."

"Ha-ha, okay bye. Just hit me back later."

"Hello, how are you doing today?"

In the sexiest British accent, she replied, "I'm doing great. I would like an Americano or a cafe latte."

"Yes, I can help you with that. Where are you from?"

"I'm from Great Britain, but my boyfriend wants me to move in with him."

"Looking that good, I bet he does." I laughed.

"Lando, leave this poor lady alone and give her the coffee," Linda said as she walked back into the shop, laughing at me.

Now Linda could've been my mom's twin, because she is a very sweet older black lady that was a 100% Christian. I liked working with her, because she was usually in a positive spirit and willing to talk to me about church and relationships. She is about the same age as my mom, their birthdays are days apart, and both married men that worked for Ford, so it was funny to me. I walked down to the other shop and saw Moe working.

"What's up my, Arabic brother?"

"Nothing much. You know they fired Sahad?"

"Yeah, I heard. What's going on with the company?"

"Just between me and you, I heard Jean has a list."

"A list?"

"Yeah, a list of people he wants them to fire and your name is on it."

"Hold on, are you sure?"

"Yeah, I'm positive."

"But I am not doing shit to nobody," I said angrily.

"I know, brother. They had Brown on there. She just got fired. Sahad and some other people I can't remember are on there. Ashley told me about it, so watch your back."

"Okay, for sure. Good looking, bro."

Later on that day. I took dad over to grandma's house and could tell he was getting frustrated, since I had a lot on my mind and was rushing. I'd gotten into the habit of grabbing his shirt and leading him to the location, whenever we went somewhere.

"I hate that you gotta hold my shirt. I'm not used to stuff like this," he randomly blurted out.

I understood, because being a grown man you don't want someone holding your shirt guiding you everywhere like you're ninety years old.

"My bad, dude, I'll slow down."

We both went downstairs and as I was shooting pool, dad said, "Man, God must've had a different plan for me. I was on my way to becoming a pool champion and now I can't see, but if it's in His will, I will be back shooting. Have you heard from AirStar yet?"

"No, not yet. But I forgot to tell you that they already started to send out the rejection emails and I didn't get one of them."

"What! How you know?"

"Because people on the forums was talking about they received them already." My phone made a noise indicating I had an email. I checked it and it was from AirStar inflight recruiting. My heart completely stopped. It really felt like everything went into slow motion. "Oh my God," I said out loud.

"What?" dad asked.

"Dad, you know what? I'm in. They just emailed me. I'm going to train in Utah!"

We cheered and hugged each other. Aunt Chris come to the top of the stairs and asked what were we shouting about.

"Lake got hired, Chris! He is accepted for training."

"Woo hoo! You go! Let me go ahead and give the flight attendant a hug. So what's the next step?"

"They told me in the email that they will email me again when the next training comes up."

"Read it to us so we can hear it," dad said.

DEAR ORLANDO,

WE ARE PLEASED *to announce that you have been invited to attend our upcoming Flight attendant training class which will be begin on Thursday, March 3, 2011. The graduation date for this class will be March 29th. To accept this class date, please reply to Madison Smith at Farecruitment@AirStar.com or call her at (555) 222-4584. If you are unable to attend the March 3rd class, please still respond and let Madison know. We also have a tentatively scheduled class starting at the end of March. A confirmed date for this March class will be announced at a later time.*

Very Important *If you have been convicted or are currently being charged with a criminal misdemeanor or felony that has happened since your interview you must inform us as soon as possible.*

Once you have been added to a class list, Madison will confirm your contact information and go over when you will receive your training packet, plus all other information regarding training. We are excited to have you begin training soon!

Sincerely, In Flight Recruitment

I checked in at the front and asked for my grandma's room number. I walked in room 213 and saw grandma lying there looking like she'd lost some more weight. She looked asleep.

"Hey grandma."

She turned towards me and smiled.

"How you feel?"

She opened her mouth to talk, but I could tell that her throat was too dry, so she couldn't. "Let me give you some water, your throat is dry, grandma."

As I raised her bed to sit her up, I could see it hurt her by her facial expressions.

"I'm sorry, grandma, drink this." I put the straw in her mouth, but she didn't drink it. "Grandma, you got to drink something, that's why your mouth is dry."

She still didn't drink it.

"So, it looks like I have to sit here all day until you drink something," I said seriously.

She took a sip and said, "You're worse than the doctors."

"Ha, I bet I am, because they can't get you to do anything. I got hired with an airline, grandma. It's called AirStar and my training is in Utah. I have been going to interviews like crazy, but finally got hired, so the next step is to make it through the training process. Has anybody been up here today?"

"Buddy," she responded softly.

Buddy is my grandmother's brother. "Okay, that's good. I'm about to head out and will come and check on you soon."

"Love you," she mumbled.

"Okay, love you too, grandma.

I walked outside and once I got into the car I just sat there thinking about the times when she was fully healthy, dancing around and joking with grandpa. How I was so blessed to have both sets of my grandparents growing up, because a lot of my close friends didn't have that. *What would I do if she was gone?* I thought.

14

At home getting ready for work, I receive a phone call from a random number. "Hello!"

"Hey Lando, this is Dick. I want to talk to you before you go in to work today."

"Why?" I responded confused.

"I will tell you when you get here, but before you go in come to the office on Tyrone St."

"Are you serious?" I responded confused.

"Yeah."

"Who's gonna cover my shift?"

"Ali will take care of it for you."

The car ride there I was nervous as hell. Thinking about how John told me they wanted to fire me and how Moe said I was on that list. I just knew I was done, but the question is what did I do to get fired.

"Hello, Dick will be out shortly," said the receptionist once I walked into the office. She was also the boss's niece.

That office is was the headquarters. It was a little building about five minutes away from the airport where candidates could fill out applications and staff could perform other little duties.

Dick was our regional manager, so we only saw him once every other month when he came into the shops to take care of the meetings.

He was an Asian gay guy in his fifties, real serious, but who reminded me of Big Gay Al from South Park, because of the colorful Hawaiian type shirts he wore. He opened the door and called me into the back room. I was surprised to see Jim there.

"Hey Lando, have a seat," Jim commanded.

"No. I'm okay I'll stand," I replied, showing them I was pissed off and waiting to see why I was there. "Lando, sit down, please," he said.

I sat down and Dick said, "Lando, the thing is, somebody filed a sexual harassment claim against you."

"What! Are you serious?" *What the fuck?!* I started laughing and said, "Who and how?"

"Megan filed one."

This caught me off guard immediately, because I didn't even know who they were talking about, so there had to be some kind of mistake. How could I sexually harass some chick I didn't even know?

"Who is Megan?"

"The girl that brings the cash," he told me.

"Dude, I didn't even know her name. I never sexually harassed anybody a day in my life. Well...not unless they wanted it. But seriously, all jokes aside, are y'all sure?"

"Yeah I'm sorry. You're not fired, but this goes on your file and can be taken off in a few months."

"Hell naw. I don't want that on my record. What's your proof that I did it?"

"Here is our tape." Dick was seated at his desk and behind him was his computer. I guess they could see or review the coffee shops from there, since they had cameras all over the shops. The video came on and it showed us upstairs in the coffee shop. She was talking to another employee, but where she was standing she was blocking the entrance into the back office. So as I went to pass her, I grabbed her side as if I was sliding by and went into the back.

I yelled, "*So she said I sexually harassed her because of this!*"

"She said she was very uncomfortable when you touched her and you always call her sweetie or honey, and she doesn't like it."

"So why didn't she tell me? I call everybody sweetie and honey."

"I don't know. But from now on watch what you're saying to people. I need you to sign this here and here."

"No, I'm not signing anything. I disagree and don't want this on my record, so I refuse to sign."

"Well, can you just write in the notes section that you saw this letter. You don't have sign if you don't want to."

I did as instructed, after seeing they really didn't want to fire me and they were very timid and scary about the situation.

"Look Lando, I know you're a hard worker. But from now on you can't trust anybody, so watch your back," Jim said.

I walked out and headed straight to work. I texted Ali about what was going on and that I was on my way to give him more details.

"Lando, F this company. I'm leaving..."

"What you mean?"

"I'm quitting."

"Dude, if you're leaving then I'm gone. I can get my old job back doing valet making twice as much as this chump change I'm getting here," Ali demanded. "No disrespect to you, but you came in making more money than me and I had to train you," he said as we laughed.

"So when are you leaving?"

"In a week."

"Okay. Brother, wait until I tell you how they tried to screw me."

"I heard. Jim told me he was kinda pissed, but couldn't do anything about it. What did they say?"

"Megan said I been harassing her."

"Who?"

"Bro, that's what I said. The fucking cash girl."

"Damn, man, I couldn't even have guessed her name even if I needed to." A customer walked in, Ali went to take her order for me.

Dawn walked in and asked if she could talk to me. We went in the kitchen and she immediately said, "What the fuck happened?"

"Man, that bitch Megan said I sexually harassed her."

"Who is Megan?"

I burst out laughing. "That's what I'm saying. It's the cash girl."

"Oh, I didn't even know her name."

"Well, all I know is I have to watch my ass around her, because how many times have I sexual harassed you?" I laughed. "Me and Ali should have been in jail by now," I say jokingly, because we always flirt with her.

"Come and give me a hug, babe," she demanded as I gave her a hug and she grabbed my butt and said, "Ooo my bad, I'm sorry."

"I'm going to write your ass up if you keep it up, ma'am. That's my no-no zone."

"Lando, can you make me a turkey sandwich and help me for a second, please?" Ali asked.

I made it and went out to help him for a while. As we knock out this crazy rush of people, we got a few tips and this gorgeous chick walked in and I say, "A-ta-a-lay-ya."

He looked over and said, "Nope. She's mine, Lando."

"Ali, you have a girlfriend!" I yelled.

"F her. What girlfriend?" he said with his Arabic accent which made it funnier.

Ali started talking to her and flirting, while she was laughing and loving it. "Do you guys sell parfaits?" she asked.

"I will go and get you a fresh one from the back," he said.

I pulled out my phone discreetly and called the job phone. As the phone started ringing and I picked it up and yelled out loud, "Ali! Your boyfriend just called and said pick him up over Sammie's when you get off."

The chick looked completely shocked. He walked outside with his head down and said, "Okay thanks, Lando."

The girl looked mad and walked away. "Yes!" I yelled out loud.

"Fuck you, Lando. What was that for?"

"Bitch, for quitting and leaving me here by myself."

I WALKED into the house after work to see dad and Aunt Chris sitting at the table.

"Lake in the house!" My aunt yelled. "How was work?"

"Horrible," I responded as I sat down on the couch. "So why am I driving to work and get a call from my supervisor saying come to the main office before I go into work because we need to talk. I go there and this girl that brings us money for our drawers, that I probably see about once every two weeks for about two minutes, said that I sexually harassed her. I didn't even know the girl's name… that's the crazy part. Now you remember I told you they've been firing people left and right, dad. I think they're trying to get rid of me."

"Don't they need proof of it to fire you?" my aunt asked.

"Yeah. Usually when she comes I say thanks sweetie or something like that. She said that made her feel uncomfortable and that was part of the harassment. Then she brings in a situation when she was in my way and I said excuse me and moved her and walked to the back. I told them they needed to show me proof and that was the only proof they had. So the meeting mainly was to tell me to watch my back and to try to make me sign some paperwork."

"You didn't do it, did you?" dad responded calmly.

"Naw man, I'm not about to mess up my record with that mess. I got a copy so I can go over our policy and figure this out."

"It's about time for you to get out of there anyway," dad replied kinda upset now.

"Yeah, I might quit soon, because I have AirStar lined up now."

"And you will have loot coming in from helping me out soon too, you know from the CNA people. So just let us know so we can get Chris to write something up for you."

"Okay. Have y'all heard from grandma today?"

"Well, your dad had an appointment with Dr. Singh. He is the one Dr. Johnson referred us to up at U of M, so we are just coming back from there. We're gonna check on grandma later on. Have you been up there?" she asked.

"I went the other day and told her about AirStar and what's been going on, but she wasn't looking too good. I could tell her mouth was dry, because she hasn't been drinking nothing, so I made her drink some water. She said I'm worse than the doctors ha-ha. Yeah, I have to show you, because her throat is not as strong, so you have to dip the straw in the water and put your finger over the top so it will hold it and put the water in her mouth."

"Oh okay. But let me know if you want me to write something up for you."

∽

LATER ON I was outside cleaning the car and got a call from Krogers.

"Hey sexy how are you?"

"I'm doing good, just cleaning my car."

"What you got up?"

"Just drinking and hanging around."

"But are you home?"

"Yeah. What's up?"

"I need to borrow $10 to put some gas in the tank. Can I borrow it until Friday, please?"

"Yeah come on, baby, I got you!"

It was random for her to call and ask for $10, but hell it was a lot better than the $300 or whatever her crazy ass asked me for before. Now the real crazy part was she pulled right up after I got off the phone with her as if she was next door on some stalker shit.

"Um damn, dude, that was quick."

"Yeah. I was close by running some errands."

I pulled out $12. "You can have 10 plus 2, baby."

"Okay. You know your girls miss you," she said replied in a seductive tone.

"Oh they do, huh?"

"Yeah." Looking at me, she pulled out her breast and kissed one.

"Man, you better go on somewhere before I rip you out of this car."

"Okay, baby, I'll call you later." She pulled off. *Women are just crazy*, I thought as I shook my head and walked towards the house.

I got an email from BYB Air saying congratulations I was invited to a BYB interview in Atlanta and they were willing to fly me out. *Yes! Things are starting to work out.*

The following Monday at work I handed John an envelope.

"What's this, Lando?"

"My two week notice."

"Your two week notice! No, Lando, don't do this to me, please."

"Naw, I already made up my mind. I tried to do the job, but

since my dad became legally blind I have to move in and take care of him full time."

"So when is your last day?"

"October 14th."

"Okay. So I'm gonna get a new manager, but you will help me train him, right?"

"You will be doing the training and I'll have your back. Who did you have in mind?"

"Grayson's boyfriend."

"Gayson's boyfriend?" I replied, shocked.

"Why do y'all call him that? You know I'm gay, too."

"But at least you're manly gay, not girly gay. Don't you think that's going to be a problem?" I asked since he wanted two boyfriends to work at the same place.

"Nope, because I'm switching him to Caliente to take Brittany's spot."

After a few days of thinking about everything, I felt this was the best thing for me to do. I liked the job at the shop, but I got tired of being unappreciated and underpaid. They started firing all my close friends daily, and it just wasn't fun to go to work any longer. Also the bottom line was I didn't want the company to have the enjoyment of firing me if I could do something about it. They let Megan pull that fake ass trick. I had a few dollars saved up and since I was hired with AirStar I could get focused and ready for that.

"Dépêchez-vous, Jamie!" I yelled as I entered the shop upstairs, telling her to hurry up in French.

"Lando, that's the only word you know. You can't keep on just telling me to hurry up."

"Salute!"

She shook her head as we both noticed a new guy standing nearby watching us argue.

"Hey, you must be Lando. I'm Phil." Phil was the guy that Jim wanted me to train and take my spot. He was a white gentleman in his late twenties. His voice was real dry and his demeanor lacked confidence.

"Hey. What's up? What time did you get in today?"

"At 2," he replied, studying me.

"Okay, so this is the deal." I took a deep breath before continuing, "I'm leaving the company, so my job is to train you to be as good as me within two weeks." I gave him a smirk. "That's impossible for you to be as good as me, but I'm gonna train you to be great in four days. Two weeks is for pussies and you don't look like one."

"So why are you leaving?"

Jamie started laughing and said in her African voice, "Because this is the best company in the world. He will be back." She really didn't want me to leave.

"You're right, Jamie!" I responded in my African voice. "I will be back! But in my flight attendant uniform. Come on, Phil, there is a lot I have to teach you."

Since that was his first day, I gave him a tour of the airport and had him work the cash register all day. As he worked the register, I made drinks. Cash registers were kinda easy as long as the person is over the age of sixteen and can pay attention.

On the second day I showed him how to make all the food and become a cook, because with that job the manager had to know everything. The coffee shop was more than making drinks and ringing sales. It also entailed knowing how to clean the kitchen, prepare the food, and stock supplies.

"Have you ever bartended before?" I asked.

"No. Why do you ask?"

"Because you also need to know how to make drinks, just in case one of these chicks call off and you're stuck by yourself. Last, but not least, is becoming a great manager. But let's get started on the food for today, my friend."

I started showing him how to cook the food and count money. We were actually having fun doing it. Once I got to know this guy he was goofy as hell. He told me about his relationship with Gayson and how he was an asshole.

Attention: Sorry readers. I'm calling him Gayson, hell that was his nickname so don't be sensitive. His real name is Grayson and everybody at the job hated him. He was a know it all, tell-the-managers-if-you-did-something-wrong type of guy, so it didn't really bother me to put him in the book.

15

"Lake!" dad yelled from his room. "What you gonna wear out there to this interview?"

"Since their colors are like Delta's: red, navy, and white, I'm gonna wear the same suit with a white shirt and red tie. Les Brown style."

"Okay, you got it all set then. Some money should be coming in soon. The adjuster that's on my case sent us a letter saying he is on everything."

"Cool." I gathered all the clothes I needed for the interview.

Since it was just me and dad that lived there and we were always in different rooms, it was normal to catch us yelling back and forth in the house. It was comical whenever a new person came over and got a chance to see how we operated, because we had no filter, especially when sports came on.

The next morning I was on the plane and looking at the flight attendants, listening to their announcements, imagining me doing the beverage service, laughing with the passengers in my little uniform with my wings on and just loving the glamorous lifestyle.

"Hello sir. How are you?" the forty-something white flight attendant said.

"I'm doing fantastic."

"What can I get for you?"

"A cranapple would be great, please."

"Here you go." She walked away as I admired her beautiful coke bottle figure and golden hair.

I called my homeboy, Squeeze, to let him know I'd just landed. He was from Detroit, but had been living in the A for a few years. We were gonna hang out while I was in town. Taking the shuttle to the hotel, I walked in and was greeted by a lovely woman working the front desk.

"You must be Lando," she said as I admired her hazel eyes and perfect caramel skin. Her weave could have been a little better, but F it.

"I'm whoever you want me to be," I flirted with her.

She smiled. "You're so sweet. I need your ID and you're in room 212." She put her hand on the desk to give me my room key and I saw a big ass rock on her ring finger.

"Jesus Christ! Somebody loves you *a lot* woman!" I blurted out as we both laughed.

"Yeah, my husband is great."

"With a ring that bad you better be cooking, bringing home beer, and letting that brother watch nonstop football."

"Boy, stop it," she responded blushing.

That night I did some more studying and went to sleep kinda early after catching up and hanging with an old friend.

I walked into the BYB and there was one white lady sitting down in the lobby. I introduced myself, reaching out to shake her hand.

"Hey, I'm Brenda, you're here for the interview also," she said as she shook my hand.

"Yes I am. Where did you fly in from?"

"Detroit and you?"

"I actually drove. I live about three hours north of here and have a few friends that don't stay too far away."

"I bet that worked out a lot better than flying. It's nice to meet you."

As we waited more people started to come. It was a total of about eight of us only. I guess if the cost was on their dime, they were being more selective about who they were willing to fly in.. As we were sitting, an attractive German woman walked down the stairs and introduced herself. She then took us all upstairs into a room.

"Welcome everybody. I know you guys feel very lucky. We've had over 3,000 applications and brought in only a few qualified applicants to interview. This is gonna be a little different than what you are used to doing, since we have a smaller interview. What we are going to do is go over the company and the benefits, then find out about you guys, and go from there. First off, I'm Jeanine and I've been with BYB for three years. Just last year I was picked to be one of fifteen BYB flight attendants on our All Star team, which allows us to go to Hawaii and Disney World with some kids to be a part of the company charity event." Jeanine was tall, with black hair, about 32, and had on her navy blue, white shirt, and red scarf uniform.

Another lady came into the room named Shelly. She was more on the business side of things. They started going over the basics of how the schedule looked and then asked us to stand up. "Tell us where you are from and just something about yourself. Who wants to go first?" she asked.

I raised my hand and stood up. "Hello ladies and..." I looked to the left and then to the right. "Um ladies."

They all laughed. "Lucky to be you, with all these good-looking women," Jeanine responded, since I was the only guy there.

I smiled and said, "I'm from Detroit. I have no kids, I'm a fun and outgoing person. Currently, I work at Detroit Metro Airport managing a few coffee shops and a bar. I'm just thankful to be here."

A sexy black girl stood up and said, "I'm from Texas and been wanting to become a flight attendant badly, so I've been going to different interviews. I work at a nail shop now doing nails and a little bit of hair on the side. And it's nice to meet everybody."

Damn! What's up with these woman from Texas? Wow they have bodies. This chick was black, short, and *stacked*. She didn't look like Kerry or Stacey, but she had her own style. I loved how she had her hair done, but I could tell she was a little hood by the way she carried herself.

The recruiters went through the process and asked if anyone had any questions. I raised my hand. "I was looking at the BYB route map and they are merging with New Air, correct?"

"Yes!"

"Well, if we get hired, would we be under New Air or BYB?"

"That's a great question."

"When we officially merge, there will no longer be BYB. Now you will get hired under us, but when the merge goes through then you will be an New Air employee. Did that answer your question?"

"Yes it did. Thanks, Shelly."

"Well everybody, follow me. What we are going to do is put you all in a room and will call each person individually," she stated as we went into a smaller room and everyone started to converse about which interviews they'd been to and how hard it been to get the job.

Brenda, a cool older white lady, said, "Hey Lando, you did good. I know you will get it."

Everybody started agreeing with her and I followed with a smile. "I hope so. Y'all nobody really did bad."

One of the recruiters came in and called a name out. The black girl said, "Wish me luck."

About every 15 minutes they would call a new person. It was only Brenda and I left.

"Lando, looks like it's just me and you buddy."

"Yeah, you're right. Have you noticed when they take people they don't send them back?"

"Yeah, I read on the Indeed forums that they let you know the day of your interview if you're hired or not." "You know what would be bad is if they had a camera in here and were listening to everything we've been saying."

"Hell, if that's the case then everybody is getting sent home." I laughed.

Shelly, the recruiter, came for me next.

I looked at Brenda. "Wish me luck."

"It was nice meeting you, Lando."

I walked into the room and it was set up like a small office with three chairs - two for them and one for me. Shelly was already sitting with a smile on her face as she directed me to take a seat. She grabbed my application, looked at it and said, "In the other room you said you currently work for a coffee shop in Detroit, right?"

"Yes I do."

"Oh my god, we love our coffee," Jeanine interrupted with excitement.

"Every morning, one or the other of us has to go out on a coffee run. My favorite is the caramel mocha."

Shelly responded, "I love just keeping it plain and getting an Americano."

Looking in her eyes, I responded, "Yeah, when I first started working there, I had never been a big coffee fan and didn't know what the heck a mocha frapalatte is, but now I can make them with my eyes closed."

"What do you think will be the hardest thing about becoming a flight attendant?"

"I would have to say probably..." I paused for a few seconds, smiling inside because I was so prepared there was not a question a recruiter could ask me without me giving a great answer. I looked up and finished, "...the weather differences. Because let's say you're based in Atlanta then you fly out to Chicago and it's freezing cold. I would say adjusting to the different temperatures would be very hard."

"Oh my god, that was my *number one* issue when I got hired was to stay healthy, because I kept on getting sick with the weather changes. I would say that was my hardest problem when I first got married. Oh I mean got this job." Shelly had been looking me in the eyes as she spoke.

"So are you married?" I asked.

"Oh lord no."

"You're telling me you are that gorgeous and not married?"

The other recruiter said, "I was telling her that last night, but she keeps on getting the wrong guys."

"Shoot, you're lucky I don't have a ring on me right now," I said and they started laughing.

"See Lando, you got me being all unprofessional. I'm so sorry."

"No, I'm sorry."

"We are about to go over your application and next we will decide the next step for you."

They walked out and I said, "Yes! I got them." I'd been doing interviews long enough to know when I had the recruiter hooked.

By the age of twenty-five I'd had over fifteen different jobs from working in the cemetery, driving, and fast food to working in the airlines. But I hated having a boss, so it would only last a few months to a year. I looked at my reflection in the mirror and said, "Lando, you're the fucking man! That's how you're suppose to do interviews!"

Jeanine walked into the lobby area where I was standing. "We decided we like you and want you to go downstairs to get finger-printed and then a shuttle will take you across the street to get drug tested. It was nice meeting you. And do me a favor and make sure this meeting stays between us that you made it this far."

"Okay thanks," I replied.

I was now understanding why they didn't send people back to the room after they interviewed them, so we couldn't share tips and any information on what they're doing. I walked downstairs and saw a cute pregnant white lady as she introduced herself and showed me the process of getting my fingerprints done. We talked about her being pregnant, but she was currently working in that department since she couldn't fly. Next, she told me which shuttle to take to get my drug test done as we parted ways. As I was walking out of the building, I saw this gorgeous Japanese chick sitting, so I introduced myself. We started talking for a little bit and she said she was there because they needed to redo her fingerprints, for some reason they hadn't come in right or some-thing like that.

We small talked for a while and I said, "I hope to see you in the next training." She was honestly the best looking Japanese woman I'd seen in my life.

I was standing at the bus stop and Brenda drove up in an older all white Oldsmobile. "Hey Brenda, how did it go?"

"Great! I'm about to go and take my drug test."

"Me too. I'm taking the shuttle over there now."

"You can ride with me over there. Hop in. I'm sorry my car's a little messy. Just throw everything in the back," she said as she mettled with the clothes in the front seat tossing them in the back.

"Okay thanks, I appreciate it."

"So they liked you, huh?" she asked.

"I guess so, because I think if they didn't like you they sent you straight home. I saw that black girl that does nails going home, because I went back to use the bathroom and saw the young one from Indiana coming up as I was going down to get my fingerprints done. So I'm assuming they hired her also. Now, Lando, I'm scared doing this drug test."

"Oh lord, don't tell me your old ass been smoking."

She started laughing and said, "No, Lando, I'm on a lot of different pills and I hope it don't come up in my drug test."

"What type of pills are they? I think you're just over exaggerating. Just show them what you're using when we go in and they will tell you."

"Yeah that's what I need to do, because I have them all with me and the paperwork for them." We walked in and filled out the papers. It was a basic routine. I took my drug test and got her number so we could keep in touch. I was happy they were able to fly me back home to Detroit the same day.

Aunt Chris and dad came to pick me up from the airport. "Hey! How did the interview go, son?" dad asked as I climbed into my aunt's red and black late model Mercedes Benz.

"Man, it went great. They didn't fully tell me yet if I got the job. But I got it. They loved me in the interview and I already went to get drug tested and fingerprinted." I felt cocky and confident.

"Did they fingerprint everybody that came?" he asked.

He was just asking to hype me up because he knew damn well they didn't fingerprint everybody, but this is what dad liked to do to keep us talking.

"Naw. They did it kinda slick and divided us up so we wouldn't know who made it and who didn't. But at the end we kinda figured out who did and didn't."

"How did you like the airline?" asked Aunt Chris.

"I loved it. The recruiters were real nice and professional. I would be based in Washington D.C. at first, then probably have a chance to go to Atlanta. And you can move up in the company quickly. They have a thing where if you're good enough you can make the BYB All-star team and do special assignment trips to Hawaii or something like that."

"Wow! It's looking like a winner. So if you had to choose between AirStar and BYB, which one would you choose?"

I looked at the sky as if it had some answers. "AirStar is overall the best of the best of the regional airlines, but I can be based in Atlanta, so I don't know yet. I really don't know. But probably AirStar because it's more my style."

"Since you're about to leave your job, me and your dad decided, if you're up to it, we will pay you $150 a week, $75 each, to go see grandma a few times a week and to also help you keep some money coming in until training."

"Yeah that sounds great. I'm down." I was thinking, *This would work out perfectly, because I love my grandma. I would go and see her everyday if I could, but she isn't the closest to our house and it requires gas, so I'm blessed to have family that can give us both a win-win scenario.*

Walking dad in the house by grabbing his shirt started to become our regular routine and he complained less and less.

"Oh yeah, dad, it was the baddest chick at that interview. She was Japanese. I'm just praying we would be in the same training if I go. She went to that school in Florida that you wanted to send me to become a flight attendant. I think it's like an academy."

"Did she tell you if she liked it?"

"Yeah, she said it was worth it. See that's why Stacey won't ever get hired anywhere, because she's scared to take the required steps you need to get hired, like buy that book you have or go to that training. Because there is no way you can tell me going to that training won't help one's chances with getting hired. You just can't tell me that."

Me and dad ranted back and forth as we watched some football, yelling throughout the house like we did regularly.

A few days later at work, I was talking to everybody and

laughing because it was my last day. It wasn't really a bittersweet moment, because all of my original friends had either left or gotten fired by that time. I was upstairs helping out and I saw Debo, the bully from the movie Friday, walking past.

"Hey. What's up, Debo!" I yelled as if I was in the streets and seen one of my old childhood friends. He looked over and said, "Nothing much, brother" and kept on walking.

Darelle, a friend from high school who worked at the airport, walked into the shop, "Aye Lando, You know Debo here walking around?"

"Yeah, I just seen him and said what's up."

"He was at my old high school in Detroit. He did a speech and some program there. Did you see his little, cute, skinny wife?"

"Yeah, I did I feel sorry for her little ass. I bet she be getting broke down. It's crazy how he act tough in all his movies, but I heard in real life he's a straight Christian and a great guy."

"He is. One of my boys from back home know his people. That's how I knew he was going to be out here. Aye man, I'm going to miss you and that free coffee, but do your thing in that air and leave some hoes for me."

"Okay, I'll see you around." We departed from each other for the last time as me being a coffee shop employee. This day I just walked around and said my goodbyes to everybody. Now to be honest I did get emotional with Jamie, because she never worked on Wednesdays, but she did just so she could see me. Even though we talked trash to each other all the time, I love that chick to death and she knew it. As I gave her a hug, she wouldn't stop saying, "Lando, make sure you have my right number. Take down my Facebook info. When can I see you again, don't forget about me and so on."

I'm in the coffee shop with Phil and we're standing there and he said, "Lando, I know this is your last day and I mean this in the most respectful way, but can I grab your ass before you leave?" I started dying laughing as he continued. "Well, that thing is always ready to explode out of those pants and I always wanted to grab it."

I looked at him and said, "If you had enough nuts to ask that crazy question then gone ahead, brother."

"So you're saying I can?"

"Yep better do it before I change my mind."

16

I love my brother, OC. I remember when we were young, he would promise me and Keke that he would drive us everywhere once he got his license and a car. He stuck to his word. Every weekend we were at Fairlane Mall and he was buying me the newest pair of Jordan's with a matching outfit or going to Toys R' Us to get the latest Power Ranger toy.

He was raised in the same circumstances as my other siblings. But on the other hand, he had it better, due to him moving out and living with my grandparents at age fourteen. He was spoiled over there. They made sure he stayed wearing Tommy Hilfiger or Ralph Lauren, everything from head to toe.

Things went great until after he turned sixteen. He was always bad. Keke and I figured that out when he taught us how to steal radios out of this limousine service's parking lot, right after we left church. Years later, that parking lot became part the of church we built. Ironic, right? He would go in and do the job, while me and Keke were his lookouts. Back in those days, car lots didn't lock the car doors. Even during those times, you were able to go to a gas station and pay *after* you pumped your gas, such was the honor system. But I'm probably the one who messed that up for the rest of the world, being broke filling my tank up, and speeding off with Sean.

Once I became a teenager, my brother was already a hood nigga. He loved the streets, selling drugs, and fast, expensive cars. It's weird, because that should've never happened, considering the way he was raised. But I guess everybody gets to choose to live the way they want. So growing up, I was used to my brother being in and out of jail. It was kind of a regular thing for him to go in for at least a few months out of the year.

Criminal or not, he was still my older brother by seven years. Most people thought we were twins, since we both have the same mom and pops. Dark skin, short, we were both crazy and always fighting. I always believed me and him both had the same mindset, we both wanted to be rich, successful, and both wanted to take over the world. OC the Third just preferred route A and I preferred route B.

While I was at Sean's house, I got an email from AirStar saying *'training will be postponed due to low attrition.'*

"Low attrition?" I repeated aloud, kinda confused, since I didn't know what the word meant. I decided to call dad and ask. "Aye, dad, I just got an email from AirStar saying training is postponed due to low attrition. What does that mean?"

"That means the turnover rate is low and people are not quitting or something like that. Did you look on your computer about it?"

"Yeah, it said something like that."

"Man, see God is good and was able to set you up with that other interview you just had. In this crazy industry, you never know what can happen. But I got Rob Green on the other end." Rob was dad's best friend.

"Okay, dad, I'll hit you back."

Sean's dad walked downstairs. "I smell a stewardess in my

house," he shouted with his squeaky voice wearing some tan shorts and a racing t-shirt.

"What's up?"

"Oh nothing much. About to show you how grown men play pool. Rack'em up," he demanded, while looking at the pool table.

We started playing and he whooped my ass for about five games straight, barely letting me shoot. I loved playing his dad or my dad, because both of them were on the pro level and that was the only way I could get better was by watching them play. Sean walked down the stairs with his Comcast uniform and said, "Whoa, I don't like how you get to walk in my house, play my games, play with my dog, and eat my food while I'm not even here."

"Sir, your family loves me a lot more than they love you, señor."

"I just want to know have you beaten this man once in pool yet?" he asked as he looked at his dad.

He asked, but he already knew the answer, so I just walked away and ignored the question. We settled down to play *Call of Duty* for a while.

Afterwards, I hopped the gate and went over to mom's to see how she had been doing. "Hey, baby, you got a lot of mail over here," she said as I walked through the back door. She was in the kitchen washing dishes.

"How has your dad been doing?"

"He has been okay. He is getting better. The process will just take time."

"Do you have a few dollars I can have, son? I been so broke. I can't wait until tax season comes."

"Yeah, I got 20 dollars." I reached for my wallet and gave it to her.

Keke walked in through the front door, "I knew I could find you."

"How did you know he was over here?" mom asked.

Then Mary walked upstairs and said, "Because of Facebook. He posts something every two seconds."

Keke got into a long spiel about my flight benefits. Apparently she had been researching again. I hadn't even started the job. Mom and I just shook our heads.

In the car driving back to dad's, Brenda from BYB called. "Hey, did you get the email yet?"

"Naw, what did it say?"

"It said I was hired and training starts the 25th!"

"What! Congrats! I wonder why I haven't gotten it yet. I made it through the process. Okay, I will keep you updated. Thanks for the call, Brenda, congrats again." I quickly double and triple checked my email to see if it was in my spam file, but didn't see anything.

Wonder why I didn't hear anything back, I'm just about sure I was hired.

Over the next few weeks I went to a few other interviews in the area and did the same process, overview, they like me, drug test and we will call you soon, but all sent me a thanks, but no thanks email.

While sitting on the couch, dad walked in and asked, "Have you heard anything yet?"

"Pops, it's been a week since they emailed Brenda that she got the job and I still haven't heard nothing. I just don't understand what's the deal. I'm confused."

"Wow." Dad shook his head. "Man, in this industry you never know what can happen. One day you're hired and the next day you can be fired. Have you heard from AirStar?"

"Naw, the last thing I heard we are just in the waiting process. There are a few more interviews going on, but I really don't feel like going, since I have a few I'm waiting to hear from."

Changing the subject, dad said, "They transferred grandma to a place in Canton off of Lilly road. She is doing a little better. It's like a healthcare place in a little hospital, so they can monitor her better."

"Okay, I will go and check on her tomorrow."

As I'm sitting there watching some football I get the email and check it. I pictured myself throwing my phone all across the room. But instead, I just took a deep breath and laid out on the couch. Yup, I was denied from BYB, the airline I knew they completely loved me. *I was the only guy. Brenda got hired. And why would they send me through the whole fingerprint and drug process if they didn't want to hire me. Damn, was it a mistake?* I thought. *Did they mistakenly use somebody else's piss with mine?*

I decided to email them back, since I didn't have anything to lose. "What's the problem? I did great in the interview and I just don't understand what's going on. I knew I wasn't going to get a response, so I did some research to call in and ask somebody personally. I eventually got the right number and called to talk to a representative who told me, "We can't disclose why we didn't hire you."

"Ma'am, please," I said with a depressed, frustrated, and tired voice. "I just don't know what's going on. I have been outperforming people during interviews. I'm making it to the next stages and I just don't understand how I'm not getting hired."

There was a brief silence on the phone for a moment. You could hear her take a deep breath over the phone and said, "I'm sorry, but all I can do is say check your overall information about yourself deeply," and she hung up the phone.

"Check your information deeply," I said out loud. "*Fuck!*"

"Watch your mouth in my house. What's wrong with you?" dad said, walking into the living room.

"I didn't get hired with BYB, so I called to see what's going on. The chick said within their rules they can't tell me the anything, but check my information deeply. So I'm thinking what could that mean. I thought of the reasons I couldn't get hired, especially if I been making it this far. Couldn't be my drug test, because I don't smoke. But could be my background with OC using my name when I was younger."

"Wow, I think you could be right on this one, son. So the first thing in the morning you need to get working on that ASAP."

The next day at the library I went to Michigan.gov/ichat and put in my info. I had to pay $10, so I put in my card information and as soon as everything popped up all I could say was wow.

I called dad soon as I got into the car. "Dad, you won't believe this crap, man. I looked up my record right and why do I look like America's top criminal on there.

"What!"

"Yes, I got felonies, about three DUIs. I have a gun charge and all."

Dad burst out laughing. I said, "Calm down. I don't think it's that funny, sir."

"Man, the thing is I know them recruiters was like..." he paused to catch his breath from laughing and changed his voice to sound like a female, "Orlando, is such a good kid, a hard worker, I really like him. And then they pulled up your background information and got scared as heck. 'Oh no, Becky, this nigger got a felony gun charger and all.' The other one says, 'Hey where is he from again, Becky?' They pull it up on the computer and she says Detroit ahhhahahaha."

I just hung up on that fool I was so mad, but after a while all I could do was laugh with him.

I decided to go see grandma at the healthcare facility.

I walked in and spoke to the lady at the reception desk. "My grandmother checked in not too long ago. Can you tell me which room she is in?"

"Yes, what's her name?"

I gave her name and she told me grandma was in room 417.

"Okay thanks."

I walked in the room and saw grandma's nurse changing her. "Oh, I'm sorry." I'd walked in the room without knocking.

"It's okay. Actually, can you help?" he asked.

"Yeah, no problem."

"Wow, you're good. You might take my job."

Smiling, I replied, "I'm a certified nurses assistant."

"What, are you serious?"

"Yeah, I took my state exam in Lansing."

"That's great. I did too. So where are you working right now?"

"Umm, I just quit my job and I'm becoming a flight attendant."

"That's awesome." Changing the subject as we finished up, he said, "She is good to go. See you later."

"Hey grandma. How are you feeling today?"

"I would be a lot better if I was out of here."

I spoke in a whisper close to her ear, "Want me to sneak you out, grandma?" She smiled. "Who all has been up here to see you so far?"

"Umm nobody. I think your grandpa and Buddy came today or yesterday."

I glanced at the TV and noticed she was watching the news. They were talking about some type of catastrophic event.

"Grandma, we have to turn this stuff off. You're supposed to be getting better. I don't see how you can watching all of this negative stuff. You need to be watching something that makes you smile and happy."

"I know that's right," she responded smiling as I changed it to some George Jefferson.

"Now this is better for you, grandma. Have you eaten yet today?"

She looked at me as if she wasn't sure. I went in the hall and asked one of the nurses when was the last time she'd eaten.

"We tried to feed her a little over an hour ago, but she

wouldn't eat. Do you want me to bring some more food out and see if you can get her to eat something?"

"Yes please," I responded as my phone rang. I told the people at the desk that I would be right back since I had to make a quick run out to my car.

"Hey, grandma, open your mouth. You have to eat for me. Baby, come on." I held the spoon up to her mouth, as if trying to get a small child to eat. "What's the problem, grandma, is it that you're just not hungry?"

"I'm just not hungry." Her voice was so weak. "I will try for you," she said, attempting to sit up.

I started feeding her, she was so happy to eat she didn't want to stop. Once she got finished, she immediately started to throw up. I helped her out and put the call light on for someone to help clean her up. I texted Aunt Chris to update her on how the visit went.

I really didn't want to think about grandma being sick. I'd never seen her in a hospital before, but I had to stay strong and positive for her. To watch the woman who raised me to not be able to eat and struggling felt terrible.

The next day I woke up to an email from AirStar saying the training was delayed and there was no update, but if the candidates had a misdemeanor or anything on their record to let them know ASAP so they could fix it. I walked upstairs and told dad about the email.

"So did they email everybody or just you?" dad asked.

"This is for everybody, so they didn't single me out."

"How random is that?"

"You think I should email her and tell her the deal, so they can know what's up?"

"Heck naw," he responded as if I were stupid. "You need to get on that computer thing and call who you need to call so you can get this taken care of before you go to training. This is a gift from the Lord trying to give you some time." I immediately got on the job.

"Hello, can I speak to Laura Michfield, please?"

"She is busy right now. Can I get her to call you back?"

I gave my information, hung up and immediately told dad about the call. We got interrupted by my phone ringing. "Hold on, this might be her now."

Picking up the phone, I said, "Hello, Orlando speaking!"

"Hey Orlando, this is Laura. What can I do for you?"

"I checked my background information on iChat and it's saying I have felonies and everything on my record, but none are from me."

"Tell her you're trying to become a flight attendant," dad whispered in the background. As I was trying to talk to her I heard his ass whisper something else. "And tell her it messed up your job interview."

I got up and walked away from him so I could focus. She asked for my information so she could look it up. Once I gave it to her, she said, "It's showing a lot of stuff on here." I was surprised when she asked me if I knew my brother OC.

"Somehow the system has you two guys' information switched up. Okay, now I see what we have to do. You have to go to your state police station and request to get your fingerprints sent here. It should take a week to get everything handled, because I'm kind of backed up. Just call me a few days after it's sent and you should be okay."

"Thanks, Laura, I really appreciate it."

I walked in the police station and there were a few people waiting in line. So I went up to the counter and requested a fingerprint form.

"Just fill out this paperwork and I will come out to take your fingerprints," the black officer stated as he handed me the paper.

We went through the proper steps and he said he would try to expedite the process as soon as he could. Sitting in the car I was thinking, *Why is all this crazy stuff happening to me? I could have already been hired with multiple companies. I could probably have been in Atlanta right now dating that sexy Japanese chick and traveling the world.*

For the next few days I moped around the house doing nothing but being depressed.

"Have you heard anything yet?" dad asked.

"Nope. I done quit my job and now possibly don't have another one. I hope this all works out."

"Well your aunt got some good news for you, call her."

"I have two tickets for you to go to the Thanksgiving game on Thursday, but I think Keke wanted to go also," she told me.

"Yes! I get to see my boy, Tom Brady, a Michigan Man, playing for the New England Patriots versus the Detroit Lions. I can just call Keke and see if she wants to go with me."

"So what's the plans for Thanksgiving this year?" dad asked.

We agreed to have the meal at grandma's anyway to keep the family together. My brother, OC, and I got into a contest to see who could barbeque the best ribs, since dad couldn't do it this year.

I stopped over OC's one day. "So what's up with your background information? Keke told me what happened. Why you ain't tell me?"

"I don't know. It's nothing really you could do, but basically I looked up my background information and it showed all of my and your information together. I need all my stuff as clean as possible, since I'm trying to get in with the airlines."

"Yeah, I got you. I decided to clean up my record so I can be out here legit by the end of next year." I was glad to hear that my brother was making moves in the right direction.

Keke and I had a blast at the game at Ford Field Stadium. It was her first time going to a pro football game. She was like a kid in a candy store. The energy in the stadium was electric.

"I'm trying to tell you this is why Aunt Chris gets season tickets and we play my favorite quarterback today."

I got Keke to drive on the way back, so I could look at YouTube of how to make the best barbecue ribs. I knew how to cook chicken and basic stuff, but never really cooked some ribs, so I went to a local store and started picking up all the good spices and stuff that I needed, including Sweet Baby Rays sauce and brown sugar. You gotta have Sweet Baby Rays. I was not going to let OC beat me!

As we were heading to grandma's house, OC called. "If you're scared then don't worry about the bet. You're the younger brother here, so I don't wanna take your money. I already feel bad that you don't have a job and got to hustle as much as you can."

I cut him off. "Bye, negro, just have my $20 ready." I hung up. Twenty dollars is the amount we agreed to bet.

Once I made it to the house, grandpa asked me to show Mary how to get the lemons ready for him to make the lemonade. Grandpa, hands down, makes the best lemonade. He usually made it for a special event like Thanksgiving.

Now our family loves sweet stuff and he made sure to put enough sugar in his lemonade. I honestly think his secret was the big ass stirring stick he had for like twenty years. It was a big wooden stick, kinda like something an old person would use for a cane. I'm not even sure if he even washed it as I think about it, but hell it got the job done.

I set up shop getting all my sauce and stuff ready for my ribs and Aunt Chris walked in with some food, greeting everybody.

"You look like you actually know what you're doing over there, Lake," she commented as she unloaded the food.

"I know a lil' something."

"Where is your grandpa?"

"Outside getting the grill ready." I walked outside and saw OC walking in with his lady Tiff. Soon as we crossed each other's path, we looked at each other ready to fight and talk smack. It's always been that way. If one looked at the other person the wrong way then thirty minutes later we would be sweaty, hot, and getting cussed out by mom for breaking something.

The contest ended up being a draw, despite the fire to the ribs. His sauce was more on the spicy side, mine was more sweet. We had a wonderful time that day visiting with family, in spite of grandma's absence. Aunt Chris visited her and took her some food.

The next morning, I went on the internet, and paid the fee again to see if all that stuff on my background was removed.

Yes! I noticed that all of my brother's stuff was gone off my record. Now that was the good news, but the kicker was it showed that I had a misdemeanor on my record for what happened on my boy Yan's birthday.

My phone rang, and ironically, it was the lady from Lansing. "I was able to take care of everything, but you do have a misdemeanor on your record that happened in Ypsilanti, Michigan."

"Yeah I'm looking at it now. I did not know I had that on my record," I said to her kinda in shock. "Is there anyway I can get that off, because I still think that messes me up from becoming a flight attendant?"

"The only thing I can think of is if you go to the court in Ypsilanti and get them to fax me something saying it's off your record."

"Okay, what's the fax number and I will send it over as soon as possible."

I began to fill my dad in on the news I just received.

"I talked to ole girl in Lansing, dad, and the thing is she got all that crazy stuff off my record, but I have a misdemeanor on my record from what happened in Ypsi a year ago."

"If you would've just told me and Chris instead of trying to do it yourself we would've gotten you an attorney so they could made sure nothing was on your record," he yelled as he shook his head in disappointment.

"Well, I can't do nothing now, but I'll will know next time. So at this point it is what is it."

"Can we get her to take it off, like pay her some loot or something?"

"You know that was the first thing I thought of, but she said go down to the Ypsilanti court and if I can get some type of paper saying it's off. Then she can remove it. So I'm gonna go down there and try to make some things happen somehow."

Driving to the court, I started to think about what happened on Yan's birthday and how many times I had to drive to this courthouse, to end up with a misdemeanor on my record. Fourteen. That's the number of times I'd been down here over this small infraction.

I got to the courthouse and the lady called me up to the desk. "Hey, how are you doing today, Jackie?" I asked, looking at the name badge she wore.

"I'm doing great. Just ready to get off. What can I do for you today?"

"I checked my record and noticed I have a misdemeanor on there. My caseworker in Lansing said to get it off I would have to show some type of proof saying I'm clear."

"Let me put in your information, sir, and we can see what I can do. You already went to trial and were guilty, so you and your attorney were supposed work that out," she said as she looked at the screen.

"So it's nothing you can do." I was so disappointed. I'm sure it showed on my face.

"No, I'm sorry, but your case is still open and to close it you have to pay $210."

"Now what do you mean by closed?" *Just when I thought it couldn't get any worse.*

"To get this off of your record, this case has to be closed for two or more years from the date you have officially closed it by paying the rest of your money. Your attorney should have told you all of this."

"Wow, that bi...that lady didn't tell me nothing, but I guess I will pay it now. Can I do debit card?"

"Yes, you can."

"Can I have some type of paperwork saying it's closed, please?" She handed me a receipt showing I had paid, but I preferred paperwork showing that it was closed.

Driving home, Stacey called sounding excited and talking about she got hired with Logan Airline and was waiting for training. Unfortunately, Kerry had been acting real jealous lately. It was just female drama, probably about them banging the same man or something, so I was saved when my dad called and I had to click over.

"Hey, boo, let me call you back. This is my dad calling," I said as I rushed off the phone.

"Hey. What's up, dad?"

"Hey, son, have you seen some of my dirty tapes? I know I'm not the smartest man in the world, but DVDs can't move themselves, can they?"

I guess he called himself being sarcastic, since he was assuming that I took them. Being goofy, I told him, "See what it is, we have a porno ghost in the house and he always *loves* to watch them in my room. So I'm not sure if they are in there, but I would assume he put some in my room. One is probably even in the DVD player as we speak."

He burst out laughing. "You're a funny guy. How did it go?"

"It went okay. I had to pay $210 to close the case."

"You better pay that with the quickness. I will give you the money."

"I already paid it and used your card," I said, sounding a little sheepish. "I figured that's what you'd want me to do. I'll pay you back later. I was able to get her to give me a copy that said that my case is closed and if I fax that over to Lansing, she might take that off my record."

"Yeah, son, it only took her a night to take all that stuff from OC off. All she probably have to do is click a button on that computer thing and you're good. But you have to convince her to do it."

"I will be at the crib in a minute."

"Okay. Since you spent all of my money, bring me some McDonalds. I want a double fish with extra tartar."

"You're just crazy. You know I'm allergic to fish, but you still continue to eat it, bye man."

While I was getting his food, I received an email saying how training is still pushed back, but if you have a misdemeanor on your record let them know, so they can take care of it in the meantime. *Damn, what're the odds of this shit?* I thought.

By the time I made it home, I was more confused than ever. "Dad! What're the odds of this?"

"What's up?"

"I got an email from Billie saying this..." I read him the email.

"I don't know what to do. They said if you have a misdemeanor you better say something."

So dad sat down. I could tell he was deep in thought, because it took him a while to speak. "Have you ever been putting it on any applications that your record is messed up?"

"Naw, I didn't know, so I haven't."

"Okay, but you made it this far. It's a big decision to make and you can look at it both ways. If you do tell them, she said they will send it to some high up people and try to save you, but I'm not sure about that because as soon as they find out you have one they might call somebody else that doesn't. And you did say it read, 'If you have had a felony or misdemeanor since the interview let them know,' right?"

"Yeah."

"Have you received a felony or misdemeanor since the interview?"

"Naw, I got that a while ago."

"Okay then you're not necessarily lying. Now if you don't tell them at least you can go to training when it starts and try to wing it from there, because this is the hardest industry I have ever seen in my life to get into. I'm 55 years old and I personally only know two people who work in this field. So what I'm trying to say is, it's a hard field to get in and if you have to say nothing to get in, then you have to do what you have to do."

I thought about what he was saying for a second and responded. "Yeah, you're right. I guess I will have to just figure it out then. But in the email it mentioned about not getting into Canada. I have to look up which forms I would need if I would want to check into it myself. Maybe I can fly, but just can't go into Canada, you know?"

"Do your thing. Have you checked up on grandma this week?"

"Naw, not yet, but I will go up there today."

Immediately, I got on the computer and started looking up all the rules going into and out of Canada. There were stipulations on felonies and misdemeanors, but it wasn't totally clear. "I'm gonna call my attorney and get him to explain it to me."

"You still have Prepaid Legal?"

"Yep, still got it. Since I moved in with you I haven't been able to go as hard as usual, but I will get back in the flow soon."

Within an hour my attorney called me back telling me which numbers to call and which forms I should print out. I did as he instructed and as I started to read all of this crap. I honestly didn't think I qualified, because these were for more serious criminals or things like DUIs, and gun charges.

I walked into the nursing home to see grandma and saw the sexy girl that worked at the front desk.

"Hey Lando, how are you doing?"

"I'm doing better since I get to see a gorgeous face." I flirted, as usual.

She smiled. "Your grandma is like the most popular person in this place. People keep calling and she has a group of people upstairs now."

I walked into her room and saw a lot of her church friends in the room holding hands and praying. I greeted everybody, mostly people that have known me since I was barely walking. Grandpa was there having a good time joking around with one of the deacons, asking him how much did he pay his wife to marry him. The women from the church started to sing grandma's favorite song and I was surprised because she sung along with them. It was an awesome thing to see since lately grandma hadn't been too active and was barely talking. So to see her singing made my day.

Once Christmas came around the majority of the family was in good spirits. But since I was a little broke that year I didn't buy anybody anything. Actually, that year my aunt made everybody pull names on Thanksgiving. The rules were plain and simple, we couldn't spend over $20. So the plan was for everybody to meet up at the nursing home grandma was at so she could be part of everything.

"Merry Christmas, grandma!" I yelled, walking in realizing I was the first one there.

"Hey hey, Lando. Is it Christmas?" Grandma was playing around as if she didn't know.

"Yeah today is Christmas. That's why we have to get you out of here, so you can remember your days again."

Everybody started to walk in with gifts, as we all greeted each other. I pulled out my camera phone and started recording everything. First, we grabbed hands to pray before exchanging greetings and jokes. Come to find out Aunt Chris had brought everybody iPads and dad bought me one. I noticed grandma over there looking mean, so I asked her, "What's wrong?"

"Y'all need to calm down. Y'all over there doing too much."

"Grandma, it's Christmas. What do you want for Christmas, grandma?"

"Some money," she said with the most serious face.

Laughing I asked, "Grandma, what are you gonna do with some money?"

"The same thing you will do with some money," she replied laughing.

"I hope you all received my text. What we're going to do is everybody that brought a gift put their name in a hat and we will pull to see who you have to give your gift to." Aunt Chris then pulled out this big ass jar full of coins and said, "The person that can guess the correct amount of money gets to keep it."

Uncle Buddy, grandma's brother, said, "I didn't get the text message, but I wanna play."

"Okay, you can get in, Uncle Buddy. So who wanna pull first?"

Kelly walked up and she pulled OC's name, I pulled Kelly's and dad pulled grandpa's. OC pulled Aunt Chris, and she pulled Keke's. We exchanged gifts and then everybody put their guesses in for the money jar. Kelly ended up winning because she picked the number closest to what was in the jar, without going over the amount.

"If I would have known that from the beginning then I would have won," I said.

"You wasn't gonna win nothing over me if I knew we couldn't go over," OC said to strike up an argument.

"First thing, I worked at a coffee shop and bar counting money on a daily basis, so I know *all about money, boy!*"

We go back and forth with our usual brotherly feud. Overall, we had an amazing Christmas. I was able to spend it with all my family and was extremely hyped to have the brand new iPads.

Since dad knew I needed a "computer thing," as he liked to say, it was the perfect gift.

Some days later I walked into the library to get some materials to help me learn another language.

"Hello, what can I do for you?" the librarian asked me.

"I'm looking for some way to learn Spanish. I would prefer books and audios."

"Follow me, we have lots of them. So, what's making you want to learn Spanish?" she asked.

"I figure the more value you bring to the world, the more money you can make. I'm about to become a flight attendant, so it would also help in that field."

"Wow. I always wanted to become a flight attendant. I applied for Mesaba once, but didn't get it," she exclaimed with excitement and a ready to talk expression.

"Yeah I did too. It's a hard field to get into though."

"Well good luck."

"Oh I'm sorry. I'm Lando."

"I'm Amy. Come back, Lando, and let me know how the career is going." She smiled and directed me to a few good books, but most of the audios were checked out. I had to just make due with what I had.

Once I got home I started hitting the books like crazy. First, I would do an hour of learning the basics of Spanish, and once I got tired, I started listening to audios.

"I see you're learning Spanish," dad said as he walked into the living room.

"Actually, you can't *see* nothing, big fella," I responded smiling.

"You got jokes today, huh. I actually know a little bit of Spanish." He smiled.

"Oh you do, dad? Let me hear some."

"Si."

"Okay, what you got?"

"Si." he responded. "Si, I got jokes, too." He laughed at his own joke.

I shook my head as I looked at the website that had all of the job postings and saw that Samer was hiring again. I went back to the forums and read how badly people were talking about the company and just closed my iPad.

"Your aunt said it's a nice place over by her house that's going for a good price."

"A house?"

"Naw, it's a Condo. She is gonna take me by it tomorrow and look into it. She said we need to get the heck out of this hood. Every time you leave the house you gotta hope you have a gun with you. Speaking of that, you need to hit up your boy Wade so we can get our CCWs. You be playing around too much. You suppose to have been did that."

"I will hit him up tomorrow."

"Have you heard from AirStar yet?"

"Nope, not yet. Just looking at all these job postings the airlines been putting up, but I'm not gonna do any more until I go to this training and see what's the deal with this misdemeanor."

"Yeah, I understand you on that one, son. But tomorrow we gonna go check out that house, so be ready."

"Just let me know what time."

The next day we drove around my aunt's neighborhood and saw a few different houses we liked, taking down the realtor's numbers. Now the last one we went to visit was a condo on the end of the street.

"Aye, dad, the price is good on this one and it's not too big. But where are we going to get the money to pay for this?"

"Hopefully, my lawsuit money will come in soon. God willing everything will work itself out. We would have association fees and other stuff to pay."

"What's an association fee?" I asked.

"It's a fee you have to pay for the people to come and cut your grass, shovel your snow and maintenance really since it's a condo."

"Do you want me to call the realtor so we can set up an appointment to go inside?"

"Yeah. If she don't answer just leave a message and let's go get something to eat. I'm hungry. So where have Kerry and Stacey been?"

"Oh, I forgot to tell you Stacey got hired with a regional and I think she starts training in a few days."

"So the three musketeers all got hired with somebody. That's a blessing," he responded, smiling.

"All they do is take turns calling me talking crap about each other. Both of them females are crazy, man. You wanna go up to Coney on Ecorse, pops?"

"Ummm, yeah just call and order for me and we will pick it up today. It ain't my day. I just wanna chill."

"So have you heard from grandpa lately?" I asked.

"Yeah, he called this morning talking crazy. Saying I went into his bank account and stole his money."

"Umm, why would he say that?"

"Because on one of his accounts my name is on there also, just like you and me have one with the credit union."

Right then his phone started ringing. "Hello! Daddy, it's no way I can steal money out of your account. I would need somebody to literally drive and take me up there. I'm blind! How can a blind man steal some money? Okay, okay don't worry about it. Tomorrow we can go up there and take it off. Okay bye, dad." He was angry when he ended the call.

It was quiet in the car and I looked at dad and said, "Why you keep stealing from my grandpa?"

He shook his head. "I don't know. I get in the car when you're sleeping, drive up there, and take all his money out before he goes up there. You caught me, Lake." We started laughing.

Later on that day I needed to go over mom's house. I went into my old room looking at some of my books I'd left over there and my Prepaid Legal accolades I had lying around the room before checking my email. I saw the official training invitation email from AirStar and I went crazy.

"What are you quacking about?" my nephew said as he came into my room.

"I'm going to training in *March*!"

"Where you have to fly to?"

"Utah."

"Ain't that all the way on the east coast?"

"No fool, that's the west coast." I read over the email to make sure I was not crazy or overacting then called dad.

"When do you leave?" he asked.

"They said probably March 3rd..."

Aunt Chris cut me off saying, "Read the email out loud, Lake, so we can all hear it." I heard a third voice in the background, already knowing it was Keke.

"Don't tell me y'all got Keke over there, too."

"Yep, I'm here," she responded in excitement.

I read the full email. Dad asked, "Have you emailed them back yet?"

"Naw, I haven't yet. I just got it."

"Man, get off the phone with us, you big dummy, before you be a day late and a dollar short again."

"Okay, I'll call y'all back." In the email it said notify them ASAP if I was willing to accept the date, first come first served. I send the email to Madison telling her I was excited and ready to get started.

Mom came downstairs. "Hey, son. I miss you."

"I bet you do," I respond, "since nothing has been getting done around the house since I haven't been around."

"How is your daddy doing?"

"Good. That was him and Keke on the phone."

"Now you said you been trying to learn another language, right?"

"Yeah!"

"Come upstairs to get your mail. By the way, I was at a garage sale and was able to find a good Spanish tape and some other ones for you only for 25 cents."

"Thanks, mom, I will be up in a minute."

"Well, son, I'm proud of you," dad said randomly as I was cleaning the house. "Many people have been trying to get into this industry and it's just too hard, so you need to be really focused going down to Utah."

"Yeah, I'm waiting for them to send the training packet, so I can start studying soon."

"Who all is coming over tonight?" he asked.

"Ashley and Slim hit me up so far. I think Yan is out here too. I have to hit him up," I said referring to some of my longtime friends.

"Does anybody know you're hired yet?"

"Naw, I will tell everybody tonight."

I was having a few close members from the group to come over and kick it for the night. Since I'd been busy doing the flight attendant stuff I felt it would be a good day to invite everybody over to come play cards and kick it.

After a while everybody showed up and I decided to tell the group that soon I'd be leaving for flight attendant training.

"Low key, I'm proud and jealous at the same damn time. Naw F that I'm hatin.' Fuck you," Slim said.

I laughed and asked, "Why you gotta be hatin' on ya boy, Slim?"

"Man, you don't have kids and you think you can just fly around the world fucking bitches and stuff. I ain't having it. I'm gonna get pregnant, nigga," he yelled, using his best female voice impression.

We ended up watching a basketball game while having drinks, pizza and play some spades.

"Lando, you know we have to party hard before you leave," Steph said, looking at me with a smile.

"You think so?"

"Yeah, I know so."

"You know what I'm thinking, your birthday is coming up at the end of this month, right?" said Yan. "We can go hard on your birthday. We just gotta figure out what you want to do."

∽

WE WALKED into Lucky's and I asked for Kim, the lady I spoke with over the phone.

"You must be, Lando."

"I'm whoever you want me to be, baby," I responded to the beautiful, thick black female named Kim. She wore a sexy, short hairstyle, an all black Lucky's shirt, and black leggings that showed all her curves.

"You got jokes," she replied with a smile. "Have you guys ever been here before?"

"No, only to the one downtown."

"Alright, I'm gonna give you guys a tour." There was something there that would appeal to all of us. From live comedy to good food to a sports bar with lots of TVs, Lucky's had it all. We were looking forward to hanging out with the crew there.

Thanks to my boy Biscuit, he was able to pick me out the outfit I needed. I loved looking good and dressing up when I went out, but I was really not a big shopper. At that time in my life my friends dressed good enough, so I preferred to just let them pick it out and I would decide if I liked it.

A FEW DAYS later it was go time. I put on my brand new Cole Haans with a Rocawear outfit that match my shoes and I even wore a hat that night. I never wear hats, my head is too small and don't look right in them. One thing about hosting a party or an event, different people were calling me nonstop, as if I hadn't given them the full information already. All those damn distractions! I was trying to get ready before my boy Bob came to pick me up so we could head out.

'Hey Lando, where the place at again?' 'How much does it cost to get in?' 'What's the dress attire?'

"Wow! Y'all done hooked up the crib since the last time I been over here," my boy Bob said, looking around with approval.

"I know that's not my boy Bob?" dad said walking out of his room.

"Yeah man, how you been? I heard you had surgery on your eyes. I hope you can still see."

"My eyes are getting better. But no matter what, there is one thing I will always be able to see."

"What's that, pump dawg?"

"Some pussy," he said with a straight face. All we could do was shake our heads and laugh.

"That's one crazy old man. I tell you the older they get the worst they are."

"You two gone ahead and have a good time. Bob, you driving?"

"Yeah, I'm looking out for the birthday boy. See you later, pump." Dad walked away and put up the peace sign. Bob was my boy who'd gone to the army, did his four years, and got the hell out of there.

"Aww shoot! I get to ride in the new boy, huh?" I asked as I looked at his shiny new Taurus Sho.

"Yea man. We gotta pick up Sean. He called and said he's rollin' wit us."

"Okay cool."

"Lando, I'm going ham tonight, bro." He told me, smiling, as we waited for Sean to return from the store.

"Aye, I need you to calm down. I thought you was on your holy man and not drinking."

"I was. Well I am, but it's my boy's birthday, and for me to get loose you know ya boy need that goose. Ya know what I'm saying, bro?"

I already knew what time it was, because he hadn't hung out with his real friends in a while. With him being around everybody and feeling good he was ready to have a drink. He was a few years older than me, but was raised by his grandparents, so he'd always had an old soul.

Once we got to the place, we walked pass the long line telling the security I had a booth.

"What's your name, sir?" Before I was able to say a word, the chick that hooked us up grabbed me.

"Hey Lando, come on in, sweetie. James, don't worry he is with me," she told the guard.

The venue was looking great, as it started to fill up we saw good-looking women, beautiful bartenders, they even had a camera man in the corner taking pictures. And to top it off the DJ was on point, so I knew it was about to be on and poppin' all night. And apparently it was!

Early the next morning I was in the bed laid out when Carlton called. I put him on speaker. "Yo!"

"Haha nigga are you alive?"

"I don't think so. What happened last night?" I said laughing, barely able to speak.

"Dude, we partied hard and soon as Kiki and Rob brought some Moët shit got real, bro. But I'm so pissed we lost all that money last night."

"What you mean?" I responded confused.

"Nigga, you don't remember going to the casino?"

"What! Hell naw I don't remember that."

"Keke got drunk and hyped everybody up to go to Motor City. Me and you was on the crap table going in."

"All hell naw. Hold on, this is Sean calling."

"Hello."

"Man, why you go so hard on that girl last night?"

"What the hell? What girl?" I said as if they were playing a joke on me at this point.

"You're telling me you don't remember getting kicked out of Motor City?"

"Oh boy, I was that drunk? Carl is on the other end talking about we was playing craps and stuff."

"Y'all was. He lost all your damn money haha."

"Wow I guess I had me a great birthday." Funny thing was, I didn't remember any of it.

I went over to my aunt's house and soon as I walked into the kitchen, I was greeted with, "There is the drunk birthday boy."

"Awww, man, not you too, Aunt Chris."

"You need some coffee. I just brewed some and we need you to sign your attendant care paperwork so we can send it in to the state. They decided to stop paying us and your dad has the information about that."

I asked, "Has anybody heard from grandma today?"

"Yeah, they just called me a few hours ago and said she completely stopped eating and her bed sores are getting worse, so they transferred her to St. Mary's Hospital."

"Oh okay. The one on Levan? I will go up there tomorrow and check on her."

"When you do go, put these scarves over her head. I bought a few of them and you know she don't like to not have herself up to par when people come visit her. Also get some chapstick, because her lips been really dry." Changing the subject, she asked, "So what date is your training?"

"Some time in February and will finish late March. They emailed me my training packet, so I can finally start studying now and just be in a zone for the next few weeks."

"You know we need to get that house cleaned up before you leave," dad replied as he took a sip of his coffee.

"Aunt Chris, do you have a binder upstairs I can use to put my training packet in, so it'll be organized?"

"Yeah, just leave it over here and I will get it back to you."

"Hey grandma," I said quietly as I opened her room door.

She was asleep and gave me no response. I saw they had her hooked up to a liquid only food system, because she hadn't been eating. There were IVs everywhere. She looked bad. I turned on the TV and pulled out my iPad, so I could start working on my training packet. After a while a nurse walked in and introduced himself, asking if I could leave for a little bit so he could change her. I complied, leaving the room to look around the hospital. It felt sad and depressing. All I saw were sick people, families bringing in flowers, doctors in the halls conversing with angry families.

"Okay, Lando, she is awake now," the nurse said as he left the room.

"Hey, grandma, how you feeling?"

She opened her mouth and nothing came out.

"Does it hurt when you try to talk?" She nodded her head in response.

"Look what I brought you." I grabbed her hair cover out of the bag. "I can't have you up in the hospital looking all crazy. See, grandma, you're looking better already," I told her, placing the scarf on her head. "All we have to do now is put some Chapstick on those ashy lips of yours. My birthday was the other day and we all went to a very nice bar in Southfield and also a comedy show. I ended up getting hired with AirStar and my training starts in a few weeks, so I'm going to be studying a lot and hopefully when I get back you will be back home." She just looked at me as I talked to her about the goings on in my life. She always was a good listener. "Grandma, since you left grandpa's been acting crazy, the house is looking crazy. I'm not supposed to tell you this, but I hope it's some motivation to get out of here. Let me change this channel to your favorite show, Jeopardy." She smiled and I gave her a kiss.

17

When I first joined a network marketing company called Pre-Paid Legal I was young, ambitious and hungry for success. My friends and family all told me "It's one of those pyramid schemes." But one thing I learned from a mentor is if you buy somebody else's opinion then you will sooner or later have their lifestyle. If they don't have what you want or aren't where you want to be in life, then who cares?

When I used to attend our local events I would sit in the front furiously taking notes. I analyzed each speaker and thought of the things they did right versus the things they did wrong, so I could use it to my benefit and learn from them. I started reading self-help books every day, listening to audio books, and just brainwashed myself for success. Every life experience, whether good or bad, is there to learn from.

It was now time to start studying now that I'd seen all of my friends, kicked it with grandma, and had my training packet in hand. If I was gonna do it, I wanted to be the best in the class was my mentality. One the first pages in the manual was AirStar Initial Hire Training Packet. As I skimmed through everything, I couldn't say exactly what was in the packet, but there was an announcement I needed to learn verbatim, all the states, different airline jargon and a lot of definitions. And I mean a whole lot we needed to learn.

I studied day after day, not picking up my phone nor eating as much. The hardest part was learning those announcements verbatim. As I was sitting on the couch studying, dad walked in and asked me to go outside and grab the rest of everything from the car. I assumed he and my aunt had gone grocery shopping. One of the boxes was a karaoke radio type of thing and I had to ask what were his plans for it.

"You know while you're gone I might have a party or two. I heard you the other day working on that speech you're gonna be using a microphone."

"Not a microphone, but an intercom, dad."

"Yeah same difference, but the thing is, what I'm trying to tell you is that you need to use this here to practice," He pointed towards the toy radio. Plug it up and let's try it. I bought a karaoke CD that play the words on that screen right in the front."

"Ladies and gentlemen, welcome inboard flight number 3333 en route to Utah."

"Yeah, keep on doing that and you will come along."

I got a call from Stacey. "You won't believe this shit! So I've been doing great this whole training, right? I mean 100% here, 98% there, on these test."

I could hear how angry she was, because her voice would switch to a Brooklyn accent as she spoke.

"But I was having a hard time learning all the different aircrafts, so after class I asked the instructor to help me a little bit because I didn't understand. She looked at me like I was crazy, and gone say, 'You should've been paying attention. You're the only one that's not getting it.' Lando, I was about ready to bitch slap her ass. So I go and take the test today and fail it."

"Damn, so what's next? Don't they give you another chance to pass?"

"Yeah, they do. But if I fail it I'm out."

"Well, you need to take your time, sit back, and study. It's not that hard. You're just thinking too much on it."

"That's what Kerry said. I will call you tomorrow and let you know how that turns out."

"Okay, babe, good luck." Her call made me that much more determined to be success on this journey.

"Hey dad!" I yelled.

"What's up, son?"

"It's not looking good for ya girl."

"Who? Stacey? Awww man! What happened?"

"She's been in training doing good, and all of a sudden, failed her test. And if she fails it again tomorrow she gets kicked out."

He silently shook his head. "Lake, this is a hard industry to get in because you need discipline. If she go to training partying, giving up pussy left and right, that can happen. You know it's an industry with gay girls, too. Right? I wouldn't even doubt it if she went both ways."

Looking at dad like he was crazy, I asked, "Why, no matter what, women always have to be giving up some pussy in your mind?"

"Because they are! Listen here, since you are afraid of the truth, let me explain. Since the beginning of time what did Eve do?" he asked rhetorically.

"She gave up some pussy."

"Right! Now it's not their fault because the thing is pussy was made to be got. Why you think one of the highest industries are strip clubs? People fly from around the world to get to Brazil, just to get some pussy," he started laughing at himself.

"Man, you are one crazy old man. So what're the plans for the day?"

"Your Aunt Chris is getting everybody together, and we are all going to the hospital to see grandma, because she hasn't been doing too good."

"Yeah, she was kinda bad when I went up to St. Mary's."

"Well, Chris gonna let everybody know what our options are."

ONCE WE ARRIVED at the hospital, we all sat in the waiting room. The same family members that came together for Christmas were sitting, conversing, waiting for my aunt to give instructions.

"They have momma on a breathing machine and me and Ocie were debating if we should take her off of it or not. We haven't made any major decisions, but we are just throwing ideas out there."

"What exactly do they have her on now?" my brother OC asked, scratching his head.

"We know they put her on the liquid foods. We need to get the doctor or nurse to elaborate a little bit better on why they have her on the oxygen."

"If they take her off, will she be able to breathe on her own? What's the deal with that?" my sister Kelly asked, concerned.

My brother jumped in and said, "We don't want to take her off and she can't breathe."

Everybody talking at the same time frustrated dad. Since his eyesight had been going bad he started to speak mostly with his eyes closed. I guessed it made him more comfortable as he did it.

"Okay, okay. Y'all not getting what your Aunt Chris is trying to say. She didn't say nothing about pulling the plug. We are just throwing some ideas out there, because she hasn't been responding to anything. I know if I could breathe on my own, without a machine, I would." Dad responded with frustration.

OC asked grandpa what he thought, since he'd really been just sitting there, soaking it all in. He looked around slowly as he played with his cane. "We are going to talk to the nurse or doctor. We should see what they say first. Until then, all we can do is pray for her, because y'all kids don't know how to act!"

The nurse walked in greeting us. "Hello everybody. I'm your mother's, and I guess grandmother's, nurse. I would like to first say, in all my time working here, I *never* had a patient with this many non-stop visitors. So I can tell she has a lot of love surrounding her. Now Christella and I..."

"Chris," we correct her.

"Oh, I'm sorry everybody. We've been communicating the most. The thing is Aletha is on a feeding machine and has been on one for a while. Since she is not eating solid food, she is lethargic and not as strong. We have her on a breathing unit, because when she sleeps she skips breaths. The machine balances her out. She should be able to breathe without the unit, but I would recommend keeping her on it for now."

"Okay thanks, that's what we needed to hear," my aunt said.

"Is it okay for us to go in there and see her?"

"Yes, just make sure you guys put on a gown, which is outside of her room, and wash your hands before and after you go in there."

When I walked in the room, I just started talking to her. I don't even remember what I said. But I do remember giving her a kiss and saying, "I'm about to go to training and all I ask is for you to stay alive while I'm in training. Grandma, don't leave me, while I'm gone." I prayed, then walked out. I couldn't stand seeing my grandma lying in a hospital bed, helpless. Something told me that might be the last time I would see her, but I shook it off.

I went home and got everything packed, making sure I didn't forget anything, like I usually did whenever I traveled. Keke and grandpa came over to take me to the airport. I got Keke to take a picture of us, dad on the left side with his blind man glasses, grandpa on the right, and me in the middle with a suit on. As we rode to the airport, Keke asked if I was ready for the *Utah* lifestyle. Yeah, I was ready to get this show on the road.

"Dad, I forgot to tell you Stacey got kicked out of training." She called and told me the other day.

"She that's why you have to go down to Utah and be serious. I bet she got kicked out of training for doing too much partying and not being focused," dad said in a serious tone.

We got to the airport and everybody said their goodbyes. *Lando, it's game time. Let's do this for grandma.*

PART II

...To the Sky

18

I flew Delta to Utah and had very nice flight attendants. I sat next to an older white lady and her husband.

The lady and I started talking about why I was flying to Utah. Once I told her, she went crazy, moved her husband out of her way, who had been sitting between us, and sat right next to me. We had one of the greatest conversations I have ever had in my life. We talked about her grandkids, how she applied to become a flight attendant in the 70s, and how much she and her husband travel everywhere. We even talked about God and how proud she was of me, even though we'd just met. The last words she said, "No matter what, I know you will be successful in whatever you choose in life. I know you will do great in training."

AirStar gave me some type of voucher for the hotel shuttle to pick me up from the airport. I really wasn't nervous about anything, just the excitement about starting my new career and meeting everybody. Actually, there was one thing that had me a little anxious. Not being able to do the announcements could get a person kicked out the first day.

As I was waiting for my luggage in baggage claim, I saw a guy I met while I was at the AirStar open house, Kurt. He was a gay, white guy from Canton, Michigan, not far from me at all. Spotting me, he walked up and said, "Hey! Oh my god, we both made it."

"How have you been?"

"I have been running around like a chicken with my head cut off getting everything ready for this darn training. I'm just happy that I'm here!"

"Let's go find this shuttle." We walked outside and saw a few girls waiting for the shuttle. We met and greeted them as well.

The shuttle came to pick us up and I decided to sit all the way in the back as I started talking to this girl named Veronica. Good-looking white chick from Portland, Washington. Her mom was a flight attendant with Toronto Air. We mingled, getting to know one another and having a good time. For some reason we instantly connected, so we exchanged numbers and decided to go over our announcements and help each other study. We got to the hotel and I saw a decent looking black chick at the front desk. I was thinking, *what the hell is a black person doing here?*

Veronica and I walked to our rooms that we located literally right across from each other. I thought they would have put me and Kirk in the same from since we were both from Michigan. He was cool as hell, so it wouldn't have bothered me.

So this is my philosophy on gay people. I respect gay people that are themselves and who don't hide that they're gay, because if that's you then that's you. Just don't be on the down low trying to lie and hide it. I don't respect that. There is no reason for non-gays to be homophobic, because most of them won't mess with you if you're not gay.

I walked in the room optimistic to see if my roommate had arrived yet. I saw luggage and the room had a strong scent to it. Not a bad smell, but more like too much cologne. There was a couch to right with a table and chair next to it when entering. The room also had one mini fridge, two queen size beds, a big closet and a unique shower. But the toilet and shower were in two different rooms. I saw a book on the dresser with a white lady on the cover and some kind of grease case that said Lush. The more things I looked at, I started thinking, *oh shit this motherfucker is black*. I laughed to myself because that never even crossed my mind.

Benjamin walked in the room and we greeted each other. Ben was about 5'7, 120 pounds, and he was gay. He had a curly 'fro and was very well groomed. I could tell he liked to take care of himself.

"So where are you from?" I asked.

"I'm originally from Michigan, but now live in Chicago. What about you?"

Laughing I said, "Wow, I'm also from Michigan. It's a few of us here. So have you been studying?"

"No, not at all. I'm happy I'm here, because I really need to study the announcements."

"What! You mean to tell me you don't know the announcements verbatim by now?"

With an I-know-I-fucked-up smile, he said, "See, the thing is, it was my birthday about a week ago and we have been partying like hell and just this week it was my best friend's birthday. I looked over everything a few times, but need to practice."

"So let me hear what you got."

"What you mean what I got?"

"On your announcements."

"Oh hell no. I told you I don't know them," he responded with a very feminine voice.

I shook my head, laughing and said, "We can split the closet in half. I'm not planning on watching too much TV, so here is the remote." I threw it on his bed. We went back and forth talking for a while.

I went downstairs to tour the hotel and called Kirk to see who his roommate was. He picked up the phone and had Hoochie Momma blasting in the background. I started dying laughing.

"Dude, is that Hoochie Momma in the background?"

"Honey, I'm up here shaking my ass. I feel sorry for whoever got to room with me."

"He still hasn't come yet?"

"Nope, how is yours?"

"He is cool…a black guy also from Michigan."

"Wow is he gay?"

"Hell yeah, gayer than my mans off the Low Down Dirty Shame movie." He laughed.

"Okay, I will call you when I'm ready to study."

I checked out the workout room. It had a glass see-through window where people could see you working out if they walked past. It was very clean with about four treadmills, with a TV on each, and some weights. The indoor pool was to the left. Overall, they had put us in a great, clean hotel.

As I was running on the treadmill, Veronica came in. I looked at her and said, "You work out, too?"

"Yeah, a little bit. I can't be down here getting all fat," she responded with her girl-from-next-door smile.

"How is your roommate?" we say at the same time.

"Mine is the sweetest little lady, I swear. She is from Florida and is a sweetheart. She drove here, so that's cool to have a roommate with a car."

"Yeah, mine is cool also. He is a black guy from Michigan. But I'm going to have the room to myself starting on Monday." I laughed.

"Why you say that?"

"I'm sorry, how do you say your name? I'm going to forget it a few times."

"It's Veronica."

"So like Monica with a V right."

"Yep, that's it."

"Well, back to my roommate, I met the guy and I asked if he

had studied and was ready. The boy doesn't even know past the first line of the announcements."

"What! He must have been lying to you."

I gave her a blank stare. "The motherfucker is finished tomorrow. You will see, unless God shows him favor. He said he is going to study tonight."

After she left, I called dad to update him.

"Hey! The flight attendant."

"Hey, dad, how is everything going out there?"

"Things are going good. How you like everything?"

"Dad, I'm loving it. The hotel is out cold, got an indoor pool and a workout room with weights."

"Chris, Lake said his hotel is really nice, has a weight room and an indoor swimming pool."

"Tell him to take a picture for me." I heard my aunt in the background.

"Did you meet your roommate yet?"

"Yeah, he is cool, he is from Michigan too."

"Which part?"

"I'm not sure somewhere far out, but he is staying in Chicago now. But that fool will be gone tomorrow though."

"Why you say that?"

"Because I was trying to go over the announcements with him, dad, and the boy hasn't studied nothing yet."

"Oh wow, are you kidding me?"

"I wish I was. We will see what he can do. He said he been partying way too much. You see how everybody wanted to hang with me every day before I left?"

"Yeah, son, with this type of job you just have to buckle down and take care of business or you're not going to make it. Flat out. Chris, Lake said his roommate hasn't studied nothing yet, so he has to cram everything in by tomorrow morning."

I heard her laughing in the background. Dad said, "Well, get some studying in and hit us up later."

I went back up to the room and Ben was on his phone talking. I decided to sit on my side and do a mixture of texting, studying, and Facebooking. After a while I doze off. I woke up during the middle of the night. I noticed Ben pacing around the room practicing his speech. I promise y'all it was about four in the morning. I was too sleepy to even say something. So all I did was laugh and shake my head. *Good luck, my brother, good luck.*

The next morning, I woke up and the boy was still up studying. "Benjamin, did you stay up all night studying?"

"Yeah." He looked exhausted.

I got dressed and went downstairs to get breakfast. Eddie B from the Miracle and AirStar interviews was there. We greeted each other, excited to know we were in the same training and had made it that far. Veronica introduced me to her roommate.

It was so many people we had to take two different shuttles to the training center. As we pulled up we all noticed that AirStar had its own training center. The location resembled a small college campus. We went into a room where our name tags were at each desk, assuming that would be our classroom for the next thirty days.

A Korean guy named Levi introduced himself and told us the agenda for the day. He and another instructor would test our announcements in two different rooms, followed by taking an online test. He gave us a few tips on what to do and not do.

"Don't come in talking like a robot. Make sure you take a deep breath before you start so you won't pass out."

They split the class in half and that's when the pressure and nerves started to kick in. I saw people go in one by one, Ben went before me and I knew he was going to fail since he just wasn't prepared.

"How did you do?" was the first thing I asked once he walked.

"I passed, of course," he responded, looking at me like I was dumb.

I heard Levi scream my name. As I walked slowly into the room, I wondered, *How the fuck did Ben pass that?*

"Do you need a minute to get everything together or are you ready to rock and roll?" I smiled and it was game time.

All of that studying I did paid off, as I went into autopilot mode. When I was finished, he said, "Wow that was the best one I heard so far. Congrats, Lando, you passed."

I walked out and saw a cute black girl in the hall being comforted by a few people as she sobbed. *Well, I guess she is getting sent home.* I thought to myself.

Damn, this shit is the real deal. If you're not ready then you're the weakest link. I was just thinking about all the preparation, studying, and telling everybody that I was leaving, the celebration parties hosted, all just to get kicked out on the first day. Talk about embarrassing.

I saw Veronica and we both talked about passing and getting each other hyped for the online test we had to take next. We both passed the computer test with flying colors. Now that the hard stuff was out of the way, it was good to know I survived and could keep everything moving forward.

Our first day was mainly all paperwork. We had to fill out all our information a million different times, but the fun part of the day was when we went over our flight benefits. That was by far the part we all were waiting for.

To clarify the airline world, AirStar is a regional airline. Meaning they are small commuter planes with 50 to 70 seats and they do work for mainline carriers like United and Delta airlines. The goal is to get hired for a mainline carrier or start regional and move up. Since AirStar works for United and Delta we got flying benefits with them.

Next, we took a break, took our drug test, and got fitted for uniforms. Now the crazy thing is that I was mingling with all of the ladies and everyone was terrified about the drug test.

"Why y'all scared? It's not like anybody been smoking some weed or something."

They looked at me like I was crazy. One chick even said she had weed a few weeks before with some friends and had been drinking water like hell. Another girl said, "Yeah, I had some 'shrooms like a few days ago. I hope it don't pop up."

One girl looked at me and said, "Lando, you don't smoke?"

"Um, hell naw...."

They laughed and said, "I figured you would."

"Ummm, because I'm black, huh?" I responded and they all laughed.

The funny thing was here's a nigga from Inkster who was ready to take a drug test. And we all know the stigmas that are associated with black people in this country and how whites are painted as perfect, moral, and free from anything impure. Yet these young white chicks from Denver were terrified they wouldn't pass. Wow! I guess you can't judge a book by its cover.

After the drug test we came back down to fill out our background forms. Then I saw the question. The one I'd been dreading and hoping to avoid: Have you ever had a misdemeanor before, please place it here.

So that was the moment of truth right there. I really didn't know what to do. Me and dad had been working so hard to get where I'm at and what would happen if I said yes and they removed me tomorrow? What would happen if I don't say anything and they slide it under the rug? As I sat there contemplating, I hear dad's voice. *"Well, you have been trying this hard to get the job. It's no point of saying something now. At least you can go to training and get that experience."*

Yep, so I did it, kept that part blank and turned it in. We all went in the training room and Levi told us it was a chill day. The next day there were little things to do like the physical test. Then we would start learning all the basics of what we needed to pass.

Terry, the cool ass shuttle driver, offered to take us to Target since we didn't have any food at the hotel. A handful of us decided to go. It felt like a field trip. We all got to Target and just ran wild. Everyone grabbed buggies to shop. I pulled out my phone and started recording. To one of the classmates, I said, "Yo, Krystal, how do you feel that they finally let the dogs out of the cage?"

"I feel..."

We were interrupted by the sound of something shattering. Turning around we saw a little kid, who looked to be around six years old, drop a glass vase and started running.

Brittany yelled, "Did you get that on tape?"

Kirk said, "Honey, that's why you don't let them white babies run around. You see they need to put them on leashes now."

"Hey, Ben, do you want to grab a lot of things and just split the bill?"

"Yeah, that would be perfect, but I don't eat pork or crazy things."

"Actually, I just gave up pork, so we are on the same page, sir."

We had fun shopping and taking pictures. We made it back to the hotel and the cute black girl was up front taking care of guests and being busy. She gave me a nice smile, letting me know she'd seen me. Ben and I went upstairs and put our purchases away. I texted Veronica to see if she needed anything, but she said her roommate already bought some things and was now going to a local gym since they had transportation.

I decided to go mess with the black girl, since I didn't have anything else to do. I figured I might as well try to get some play, since I was going to be stuck for a while out there.

I went downstairs and saw her hiding in the back eating some pizza. "So you're gonna order some pizza and not tell anybody, then eat it in my face, huh?" I teased her.

"Oh my god, I'm sorry. That's what you guys went to Target for. I seen you come in with like fifty bags," she replied with a laugh. "Do you want a slice? I ordered a whole box and have it to myself."

"Oh thanks, but I'm okay. I was just playing and have all types of food upstairs."

"Nope you started it, so you better take a piece."

"I would, but the thing is that I don't eat pork and don't want you to give me a slice and I'm picking away all of the pepperoni."

"I don't eat pork either. I have ground beef and banana peppers."

"What! You are the first person that didn't look at me like I was crazy. Once you say you don't eat pork, the first response is are you Muslim?"

A white guy in the lobby saw us talking, so he walked up and started asking her a lot of dumb questions. It was blatant that he was straight hating on me with his lame ass. I told her I would talk to her soon.

As I was going upstairs my phone started ringing. It was my brother. "Yo black man. What it do? What it does?" I answer excitedly.

"Man, at the crib sitting here just thinking. But I felt it was best for me to tell you rather than anybody else. Grandma just died."

"Awww man. When?" I responded, feeling like the wind had been knocked out of my chest.

"At 11:30 tonight...about thirty minutes ago."

"So what happened?"

"Everybody decided to take her off the breathing machine so she could breathe on her own. She did good for the first few hours then stopped after a while. I wanted to tell you because dad and everybody decided not to tell you since you're in training."

"You're telling me grandma just died and they wanted to not tell me because I'm in training? What the fuck? How does that sound? I'm happy at least you told me."

"Yeah, bro, I feel you. Everybody got together and said they didn't want you to try and come back home or lose focus. But at the end of the day you're grown and you were with her the whole time she was in the hospital, you know."

"Yeah, you're right."

"Will you be okay?" His voice was sad.

"Yeah, I'll be good. I'll hit you up tomorrow. Thanks for calling me. Love you, bro."

"Okay love you too."

I got off the phone and realized there was nowhere I could hide. Veronica had a roommate and I had Benjamin in my room. I really just wanted to find somewhere in this hotel I could disappear. *Fuck!*

I saw that the pool area was open, so I put on my stuff, grabbed my headphones, and sat there just thinking. How would the world move on without her? What would Aunt Chris do? How would OC handle this? Better yet, what would grandpa do? The man had been married to her for 60 years. I worked at the cemetery and knew when couples had been married for so long, usually the surviving spouse died within six months to a year. *Damn! This is fucked up.*

I thought long and hard. Then I got angry when I realized that dad and Aunt Chris weren't even going to tell me. *What the hell type of shit is that?*

Death didn't scare me. Also with my personality, for some reason, I don't cry or get too emotional. The last time I remembered crying was when I was around twelve. Grandpa went to the hospital and I thought he was going to die. Besides that, I was just not a big emotional type of person.

Since I was with grandma five days out of the week, feeding her and talking to her, I was already mentally prepared for her death. I was more worried about my other family members. I knew I would be ok. I made up my mind that I wasn't going to leave training for the funeral, nor tell anybody what was going on. I just hated the way people reacted and want to baby you once they heard bad news. I just wanted to be treated the same and needed to get through the process. I went in the room and all I could do was go straight to sleep.

THE NEXT DAY we had to take our physical test to determine if we could handle the job. Mainly just picking up heavy girly bags and putting them down. In class they switched around our names and I was sitting next to Veronica's roommate. She was a very cute older white lady, but very skinny, about 90 pounds. After I introduced myself I don't remember how we got into the conversation, but we started talking about football and Tim Tebow.

"Lando, let me tell you about him. My son is the biggest Tebow fan and was able to meet him before."

"That's amazing. How did he meet him?"

"He was in the mall with a friend in Florida, because that's where we live, and Tim was in the mall shopping like a regular person. My son walked up and said, 'Are you Tim Tebow?' He responded 'No, but a lot of people say we look alike' and they all started laughing. He was able to take a picture and he just stood there talking to him for over ten minutes."

"Wow! I'm a huge Tebow fan. I can't wait to see what he does in the NFL, because you know everybody been saying he won't be able to last one year."

This attractive flight attendant walked into the class and introduced herself, telling us our agenda for the day. Levi came upfront while we were waiting to take the physical test and had everyone introduce themselves, state where they were from and their background.

When it was my turn, I stood up and with a straight face said, "I'm Lando from Detroit, Michigan and my occupation before this: I was a former Pimp and since the economy went down I decided to become a flight attendant." Everyone started laughing.

"Pimping all over the world, huh, Lando?" he responded.

"Sit cho butt down!" Eddie B exclaimed as he threw paper at me.

In the area where the physical exams were taking place, I saw Veronica's roommate crying.

"What's wrong, sweetie?" I asked.

She wiped her eyes and looked at me with her sad puppy eyes. "They're kicking me out, because I told them my shoulder's been hurting. My doctor said I'm okay to come to training. But since I told them that they're making me leave and get a doctor's note then I can come back. I know I can lift the objects, Lando. I know I can, but he won't even give me a chance."

"I'm so sorry." I gave her a hug.

Everyone ran over to her and started asking what happened. During our next break, Veronica and I talked about it saying how sad it was she had to leave and no longer had a roommate.

Once we had a break I went outside on the balcony and called dad.

"Hey, what's up, son?"

"Nothing much. Just on break trying to see what all happened last night."

"OC called you?" Was his first response.

"Yeah, that's stupid how people thought not letting me know was the right thing to do."

"Yeah, I know. Nobody was thinking right at the time and we didn't want you to lose hope or your focus."

"Yeah..."

I started the conversation with so much anger, but once I talked to him, he really made me realized at the time they did what they thought was best for me.

"So y'all decided to take her off of oxygen?"

"Yeah. We all came to the agreement that she didn't want to be on oxygen and stuck in the hospital, so we told her the deal and she agreed. We took her off at around 8pm. Just about everybody was there. Even Leondre and Kenny came up and she was doing great on her own until about 11:30. Chris was in there with her, me and daddy already left to go home. I guess she started to freak out since she was the only one in there with her and she called me explaining the deal. Man, momma fought tough, but it was her time. So Chris put me on speaker and I told momma it would be okay and to go to sleep."

I could imagine exactly what had happened in the hospital. Since I saw the area she was in, I knew where she was laying, what she had on, her beautiful smile, and those rare blue eyes she had.

"How is everybody holding up?"

"I couldn't sleep last night, but I'm doing better today. You know Chris is taking it real bad and also OC."

"How is grandpa taking it?"

"I'm not sure. I think he is doing okay for now."

Veronica walked outside, "Lando, we have to go back to class."

"Alright, dad, I have to go back to class. I will hit y'all up on the next break."

The whole day I was kinda zoned out, didn't talk to anybody, or tell anyone about my situation. I could tell people started to notice that I wasn't my crazy, goofy, funny self.

So when class was over, Veronica's roommate came up to me and pulled me in the corner asking could we talk really quick. She said, "Lando, there is just something about you. I know you will be successful in life, and you have a great heart. Don't change for anybody and it was a pleasure meeting you."

I really appreciated that, even though it was weird that she was the one getting kicked out, but was telling me to keep my head up. "Thanks, I needed that."

The next day I was in the cafeteria texting and Veronica asked me what was up. Just by looking at her blue eyes, I could tell she was genuinely concerned about what was going on. "My grandma died the other day," I replied. "But don't say nothing to anybody. I don't want everybody all up in my business."

"Lando, I'm so sorry to hear that. Give me a hug."

"Aww thanks, love, I need it."

"I have a perfect plan to make you feel better."

"And what's that?"

"Boston plays Miami tonight and since my roommate is gone you can come over watch it. We can order some pizza and soda."

"Haha, some soda? Really. Not pop, but soda!"

"Yes, leave me alone."

"Okay I'm down, but let me call my sister and see what's been up." I cracked a smile and walked off.

When I got outside I called Keke, "What's up?"

"Man, it's crazy out here."

"What's been going on?"

"OC and Kelly got into a big fight at the hospital."

"No they didn't! What happened?"

"Man, we were in the lobby talking about grandma and OC wanted to buy the headstone. He and Kelly just went at it. She said she would shit on his grave when he die," she said dramatically.

"What?!" We were both over the phone dying laughing as she tried to explain the situation. "Are you kidding me? How the hell did that happen? Hold on this is dad calling."

"Hey, dad."

"Hey, what's going on, son?"

"Just on break talking to Keke on the other end. She has me over here cracking up."

"Is she talking about them dumb kids?"

"Yep, I have to tell you about that one, so hit me up when you get out of class."

Clicking back over, I said, "Okay, Keke, that was dad right there. So how is everybody holding up?"

"You know grandpa been going crazy crying and stuff. Aunt

Chris is taking it okay." Keke always had the funniest stories, because she would over exaggerate anything. If you let her tell the story OC and Kelly were about to get into a shoot-out in the hospital.

Later on that day I was in my room talking to Ben and making some food. I decided to tell him that my grandma died and that's why I'd been so quiet lately. He expressed his condolences and I headed over to Veronica's room.

"Your room is way different than ours." I stated as soon as I walked in and looked around.

"Really?"

"Yeah, but we have a sweeter shower." I said as I went over the differences of our rooms.

I looked at the TV and the Boston Celtics game was just was coming on.

"We need to talk," I said to her. "You're good looking, laid back and watch sports. So what the hell is wrong with you? How are you not in a relationship right now?"

"I learned to watch basketball from my ex-boyfriend. He is in love with Ray Allen, so after a while it dripped on me."

"So what happen with y'all?"

"He dumped me before I came to training."

It turned out that Rick, her boyfriend was young, good looking, and rich. An online poker player by trade. The kid even had a Porsche! Even though he knew she was the one for him, his status and just being a male had him making bad relationship choices. If it had been me, I would have had a hard time being faithful to just one woman, too.

After talking and getting to know each other, her situation was easy. It amazed me how comfortable we were with each other, especially since she hadn't grown up with many black people. Other than a few cultural expressions she wasn't familiar with, the conversation flowed all evening.

Later that night OC called me and said the funeral was going be Tuesday at 10 a.m. He asked if I had anything I wanted him to say on my behalf when he got up to make his remarks. I thought long and hard and just started writing about the good times we had and how much of a great mentor grandma had been in my life. *Wow! I love that lady.* Everybody in the neighborhood, starting with dad and Aunt Chris's friends all the way to OC's, Keke and mine were always welcome over grandma's house. She had an open refrigerator policy. If you went in the fridge and saw something you wanted, it was yours because if somebody else wanted it then it wouldn't still be there, she would say. Taking the trash out we got compensated. Grandma loved to give us money and the best Christmas gifts. Yep, that was grandma. She was the center of our family. *It's going to be interesting what happens next with the family.*

As the days went by training became more fun, but also more intense. People started to get in trouble all day everyday just for the smallest things. Our number one problem was phones. AirStar had a very strict no phone policy while in class. Even on break we couldn't use our phones. We had to go outside to use it and these fucking chicks were killing me. They could not leave their damn phones alone if their lives depended on it. I guess we were getting to the point in training where all these females were starting to miss their boyfriends.

"Hey sexy!"

"Sexy, you must be talking to somebody else," the black girl from the front desk responded, blushing to my remarks.

"Nope. I'm talking to you." She smiled.

"Well, you're the only one who thinks that."

"Hell naw. I highly doubt that."

"How you figure?"

"Think about this…just about every time I see you a random white guy is all over you, especially if they see me talking to you. So keep on talking to me and watch what happens. How long have you been working up here?"

"For over two years. I been in the hotel business for years. I've been doing this and also going to school on the side."

"Damn, you be here practically every day, so you must be a hustler."

"Yeah, I guess it's in my blood."

"What are you mixed with?" I asked, because she looked as if she could be from the islands with her perfect dark chocolate skin.

"I'm Jamaican."

"Like family from Jamaica or like you were born in Jamaica?"

"I was born there then moved to Maine to go to school."

"Whoa! Did you just say you went from Jamaica to Portland, Maine?"

"Yeah, I'm wondering what the heck I was thinking also."

"What made you move to Utah with no," I looked both ways, smiled, and quietly said, "black people." I smiled.

"Since I became a Mormon and their best churches are out here, this is where I decided to come."

I only knew one other Mormon, so I didn't know much about it. An older white male in his late thirties, early forties walked into the hotel, cutting into our conversation, flirting with her. I laughed, gave her a look that said 'see, told ya!' and went over in the corner and started studying.

Our trainer the next day was Justin. The way he started the class before getting to work was to ask if anybody in the class had a joke to tell the class. I raised my hand.

"Oh Lord." I heard a few classmates say while laughing, because I was known for being a funny guy with jokes for days.

"So I used to use to work at a cemetery as a family service counselor." Their faces dropped in disbelief.

"Now my job was not to touch dead people or anything like that, but if John Doe died, they would call me and set an appointment to fill out the paperwork for the family that will be coming in and things like that. So after my training it was my time to do my first funeral service by myself and this is the way it went." I stood up so I could get more animated. "You guys know when somebody dies and you drive to the cemetery, it's the long line of cars that follows the hearse, right? Now when they come to the cemetery my car is supposed to be in the front of the cemetery waiting for the hearse to pull up, and my job is to drive to the grave site and everybody follows me. Everybody, this the deal... we all know a big cemetery is kinda like a maze with all type of turns and stuff. Now when we know we're gonna have a few services that day the ground personnel usually pre-digs the holes and has everything ready with the tents and stuff. Now I hop in the car, freaking out and nervous, because they don't really train you to drive people to the burial site. When you start driving *the whole* line of cars starts to follow you. So I panicked and made the wrong turn. Soon as I turned, everyone followed, so I freaked out even more and needed to figure out how to get everybody going to the right place. I pulled up to the tent and I saw the ground personnel guy running towards the car waving his hands. I got out the car and y'all can probably already guess at what I did."

A classmate in the back said, "Don't say you pulled up to the wrong tent."

I pointed at her and said, "Hell yeah I did! But look... this is how I brought it back. I got out the car, smooth as hell, and did this..." I made the sign of the cross. "...and got back in the car. I looked behind me and everybody did the same thing, so I told them this is how we pay homage." The room erupted with laughter and clapping.

"Wow, Lando, great story and with that it is break time everybody."

Back in class Justin asked, "Who can tell me the primary differences between the CRJ 200 and the 700?"

I raised my hand. "Yes, Lando."

"The 200 has 50 seats with only one flight attendant required, and the 700 is a 66 seater with 2 flight attendant required and the equipment is in different places, but mainly it's the same plane."

"Wow, Lando, that's great."

Towards the end of the class he said, "Tomorrow wear business attire, study hard for the CRJ 200 test and class starts at 7:30. Don't be late."

∽

"How was the funeral?" was the first thing I asked Keke when she got on the phone.

"Grandma's funeral was off the hook, man. Everybody was there. She really went out with a bang."

"What was everybody doing?"

"Aunt Chris came decked out wearing a $10,000 mink coat with the matching hat. OC came with those glasses Mayweather had on the HBO show, and you know how I did. They were going crazy over us."

"Who all came out of my friends?"

"Brown and Alvin was all I saw. I didn't really see anybody else, because it was so crowded."

"Oh okay. That's what's up."

"Everybody missed you, but they were all happy you stayed in training to work on your goals."

"Yeah well, I'll hit you up tomorrow. I'm about to go for a swim."

Today was a sad day in class, because all we did was watch all of the different airplane crash events that happened throughout the day. Once they played the remake of the 9/11 scenario that's when everybody in the class just started to cry and tear up. It was very emotional.

Levi stood up and said, "Today is usually the emotional day of training. It shows you how important the security aspect of aviation is, because some of these crashes were from human error. Before we take a break does anybody have any questions?"

One girl raised her hand and said, "My dad works for the government and what I can say to everybody is that the people who were on flight 318 fought all the way to the end and were able to break into the cockpit and kill those men."

Levi looked up and said, "Let's take a break."

I went outside and I saw most of the girls in the class were outside smoking. "Damn, all y'all smoke?" I yelled.

"Yep, I know it's not lady like, but fuck it."

Eddie walked outside and said, "I don't know how much more of this type of shit I can take. That's some sad stuff."

"Man, hell yeah, it's too sad for me too," I agreed.

The second half of class we were able to go into a sample aircraft. Levi showed us where all the equipment was and how to get familiar with the aircraft. At the end of class they said we finally got to have a day off.

Now my favorite shuttle driver, Terry, the one who'd taken us to Target, asked, "When is you guys next day off?"

"We'll be off tomorrow actually."

His phone rang and he started talking. "I know this is very unprofessional, but my son's mother is acting crazy. Do you all care if I pick him up? It's about five minutes away." We were all cool with that. He picked him up. I told him he could sit next to me. We started talking about video games and sports. He was a cool chunky little kid around age eleven. "Since you guys don't have class tomorrow, do y'all want me to give you a tour downtown and show y'all some cool places?" he says before dropping us off.

I say, "Heck yeah. I'm down. Does everybody else agree?" He gave us his number and said let him drop his son off and he'd be back at 5:30.

I went upstairs and told Ben to bring his ass so we could get out of that hell hole. All he did was complain about how much he needed to take a nap. Veronica and I went downstairs with about five other girls who were ready to go. To be honest, Terry was the best tour guide ever, anything we drove past he knew the history of it, when it started, and all background information.

"Terry, brotha! Where are the best strip clubs out here?" I demanded from the back seat. "I know y'all orthodox and mormons have one somewhere in the hood."

"Actually, there are a few places around here. It all really depends on what you're looking for. Seagrams is expensive, but don't show ya shit, and Belly's is the only full nude place in Utah, and they have so many cool things that go down there on Tuesdays."

"Damn, Terry, you sound like a man with a lot of experience," Becca responded laughing.

"Haha. Well I do. Back when I used to drink, I was in those clubs every weekend. I used to be a real heavy drinker and my wife at the time ended up leaving me a little bit after she had my son Adam."

"So did you become a Christian or Orthodox and stop drinking?"

"Naw, they're too darn weird and strict for me. I still like my freedom, but I quit drinking about eleven years ago."

"That's great, T," we all responded as he kept driving.

As Terry drove we started going a big hill. "I'm about to take you guys to the top of Utah where we can overlook the whole city."

We went up hill after hill. It was a consistent ten minute up hill drive until he told us to look to our right and all we saw were mansions everywhere. It was like an exclusive area only for the rich. He started to explain what type of people lived there and then we went to a dead end road. He looked at us and was like, "You guys this is the Lot."

"What's that?" Ashley asked.

"It's very romantic, like in the summer to take a chick, but the cops blocked it off because they kept on catching people having sex. Haha."

We all got out of the van. I walked towards the end of the cliff and it was the most beautiful site I'd ever seen. I could just about see all of Utah from here. The downtown area was amazing. Mountains were surrounding us everywhere we looked, but I didn't want to get too close to the edge, because it was windy as hell and I sure as hell wasn't trying to fall over. Terry told us to get into a group and take a picture all jumping up at the same time. As we were heading back to the hotel, we all thanked Terry so many times for looking out for us. We all came together and gave him a $20 tip.

I really needed this to distract me from thinking about being away from my family and the reality of the situation going on back home. I kind of felt guilty that I got to be in another state for free living the dream. But that was to be my new home for the next few weeks.

19

Growing up I was always infatuated with women. I wanted to learn how they think, about their bodies, and just about whatever I could find out. My mom even purchased me a 'How to properly learn the female body while having sex' type of book. Yeah weird, right?

But once I got older I realized I wanted to know all that information only to use it to my benefit and learned how to cajole females. It also didn't help that my favorite movie was *Cruel Intentions* growing up.

By having an affable personality most women are comfortable telling me their thoughts about men and their relationships, since I actually give decent honest advice.

I remember having a white girlfriend when I was in elementary and one when I was eighteen, but she was blacker than me, so I'm not even going to count her. I never was a person that cared about race.

Yeah, I would love to marry a beautiful black woman since I am black, but if I happen to fall in love with an Asian woman, then so be it. After all that research and studies on woman, I failed to realize I never grasped the emotional part of a woman.

Why they cry, their monthly cycles, and how much it affects them. Get stuck with women from all different races for thirty days and you will learn a lot.

I started to notice as training progressed that at least once a day a different chick was in class crying about something. When I say every day, I mean *everyday!* That shit pissed me off.

I never been a big emotional person. There I was, my grandma had just died and I was still holding it together. These chicks were crying because they were having boyfriend problems and petty crap like that. After class I went into Veronica's room and she would be nagging and complaining about Rick.

There was the gorgeous Indian chick named Doll whose boyfriend had her all emotional, because he would call her every day going nuts that he was stuck at home watching the kids and she is at training skanking around and whatever. I really could go down the list with problems of everyone in class. It was just sad to me.

The only person I could vent and complain to at the time was Benjamin about how sad, emotional, and crazy these woman were. After a while we started to build a good strong friendship. All we did everyday was watch *Family Guy* and talked shit to each other. I usually complained how he never studied for a test and always got the highest grade in the class and he complained how I always left and went over to my 'girlfriend' Veronica's room.

I went over to my boo's room and she was on the phone with Rick and gave me the be quiet, don't say nothing look. While she talked on the phone, I started on my homework.

"Lando, I need your help. I just don't understand men!" She yelled as she put her head into the pillow.

"Porque chica porque?"

"Because he is the one who broke up with me, but he wants his cake and wants to eat it too. He is now single, gets to bang anybody he wants, but still texts me every day and calls saying dumb shit."

"What type of stuff did he just say?"

"He called to ask if I was watching the game."

I laughed and said, "If you give me most of the answers for the worksheet 2.1, then I will help you get him back, if you want."

"Do you honestly think I can?"

"Babe, I know you can if you really wanna go that route."

As we did homework, I started explaining how males think to her.

"See the thing is, he understands you're in training missing and still thinking about him. He has you exactly where he wants you. He can knock off his chicks without feeling guilty and have you as a back burner when he is ready to settle down."

"Umm what did you say?" she responded confused. "Remember I'm white you have to speak white lingo to me."

Shaking my head, I tried to explain again. "What I'm trying to say, Veronica, is that he doesn't have to settle down right now. He gets to be a man well... You guys been together like forever, right?"

"Yeah."

"When was the last time he had some other pussy?"

"He cheated on me once. I'm not 100%, but I'm sure he did. Remember when I told you about it?"

"Yeah I do. But basically he really hasn't had no other pussy than yours in like forever, he wants some different pussy and just wants to see what's out there in the world and come back to you after when he is ready."

"Lando, that is bullshit! I have never cheated on him." I look at her like she's crazy. "Oh my god, shut up. I haven't and why wouldn't he want to be with me forever?"

"Look lady, I don't make the rules. I'm just here to tell you about them."

"So what's the plan?"

"Every time he contacts you don't say anything to him at all unless I tell you what to say first."

"Oh my god, are you serious?"

"Umm hell yeah. If you want him back you better listen to me. If you text him once then I'm finished."

"Okay I wont....."

"*Veronica!*"

"I said I won't." I could tell she didn't like what I'd said to her.

"I'm serious. If you be on that bullshit then I'm done."

The next day in class we had to take a big test and people were praying before the test, crying after the test and some were just flat out scared. My deal is, I get a little nervous before a test, but if I studied well enough then I should be able to pass the test with no problem. In class they gave only one chance to fail and if the person failed their second try they were done. So after we took a few tests they told us to go into the lecture hall so we could meet someone. I guess one of the pilots was a motivational speaker and he was coming in to get us hyped or whatever. He was about a 40-year-old male, bald headed, and not too bad looking.

So he started with his introduction being an only child and always wanted to become a pilot and is now a cancer survivor. At the end of him telling everybody his story, he was like seeing Jim Rohn or Les brown live, but for free. All the women in the class were crying because another one of the students was also a cancer survivor, so they had them a personal moment hugging each other and that touched the class big. I was happy he came because he was one of the good guys that was just down to earth and loved life.

At the end of class before we took a break, Angie from the training department said today they were providing snack boxes for everybody and after we ate we needed to take our pictures for our badge and line up by the wall. Right before she left she said, "Oh yeah and I need to see somebody in my office."

My heart dropped. Since I knew I lied on the application, just about every day I thought they would bring it up.

"Ashley, can I see you for a moment?" she said.

Whew! That was a close one.

Now our agenda for the rest of the day was that Levi and the good-looking trainer were taking us out to the hangar so we could see a CRJ 200. We didn't go out until later and I was so excited to finally be able to do something different and go on a plane. We finally got on and Levi sat us down and gave us our agenda while we were on the plane.

We would learn what was in the flight deck, use the jump seat, and practice doing door pulls. Overall, we had a lot of fun that night doing door pulls and practice jumping out of the airplane.

Back at the hotel the other sexy chick that worked the front desk was there. Since I didn't have anything else better to do I figured I might as well mess with her also. Why not?

She was originally from Hawaii and moved out to Utah for school. I was still wondering why was everyone moving to Utah for school. Who the hell wanted to live there? Later on in the conversation she talked about basically how boring she is, she doesn't drink, smoke or ever go out and party, so I put two and two together and realized that she was also deep into religion. She was about 5'9 with perfect black curly hair. Her body was perfectly thick. I'd say about 165 pounds, but looked good since she was taller. Only thing her aura didn't show me that she was confident within herself.

I went upstairs to kick it with Veronica and she ordered some Pizza Hut online for us. This was my first time ever seeing somebody order pizza online. She kept on laughing at how amazed I was since I'd never seen it before.

"So, Lando, what do you think is gonna happen next with Ricky?"

"When was the last time he texted you?"

"Just a minute ago."

"Don't reply back and he will start to go crazy."

"You think so?" she replied with a smile.

"I know so. He is used to talking to you whenever he wants and if you change that I'm telling you he will go crazy and want you back."

"Lando, I love you. Give me a hug."

As we are hugging, Rebecca walked in. "Looks like I walked in at the wrong time."

"Shut up. You actually came in at the perfect time, baby," I replied with a deep voice, pretending to take off my shirt as they laughed. Once the pizza came we were really able to learn about each other's family background, and had a good time bonding.

The next morning, I woke up before Ben, because his lazy ass always took the second shuttle. I listened to Jim Rohn as I walked around the room getting ready. This was the seminar he did in 2003 in California.

I'd awakened on the wrong side of the bed and was so grouchy. Yeah, it was one of those days for me. I was pissed off that I missed grandma's funeral. I had a new test to take every day. I was horny as fuck and couldn't jack off, because it felt homo to do it while staying with a gay guy. And to top it off these chicks cried *everyday* about how they missed their mom, their kids, and their boyfriend is gonna break up with them. A chick even cried yesterday because she missed her dog. Yes, her motherfucking dog! So I had to put on some Jim Rohn to calm my morning nerves.

It was a calm day in class, since I was to myself more than usual. The rumor was that me and Veronica were dating. I guess folks thought that since we sat next to each other in class and hung out all day, every day after class. F it! I guess I would say that we were dating too, if I was them. Even on break one of the girls sat next to me in the cafeteria.

"Lando, I wouldn't ever have thought you would like a girl like Veronica." There was a sneaky tone to her voice. Clearly, she was being nosy.

"Umm...why not?"

"Because you know you're cool, hip and black."

I spit out my drink laughing when she said that. Shaking my head, I said, "Thanks, Lindsay, thanks."

Those chicks were crazy and nosy. I guess they felt that if Veronica was the only one in the class getting laid, they wanted full details.

Back in class Sam was in front teaching and somebody next to me pointed at Eddie B. Now Eddie sat in the same spot every day in the back corner of the class. I turned around to look at him and he was passed the fuck out with his mouth wide open. I'm not sure if Sam noticed him or not, but he asked the class what the difference was between rough air turbulence and clear air turbulence. Eddie randomly popped his head up and raised his hand fast as hell. He even answered the question and we all started dying laughing. Sam said, "Well, tomorrow is your last off day, so get lots of sleep and study, enjoy it because you guys have 12 days straight."

Soon as we got out of class we convinced one of the drivers to take us to the liquor store. It was like a circus, people were putting in orders left and right of what they wanted back from the store and the shuttle driver told us to meet back downstairs at six because the liquor stores closed early as hell out of there. People were leaving with boxes of wine, liquor from pints to bottles of different crap showing that we really just had a class full of alcoholics. The driver asked, "Do any of you guys like to go clubbing?"

"Hell yeah, we like to club. What's up?"

"Well, my friend owns a real upscale club downtown and I can hit him up and see if he can get all you guys in for free."

We all got excited telling him to please do it, we all want to get out. The next thing we know just about half of the class wanted to go. Even Ben agreed. Now I forgot to mention how I packed for this training. I'd brought so many different dress shirts and outfits. I had the pink shirt with the pink tie, blue shirts, black, brown and bought so many different ties, so I could switch it up a little. Also Eddie B was one fly brother, when he came to class he was always on his grown man Chicago swag, because he would come in with a suit and some matching gators to go with it. But what I'm trying to say is if we were to go to a club I had my Gucci's on me and was ready for whatever.

I got dressed then went into Veronica's room. She was looking confused, as if she didn't know what to wear. "Lando, you're good at everything. What should I wear?"

"Show me all your options."

She laid her clothes on the bed and I pointed to the black shirt with jeans that let me see her heels.

"Yep, you look good, so wear that. Oh yeah, have you heard from Rick?"

"Nope, he texts me all the time. It's crazy. I haven't talked to him in like a week."

"Call him, tell him you were extra busy and let him know you're about to go to the club."

"Ha-ha. Are you serious? He will be pissed."

"I know he will. Now do it and hurry up." I laughed.

We all went downstairs and Roma was looking sexy as hell. Doll looked great. Basically everybody was looking good as hell ready to go have some fun. Ben had on this crazy ass green shirt, but whatever he is gay, so I guess they can do what they want. We hopped in the van and hauled ass. The good part was we had Terry as our shuttle driver and Roma said she already texted the club owner. They were waiting for us. We pulled up and Terry said, "Nobody is opening the door, I'm going to pull up in the front and open the door for you guys VIP style."

As we pulled up, it was perfect timing. There were a lot of people standing in line so people turned to look at who we were because we were Mexicans, Blacks, Whites, Arabics and all. Oh yeah, and me, Eddie B and Ben. I was actually very surprised, because I walked in the club and they were playing hip hop and I saw black people.

Yes! This is all I freaking needed, thank you Jesus!

Now it was so funny to see all these chicks in action, they were like kids in a candy store. Everybody just about had boyfriends, but as Lil Wayne said in his song they were single for the night.

These chicks were thirsty and horny as hell to finally see some males outside our class. Hell can you blame them? I couldn't judge them, because before they came to training half of their boyfriends dumped them and didn't want them to come any way. They were now free and ready to have fun. Eddie's goofy self actually surprised me the most, because he was all over the ladies and could dance his ass off. I guess all he needed was his Patron shots to get him started.

Mary was the chick with all the money in our class and she was on the same page as me. She pulled me to the side and was like, "Aye, I don't usually club. But when I do, I like to do it big. First, we need a booth and we need a second bottle."

I was like, "Hell yeah, now you're talking my language. I'll see who all wants to go in on it."

I don't usually go out, but if I'm going to do it, I wanna do it big. Hell we only live once. So I asked a few people and everybody chipped in here and there, but mainly me and Mary paid for it. The next thing we knew they were bringing out bottles with the sparkles flaring out left and right. We all took shots and the party began. After being there for about an hour I got my groove and a feel for the place, so I started dancing and talking to chicks. I saw this good-looking black girl walking past, so I grabbed her arm.

"Hey, how are you doing tonight?"

"I'm doing great and you?"

"It's my first time here and I'm just surprised there are black people in Utah."

She started laughing. "Yeah, it's a few of us. So where are you from?"

"Detroit!"

"So I got me a thug, huh?"

"Dang, why I gotta be a thug? Why can't I be a God-fearing man?"

Ha-ha, we both laughed. "Do you want something to drink?"

"No, I'm okay. I don't drink." In my head, my cheap ass was like, *Hell yeah!*

"So do you dance?"

"Yeah, I at least do that," she replied smiling.

We go in the middle of the dance floor and start getting it on and next thing I know I pulled out that phone and pulled that number. I went over to Carolyn. She was in her own zone, but she grabbed me and starting to dance aggressively. She completely threw me off guard, because in class I would have never expected this, because she acted shy. I looked over to see what Ben was doing and I noticed he was standing alone looking confused, so I went over to ask him what was up?

"I'm trying to go to the bathroom, but these guys keep on fucking with me."

"Come on and let one person say something and watch them get their ass whooped," I replied aggressively.

He instantly started smiling, so I grabbed the back of his shoulders and guided him into the bathroom, mainly so everybody could know we were together. I could tell that was the moment when he realized I had his back no matter what. When we both came out of the bathroom, Ben started laughing and pointing saying. "Look at those horny ass flight attendants."

I looked over and I saw Becca in the corner kissing the hell out of some random guy.

Mary was sitting down with some guy and then Angelica came up to me and said, "Lando, I need your help."

"Um, okay. What's up?"

"You see the bartender, right?"

"Yeah."

"We keep on looking at each other and he is so hot. Can you give him my number?"

"Ha-ha Gelly, that's for guys to be scared to talk to females, not the other way around."

"Please..." she said as she stopped me from walking away by grabbing my arm.

So I walked up to the guy and said, "What's up?"

"Hey, dude, I see you over there with like ten bad ass women. What do you do, man? Because I'm trying to get on your level."

Laughing, I tell him, "I'm a flight attendant and we are all here for training. But this is the deal. You see the cute black girl over there? She has been talking about you like crazy, but is too shy to come and talk to you."

"Okay, tell her my name is Nick and come over here right now."

I walked away and I say to Gelly, "His name is Nick and he told me to tell you if you don't bring your sexy ass over there and introduce yourself, then y'all might have a problem."

She walked over and they start talking and next thing I knew he had about five shots lined up for us to take.

"Lando! Come over here, brother," Nick said and he gave us a round on him.

We partied all night, lots of dancing and drinking. Everybody had a fantastic time, just about every chick met their husbands that night. As I think about it there was one chick so in love and horny she begged us could she go home with this random guy. I remember the guy asking for my permission, like I was her pimp.

"Excuse me, Lando, I promise you I'm not a creeper or anything. I have a good job and you guys can have my number and the address to my house. I will bring her back safely."

So at first I was like *hell naw,* but then I thought about it as she kept begging. I'm nobody's damn daddy and if this was vice versa

I would be trying my hardest to get some pussy too. Veronica couldn't believe it, but hell she was drunk too, and got the guy's number. "So just call us when you get there and be safe, baby."

Benjamin came running up to me like, "Lando, please let's get the hell out of here."

"Why?" I responded laughing.

"These chicks are drunk and crazy. This the second time tonight Carolyn tried to kiss me."

"Kiss you?!" I yelled out loud.

"Um, yeah. She said she needed to make out with a black guy or gay guy or some dumb ass excuse."

I yelled. "What the fuck?! My black ass is the only straight guy in this class, besides Eddie, and she wants to give you some pussy?" Shaking my head. "I'll be damned. Okay, let's go."

By the time Terry came to pick up us everybody was shit face wasted, sleepy and hungry.

"Micky D's! Come on, T, you gotta make a stop for us," I pleaded for the group.

Now I felt so sorry for Terry at this point, because this had to be one of the worst fast food stops I had ever been a part of. The ride there everybody was drunk as hell and being loud, telling drunken stories and when we got to McDonald's everybody wanted something. A few people only had debit cards, others had cash, and to make matters worse, we switched up our order like ten times.

I know I'm not perfect, but I remember mostly everything that happened that night, so believe me I wasn't that messed up. Terry got so mad he just pulled out of the line and was like, "C'mon! We have to get more organized, if we really want to order."

So Roma started speaking her Spanish, or whatever she spoke, but basically she said she'd take care of the order if everybody just told her what we wanted. In my head, I was laughing thinking, *Roma already has a strong accent, and going through* drive-thru they're definitely not going to understand what she is saying.

Once we finally made it back to the hotel, we gave T some food and also a big tip for taking us. After everybody walked into the hotel, I pulled him to the side and thanked him again, telling him how much I appreciated the small things he did for us. "Ever since we've been here you been helping us out a lot, so thanks, bro."

The next day we were all in each other's rooms laughing about last night and how much of a slut we all were. How Eddie kept on dancing nonstop all night. Mary kept on having Arabic guys buying us drinks. Roma got so drunk she stopped speaking English. How this random guy fell in love with Veronica, telling her how beautiful she was and how perfect she was for him all night. Last but not least Rebecca...and speaking of Becca where the hell was she?

"Oh my god, didn't she leave with a random guy last night?" Tina asked.

"He was hot too," Shannon replied as all the girls started laughing.

"And who was that guy you were all lovely dovey with last night, young lady?" Eddie asked Shannon as he sipped some of his tea. Well, I assumed it was tea.

"Actually, he is texting me right now," she told us with a smile.

Later on that day I went downstairs to talk to Lisa the girl at the front desk. This was the first time she was not busy, so I had to make my move. "Hey, sexy lady!"

"Oh hey, Lando, how are you doing? I heard you guys had lots of fun last night."

"Oh yeah." I nodded, giving her a smirk. "It was fun to get out of this hotel. We went partying and did it big."

"What you mean by 'doing it big?'" she asked confused.

"Never mind. Just know we had some fun. So you're from Jamaica, right?"

"Yeah, you guys get free flying benefits, right?" she replied quickly.

"Yep."

"I will need a flying pass, so I can show you around, you know." She spoke in her crisp, fast-speaking way. I had never met anyone who spoke as quickly as she did.

"Lisa, what made you become a Mormon?"

"I first moved to Maine from Jamaica for school. Most of the crew I hung around was actually deep into religion. You know, so I converted over. When I finished school there I decided to come to Utah, because this is big with the churches."

By the time I went back to upstairs in Veronica's room, she and Becca were there having girl talk. "I need full details!" Veronica demanded as she waited for Rebecca to give her the full story about what happened last night.

"Well, you guys better not tell nobody because, well, mainly don't tell Sara because you know she is very judgmental, and since that's my roommate I don't want to hear her shit. He is so cute and sexy and by the time we went to his place we were wasted."

"So...did you get some?" Veronica demanded.

"Girl, hell yeah! We fucked all over his house. His cock was huge. Probably one of the biggest I ever had."

"Whoa, whoa, okay now, thank you," I said sarcastically.

Becca laughed and said, "You're the one in here invading on our girl talk." She went to touch my hand. I moved it quickly out of her reach.

"I don't know where them damn hands been, lady. And go take a damn shower with your hot-in-the-pants ass." We all laughed.

The next day in class, we spent half the time on our self-defense training and the other half practicing evacuations. One thing I did notice when we came back from our one-day vacation was one of the other ladies was gone. "Hey, Eddie B, where is that girl from Cali?"

"I don't know. Ashley just asked me the same thing. Y'all acting like I'm her damn keeper."

"Don't act like that white girl is not yo' boo."

"Shit she was crying and complaining to me and you the other day about her dog and all the other issues she had going on."

Levi walked into the class and said, "Y'all know what time it is."

Every morning in class they made us do a compliance check. Which was to make sure we had our flashlight, badge, watch and stuff like that. Each day a different person had to go in front of the classroom and read our announcements out loud. Today it was sexy Roma's turn to go up there and say her announcements.

Before she got started, I yelled, "Say it in Spanish!"

She laughed, looked at Levi and asked if he cared if she did it that way.

"Naw, be my guest. Tomorrow I'm going to make Lando say his announcements, because whenever he reads his you would think he has music going on through his head."

Roma stood up and made her whole announcement in Spanish, receiving a standing ovation from the group.

After we took our break, one of the instructors from the training department came into the class and told everybody to sit down.

"I was once a flight attendant, but this now has to stop. I know how hard it is to go through training not being able to talk to your loved ones everyday, but from today until graduation. If I see one person texting in this class or in the hallway you be dismissed from training. Good luck!"

I just couldn't understand why no one had enough discipline to leave their damn phones off until the break. Like what the hell! I loved to text, I loved to be on social media and stuff. But I was not about to destroy my dreams because of a phone. Soon as I got to class I ripped out my battery and put it in my bag. I didn't even want it to be on. I'd worry about calls after class.

For self-defense, we went to a classroom next door that had more space. Once we walked in, I noticed that one of the instructors was big as hell with a beer belly, but he looked like he could F somebody up, if needed. The other trainer was a younger man in his mid-40s, in great shape, dressed up in a karate uniform. They first started off by telling us all the different situations we could deal with on the plane with passengers getting close, passengers with weapons, knives, and all types of situations. The fun part was when they brought out Bob the dummy for us to practice beating up on. It was hilarious to me, because everyone in class was either gay or female, so everyone fought like a girl.

Benjamin was funny to watch, but Kurt was the funniest. Eddie B wasn't too bad, because he had some power behind his punches, even though he swung like a girl. I wouldn't want to get hit by him too many times. Now when it was my turn, poor Bob went down and everybody was laughing at my stance, because I looked like I was ready to box.

"Bob, get back!" I yelled. "Bob, I said *get back!*"

The only thing that could be heard was a loud thump. The instructor said, "I want everybody to watch Lando. Everybody is doing fantastic, but the thing is when you scream you want everybody to hear you. Imagine yourself on the plane and an intoxicated passenger is walking up to you." The instructor demonstrated. "If you're quiet nobody will hear you. Also when you strike I want you to step into the punches, now watch the difference."

Later on Ben and I were back at the hotel conversing like we regularly did.

"Oh yeah, I need your bitch ass to be on your best behavior," he randomly blurted.

"Why?" His comment came from out of nowhere, so I was confused.

"We are having company. One of my friends is coming over."

I jumped on the bed, started dancing and yelling, "Big booty hoes, who dat. Who's dat hoochie momma!"

"See...that Detroit shit is not cool. I need you to put on the Jesus tapes you listen to in the morning and get it together."

Later that day his friend came over. We all visited for a while, before I went over to Veronica's room. She was on the phone with Rick. After she got off, she hugged me and said, "You are a genius!"

"How you figure?" I laughed.

"Because Rick said he is thinking about coming to see me for graduation. Aren't you excited?!"

"Woohoo! I'm soooo excited," I said giving her a straight face and speaking in a monotone. She gave me a funny look as if to question my sarcasm. My responding look implied I was thinking *Did you doubt me?!* He did just what I knew he would. I'm the man!

Going downstairs for a bit, I stopped by the front desk. "Hey Lisa, they have you working late today, huh?" I asked to start up a conversation. We talked for a little bit. I'm not sure if I was just horny, but I actually was kinda feeling Lisa. It was something about her that day I that turned me on, so I was more flirtatious than usual and kinda let her know I wanted her on the team.

Once I went back to my room, I noticed Ben was all dressed up as if he was about to leave.

"Where the hell you niggas think y'all going?"

"Well since your nosey ass wants to know, I'm going to Vegas."

"Umm Vegas? What you mean? I'm serious where y'all going?"

"I'm serious. We saw a cheap flight."

"Dude, did you forget we have class at 7 a.m. tomorrow?"

"Yeah, I'll make it back." I just walked out of the room laughing.

One of the other students told me about Ben's Facebook post about going to Vegas.

I went back to my room and got on my iPad. I logged into Facebook and saw Ben's status pop up. "In Vegas for the night. Lets partayy!" All I could do was shake my head and laugh.

I heard a knock and a woman's voice at my door. Veronica walked in. "Lando, why am I on Facebook and I just saw that Benjamin is in Vegas."

"He is too crazy for me," I replied smiling. "He and his little boo thang said they were about to drive to Vegas, party, and would be back before class tomorrow."

"Does he know we have a test tomorrow?"

"Hell yeah he does." My response was nonchalant.

My alarm went off and I woke up to see an empty bed next to me. I shook my head, put on Kanye West's *Graduation* CD, and got dressed. This was before he turned crazy. As I was getting ready, this fucker walked his ass right in the room. "What the fuck?! Did you really just go to Vegas and make it back? Haha."

He looked at me with the face of a zombie who hadn't been to sleep in years and said, "Lando, I'm so tired."

We both went downstairs and got some breakfast. The hotel usually served a good breakfast for us in the morning. I would grab a few items and bring them with me to class so I wouldn't be hungry throughout the day.

Terry walked in doing his usual routine. "Whoever's taking the 7 a.m. shuttle, come on." I brought Terry coffee and a muffin, like I did whenever he was our morning driver.

"Here you go, my brother. Looks like one of those days for you." I said, handing him his coffee. "Thanks, Lando, I appreciate it."

Usually, on the van rides I would sit to myself, wearing my headset, trying to get a few more minutes of sleep as we were en route to the training center. One thing I noticed that day was that the class had become very cliquish.

There were the smokers who would go outside and smoke on every break. There were the stuck-up chicks. All pretty girls with bad attitudes. The old heads were over the age of forty. Last, there were the regular, cool people. That was the group I was in. I was cool with everybody, but never really had any important drama.

That day in class I was seated two desks away from Ben. The teachers randomly switched our name tags and seating arrangements daily, but we would switch them back anyway so we could sit next to whomever we wanted. On this day, one of the hating ass hoes didn't want me and Veronica sitting next to each other. It was obvious she was hating, so we just split up for the day.

I looked over at Ben and his head was bobbing back and forth. His ass was knocked out sleeping! We all were in class laughing and shaking our heads, since we all knew he had gone to Vegas and made it back. During break Ben walked into the cafeteria on zombie mode. All I could do was laugh and tell him that's what his dumb ass got.

"Was it worth it?" I asked. He opened his eyes, like he was high or something, and said, "Hell yeah."

Matt, the motivational speaker/pilot came into the cafeteria. A lot of chicks liked him because he was just a great guy. He came in working the room speaking to everybody and sharing his positive energy.

When we went back into class Justin and Levi were in there telling everybody after our test they had a surprise for us. Since we had such a big class every time we took a test they would divided into two groups. Group One would stay in the class and Group Two would go into the computer room to take it.

Usually, I studied hard and got a top grade on each test, so I wouldn't have any problems. I actually don't remember what test we took that day, but I had a tactic I usually stuck with. Whenever I took a test and wasn't comfortable or confident with my answer,

I would get a piece of paper and write down all the ones I assumed I could get wrong. For example, if it was a 20 question test and we needed to get an 80% or better I knew I could only get 4 wrong. So my plan logically sounded good, until I clicked my results. I got all the ones I thought I got wrong, plus more. My heart dropped because I knew I only had one more shot since I'd failed.

I just knew Benjamin would fail from not studying and getting no sleep, so he was the first person I asked about his score. "Hey, Ben, how did you do?"

"I got a 96."

"Umm a 96. What?!" I screamed back, completely shocked. I sat there with this crazy expression on my face wondering how the guy who was in Vegas last night, not only just got a higher score than me, but probably higher than anyone else in the class.

Then I remembered when I first met him and he'd stayed up all night before the first day of class and still passed everything. He was just one of those types of people who could do crazy shit like that.

"What you get?" Veronica asked me.

I put my head down, and replied, "I failed..."

"What?! How? What happened?" she asked, worried and nervous.

"Man, I don't know. I guess I got too nervous, but I will bring it back tomorrow, so I will be okay."

"Looks like we have some studying to do, because I will help you."

"Okay thanks, babe."

Once class resumed, we all sat down. "We have all of your bases today," Justin said. Everyone was so excited. That was what we'd been waiting to find out. They'd told us repeatedly that there was no guarantee we'd get our first choice. However, there were opporutnities to transfer and to move up depending on the type of base we were assigned to.

My first choice was MSP-Minnesota, because my sister still basically lived out there, I have family in the area, and kinda know my way around, so it would not have been hard to make it home. My second was ORD-Chicago, since it was close to home and I also have family there I might've been able to live with for a while. AUS-Austin was my third choice, because it was a warm climate and a brand new base, increasing my chances of being moved up a lot faster. Surprisingly, my fourth base was Utah. I kinda liked it out there and Levi had already told us about a few places we could stay.

Levi went in front of the class and gave like the longest speech trying to prepare everybody for their bases. At the time I didn't understand why, but I did soon enough.

Ashley went up and talked about how she wanted Denver, but got Utah. She and her roommate became best friends, so she was okay with it.

"Justin, what's your story?" I yelled to him.

Justin came up and said he was the only one in his class that got his 1st choice, so he couldn't relate to anybody and laughed.

"Okay everyone, these are the people that got MSP. Shannon, Benjamin, Christina, Rhonda and Kirk. Everybody else got Austin."

I thought he was playing around when he said it, but he wasn't. Honestly, it was funny as hell that only six people got MSP and the rest were going to Austin. Fuck it! I was down. At least I wasn't going by myself. That's when I realized why the trainers had tried so hard to prepare everyone before telling them. I turned around and all these chicks were crying left and right, hugging each other.

Oh Lord! I thought, *Here we go again. Hurry up and get me out of here.*

I raised my hand. "Umm…can we take a break, Levi?"

"Yeah go ahead. Come back at the top of the hour," he told the group, while looking at his watch.

I saw Sara crying and I asked what was wrong.

"I don't know what to do. I told my boyfriend that I was going to be based in Denver, back at home, he is not going to stay with me if I'm living in Austin, Lando."

I walked over to the next person crying and her story was she was paying $1200 a month in rent, car insurance and more. "Now they expect her to move to Minnesota overnight? Hell naw! I'm quitting first thing in the morning," she stated.

I just knew it was going to be a long day. On the bright side, Veronica, Rebecca and a few others weren't too mad, since we all would be together.

"We are all going to be based in Austin, y'all want to get a place together?" Rebecca asked me and Veronica as we sat in her bedroom conversing later that evening.

"Heck yeah! We have no idea where to go or what we should do, so it's better to be confused with people you know than to be by yourself," I told them.

"Alright, I'll start looking for places and let everybody know what I find out tomorrow," Becca said.

"Okay y'all do that. I got to get some studying in so I can pass this test tomorrow."

Benjamin was passed out when I got to the room. Putting on some smooth r&b to help get me in a zone, I pulled out my book and started studying, so I'd be ready to retest the next day. After a few hours I grabbed two Cup O'Noodles and went downstairs to cook them. Ramon Noodles are a broke man's lifesaver. In the lobby area I saw Catherine at the table looking as if she was crying. I put the cups down and walked over there and gave her a hug.

"What's wrong, baby?"

"It's just I told my husband I would be based in Chicago. Lando, we already been having problems with our marriage lately. Financially, we've been struggling and starting this job is not going to make anything else better. I don't know what to tell him."

"This is what you do, don't call him crying and sounding all sad. Sound excited and say 'hey baby, we got our bases today and I'm starting off in Minnesota until they switch me to Chicago.' Tell him they said after you learn the system you can start commuting to work. He will support you, so just be strong, okay?"

"Okay Lando, thanks," she replied with a smile.

Back in the room, I woke Ben up to the smell of chicken ramen noodles and a Gatorade I'd prepared for him, since he'd been asleep all day.

"Hey wake up, buddy. Get you something to eat and drink this."

"Aww thanks, I appreciate it." His voice was groggy.

We stayed up for a while conversing and watching *Family Guy* until we both fell asleep.

I went to class early on the first bus the next day so I could retake the test. In the computer room it was me and another chick taking the test. I said a quick prayer and got to work and ended up getting a 96%.

Once everyone started to arrive, I heard somebody say, "I think Sara quit."

"Who is Sara?"

"That's the chick from Denver who was crying yesterday because she didn't get her base." I looked around once we got in the class and yep we were one person short.

Billie Jean walked into the class and said, "I need to see..." She looked down at her paper and my heart stopped. "...Ashley!"

Whew! Throughout the whole process of training I was nervous, but the closer to graduation the more comfortable I became. It was always in the back of my mind that somebody would come and remove me.

Later on that day, watching the Miami Heat game with Veronica, I noticed that she was kinda down.

"What's up? What's wrong with you?"

"I told Rick where I was going to be based and he was cool with everything until I told him me, you, and Becca were moving together."

"Oh Lord. What did he say after you told him that?"

"He said 'don't get me wrong. I like Lando and feel he is a good guy, but I don't want you moving in with a guy you know. He went on about it."

"What...does he think I'm going to be getting some of that big booty?" I smacked her on the ass, laughing.

"I don't know. He was like 'he is going to have friends and people over all the time.'"

"Veronica, my dear, our mission is just about complete here."

"What you mean?"

"He is back talking to you on a regular basis. He is kinda getting jealous of me, because we cake all day every day."

"What's cake mean?" I looked at her and shook my head. "Lando, you know I'm slow. Explain it."

"No damn it. Just know he will be ready to fly out here and get his girl back."

Becca texted Veronica saying she was coming over to go over the living situation.

Our problem was that we all had different ideas. Rebecca was thinking of getting something like a crash pad and commuting. Veronica's idea was to move there, drive her car down, get a very nice three bedroom apartment. I looked at the numbers. Starting off we weren't going to be making any type of money.

Now the places Veronica liked were cool, but expensive as hell. I was not about to pay more than $300 a month to halfway live somewhere. I would be there only a few days a month and would still be going home, so I wanted to find something in the middle of what they were saying. The other thing is from what we looked up, Austin is not as big as other areas with public transportation, so we would need a car there. I wanted to take a nap, so I told the ladies to figure it out and then let me know later.

I walked back to my room, turned on Sports Center, then posted on Facebook *It's official, I'm taking my talents to Austin!* mimicking Lebron James. A lot of people were congratulating me. I sent out a mass text to primary friends and family telling them about my new base.

I called dad to check and see how grandpa and the family were doing. He asked me if there were any chicks I was liking down here and filled me in on what was happening at home.

He was hyped about Austin saying, "We should have some family members that stay down there I can hit up."

We talked about the upcoming graduation. I told him once they us knew how many people we could invite I'd have him tell Keke.

"Have you heard from her?" dad asked.

"Naw. Why, what's up?"

"She's gonna hit you up. She's in Minnesota."

"Minnesota?!" I yelled. "Don't tell me she flew already, dad." I was shocked. I wasn't even through training and already she was using my flight benefits!

"Yep." He laughed.

"Wait. Hold on. Let me call you back, this is her calling now." I clicked over to answer her call. "What's up, Keke?"

"What you know about your sister in the Minno?"

"Man, dad just told me. How did you figure out how to book a flight that quick?"

"I called the people and they walked me through how to do it. I missed the first flight, but the ticket lady booked me for the next one. It was just one seat open and they were calling the lady's name to come. The ticket agent was cool as hell and was like hurry up and get on."

"When are you going back to Detroit?"

"I don't know yet, because the people on Facebook are hating on your sis. Just wait 'til I hit them hard with our first trip. I'm thinking about doing it big and hitting up Hawaii. What you think about that?"

"Man, that would be out cold. I might need you to fly down for my graduation and take a few pictures and stuff. They haven't given us the full dates of everything yet, so I will keep you updated."

"Okay. Love you, Lando."

"Okay. Love you, too."

We got on the shuttle the next morning and Veronica sat next to me and said, "Guess what?" She was smiling and blushing.

"What Veronica?"

"Rick is coming out here."

"What! Wow that's good. Is he coming for the graduation?"

"Yeah that too, but he's coming today for a few days and coming back for the graduation."

"Are you serious? He is literally flying out here?"

"No, he is driving. You get to see his car."

"That's great," I said as all the noisy chicks butted into our conversation.

"At least somebody gets to get laid out here," Doll said.

"Who said I'm just going to give it to him that easy? We're still on bad terms."

Everybody turned around, looked at her like she was crazy, and started laughing. The rest of the day I kinda felt different. It was cool that he was coming and she was happy, but after it was all said and done, she had been my best female friend/girlfriend for the last three weeks and I knew when he came I was gonna have to accept my role.

Class that day was spent in preparation for the final exam and graduation. The ceremony wasn't going to be long and we could only invite two people. So after I thought about it I didn't want Keke to fly out for no reason. I was so ready to head back home and see everybody.

It was tradition to have another flight attendant pin on the wings of a new flight attendant at the graduation ceremony. Brittany, a friend from high school, had been hired by Jet Smile. We'd been communicating about her coming to the graduation to pin me. That seemed like the best option.

Back at the hotel I was hanging with Veronica, waiting for Rick to come. She hadn't heard from him all day and didn't know what time he was coming.

"Let's order some pizza for all of us and I'll pay for it." The smile on her face was so bright as she spoke.

Now I can't remember why she left the room, but picture this situation. I'm in Veronica's room wearing a white beater and some hoop shorts, hair looking all type of crazy, when I hear a knock on the door. I opened it and it was the pizza man. I signed and grab the pizza. Right behind him was Rick.

I paused, looked, and was like, "What's up, Rick?" My tone was surprised and excited. I'm sure he was thinking something along the lines of *I'm going to surprise Veronica by popping up, but who is this buff black nigga in her room?* The look on his face was priceless.

So I invited him to come in and made small talk. "I'm not sure where Veronica is. She went downstairs to get something. You didn't see her?"

"No, I wanted to surprise her..."

Suddenly, she walked in and went nuts. *"Oh my god!"* She ran up and hugged him, yelling, "Why you didn't tell me you were here?"

I said, "Shit, I thought his ass was the pizza man's assistant or something. I opened the door and saw a man with a pizza and somebody else standing right behind him. Haha."

"Lando, shut up."

"How has class and everything been going?"

"Man, everything's been great actually. So I heard you love sports as much as I do."

"Yeah that's all I watch here. I'm so damn lucky to have her here, because my roommate never played a sport a day in his life."

"Is he gay?"

"Hell yeah," Veronica and I said at the same time, laughing.

"So Rick, we have to sit down, because I saw your car and I will be forced to hump it if I have to."

He started laughing. "Yeah man, it's outside. I just got a full tune-up and a few things done to it so I could make this drive here. You can take it for a spin if you want."

"How long was the drive?" I asked.

"It was supposed to take three and half hours, but I made it in about two hours and forty-five minutes," he replied with a cocky smile.

"Ricky and his cars... I'm going to fix everyone's plates. I have Lando's side with no pork and Ricky you will like what I got."

Rick looked at me and said, "You're Muslim?"

I laughed. "Naw. It's a long story. I just don't eat pork. So you actually play online poker for a living?"

"Yep, been doing it for a few years and been able to make a good living, but I think I have to move to Canada."

"Why Canada?" I asked, confused.

"About a week ago they banned all online gambling in the US and froze all of my bank accounts that had my winnings from poker in there, but if I go to Canada I can still do what I need to do and make money until it's all over."

"That's crazy. I'm going to leave y'all alone and get a good workout in. See y'all soon."

"Okay, it was nice meeting you, Lando."

Ricky was a great guy. Real cool and genuine. I approved of him.

20

"Aye son, do you still have the hookup at the cemetery you used to work for? We're thinking about getting a headstone for grandma," dad asked. "And do you think we should get a header or something they was saying when we were up there?"

"Naw, dad, it's called a ledger and they're real expensive. Most of the Arabic people usually get them. For grandma, I would say get her a bench. A bench is a headstone, but in the shape of a bench. The best part about that is you know when it snows it's hard to locate a regular headstone because they are covered up. A bench is a bench and soon as you drive up you can locate that easily. That's what I would recommend, but that costs a little bit also."

"Man, I'm not worried about the price just see what you can do."

"Okay, dad, I'll hit you back."

I decided to give one of my old cemetery partners in crime a call to see if he still worked there.

"Woodlawn Cemetery. This is Sherry. How may I help you?"

"Does Mike McDonald still work there?"

"Yes he does. He is our manager. Let me get him for you."

We talked for a while and played catch up. He wasn't able to help me, but it was nice to talk to him. I hung up and thought back to how times used to be with me and Mike running a cemetery. A young black 19-year-old and a 50-year-old white male became best friends. We had some good times and lots of crazy stories.

I went to class the next day, happy there were only six days left. Veronica and I were seated next to each other and she was glowing a little bit, happy because Rick was back in her life. As we were talking she said, "I'm so happy that you guys like each other, because he is still a little bit nervous about the moving in situation. I feel it will grow on him more and more."

Nick was teaching. I just couldn't focus, so I started to draw on a piece of paper and on the top of it wrote: *Add on and pass along*. I drew an AirStar plane at the top in the clouds with a guy looking like superman flying and passed it to Carolyn next to me. She looked at it and started laughing then she added to it. The paper went around to about seven different people until it went to one of the old heads in the class. I guess she didn't like it, because her ass didn't pass it on. When I got it back honestly it was real funny. It showed how goofy and what type of creative imagination some of our classmates had. Nick told everyone to take a break and I went into the cafeteria sitting down with the girls. One of the trainers came in and was like, "Lando, come with me for a second."

I was kinda confused and took my time getting up wondering what it could be. I was taken into Kim's office and I noticed a piece of paper on the desk as they closed the door. "Lando, this is the situation," she said and gave a brief pause. "We received your background information and it shows you have a misdemeanor on your record which you never told us about."

"What! A misdemeanor? I went to court for that situation, but I don't have anything on my record that would hinder my chances of becoming a flight attendant."

"So with our rules and regulations I'm sorry to tell you, but you have been released from the training. We had Billie Jean to set up your flight back home."

I put my head down and my eyes started to water. "I can't go home, Kim. My grandma died a few weeks ago and my family begged me to come home, but I stayed so I could become a flight attendant for her. I have one of the top grades in the class and never had any problem with anybody."

"Yeah, Lando, we are sorry, but this is our rule. We have a van driver outside waiting for you."

As I got up, she also said, "Just leave your book and badge in the class."

I walked out of the meeting and I was pissed, but I was more upset to face all of my new friends and to tell them I was leaving. I walked in the classroom gathering my stuff and Veronica was the first one in with the worried look on her face. "Lando, what's wrong?!" she screamed.

"I'm getting sent home."

"What? How? What happened?"

"Some stuff on my background information came up and they said since I didn't disclose the information I've got to go."

She just ran up to me hugged me and started to cry. I went into the cafeteria and everybody ran up to me asking what happened. It hurt even worse when Benjamin came and gave me the biggest hug, crying. I talked to Eddie B and he told me good luck and to take down his number. As I was leaving, the teachers briefly shut down class to let everyone say their goodbyes. As I walked outside I saw my main man Terry outside the van waiting for me. Veronica and Becca walked me outside, both hugging me.

"Lando, what are you going to do now?"

"Man, actually I'm not sure. But y'all finish class and don't worry about me. I will be strong and come back."

"Lando, still come to Austin with us."

"Yeah, Lando, that would be great and we could help you find a job out there."

"Okay, I will think about that. Love you two. Y'all had my back since day one, ladies."

"Okay, Lando, love you too." *Cry Me a Fucking River.*

21

I was so close to achieving my dream I could taste it, feel it, smell it, and in one moment it was gone. All the hard work I'd put into it, the grind, the practice, the dedication, and now all I could do was decide my next move. Most people fail in life because they don't have faith in God or themselves. Sometimes his plan was nothing close to what I imagined it to be.

Terry grabbed my bags and put them in the back as I sat in the front seat. He looked at me and said, "Man, see this the shit I don't fucking understand. Whatever you did is whatever you did, but why did they wait until a week left of class to kick somebody out? After all these years of working here, whenever they call me to pick somebody up during the middle of the day it has never been a good outcome."

"Yeah man, this sucks, T. I'm not sure what I'm going to do. All of my family and friends are proud of me for coming out here, doing good and training. Now I have to go back home with no damn job, no nothing."

"Yeah, Lando, it's sad, man. I know this is the wrong time, but for the situation, it seems right." He pulled a pipe out of his pocket. "I doubt if you smoke, but you want to hit?"

"Man, fuck yeah! Terry, on some real shit from me to you, stay being you, man. I love your ass. Do you have a lighter?"

He handed it to me. While he was driving we took turns smoking and telling stories as we drove back to the hotel. As we pulled up to the hotel, Terry started crying and looked me in the face. "You're a good man and I know you will be successful in life. Just keep that personality you have and keep your integrity. You have my number, call me."

I walked in my room and got an email from Billie Jean saying my flight was at 2:55. It was already 1:30, so for me to pack and leave it was nearly impossible for me to make it. I took my time and packed everything up, trying not to think about the situation.

What am I going to tell dad? What am I going to tell my friends?

Finished packing, I wrote Ben and Veronica a nice goodbye letter. Benjamin's stated how happy and blessed I had been to have him as a roommate, wishing him the best of luck and to stay in touch. Now Veronica's was deeper, because she'd become a new best friend overnight. I was breaking down how much fun we had and I would definitely see her again. I slid the note under her door and left Ben's on his bed. I took one last look at the room and walked out with no turning back.

As I walked downstairs, and I saw Pattie, the sweet little lady who'd been kicked out of class in the beginning of training. I noticed she was pulling her car up and started to unpack her things. I assumed that she was able to come back with the new class that was starting in a few more days. I smiled and was happy for her to be able to bounce back, but avoided seeing her, because I was in too much of a bad mood to tell her the story or to see her start crying.

Lisa came from around the front desk and asked what was I doing with all my stuff packed up. I told her the situation and she told me to take down her number, because she wanted me to come back out and see her.

A shuttle bus came to drop me off at the airport, but soon as I got there I just looked at the time and realized there was no way I was making that flight. I found somewhere in the airport to sit down and emailed Billie telling her the situation and to re-book me. Since I used to work for the airlines I knew the ins and outs of the flights. All they really had to do was re-book me for a later flight. A random number called me and it was a lady in the travel department telling me the situation. She was going to re-book me, but all the flights were full so would I want to go back home tomorrow and stay an extra day.

That was cool with me. Now what they were trying to do was to keep me away from the training hotel and put me up in a different one so I wouldn't be close to any of the classmates. I agreed with everything she said. Sike! I had been texting Veronica all day since I left training and told her the deal. We agreed I was going to stay with her and not tell anybody, keeping it between me and her.

This time everything was weird and uncomfortable, because I was in the same location where we caught the blue shuttle when we all first arrived in Utah, so I was having flashbacks. Just my luck they had a new training class standing in the same spot we were when my class first arrived.

So what I did was sit all the way in the back and put my headphones on to minimize questions. I forgot what I told them when they asked me a few questions, but I did good to avoid everyone and went straight up to Veronica' room. It was good that Rick had gone back home for a few days and was coming back for graduation. That made it easier to stay with her. She already had the room door open and texted me that she was going out to get ice-cream with Pattie and did I want to come with them.

I wasn't in the mood. I just really wanted to hide out from everybody. I finally decided to call dad and tell him what happened.

"Hey, what's up, dude?"

"Hey, son, what you got going on?"

"Man, I'm coming home tomorrow."

"What you mean?"

"I got kicked out."

"What?! Right before graduation? That's bad. What happened?" He was shocked.

"I was called into the office and they said I didn't give a full background and lied, so they had to let me go. I tried everything when I talked to them, but they already had the van and my flight already for me."

He laughed a little bit and said, "People have no idea how hard it is to be a flight attendant. You just can't win for nothing with this job. When do you come back?"

"I'm supposed to come back today, but will do it tomorrow. So I'm just hanging out with Veronica today."

"Who is going to pick you up tomorrow?"

"I'm not sure, not even thinking about that right now."

"Okay, well hit me up."

The rest of the day I kicked it with Veronica and tried to stay low key. But that sure as hell didn't last long. People started to come over left and right to talk to me, but later that night I went downstairs and saw Eddie B sitting on the couch. We greeted each other.

"Lando, no matter what anybody says, I'm proud of you. We've been going to interviews for the last year. Just pray and keep fighting and one day you will be a flight attendant."

"Thanks, I really appreciate it. Hit me up when y'all graduate, because you know I will be in Austin partying with y'all. Did you figure out where you're going to stay yet?" I asked him. "Frank and Gelly were looking at a few apartments, so if they get one I'm just going to move in with them."

"Okay, well I'm going to let y'all get ready to study."

"What you mean?"

"Veronica told me everybody was coming down to do a little bit of studying and help each other out."

"Man, I don't have time to deal with all them damn crazy folks. I'm taking my black butt right up them stairs in a minute."

His phone rang and I left to go upstairs.

The next day went quickly, since I was so sad. I honestly don't remember the flight or who had picked me up from the airport. I didn't want to see Keke or any of my friends. I just wanted to hide out. I'd asked dad not to tell anyone, but as soon as I landed, OC called trying to hang out and cheer me up.

My first few days back home I was just flat out depressed. I stayed in the basement, didn't listen to any self-development audios, and went upstairs only to eat and use the bathroom. One day my aunt called me upstairs and told me the plan.

"We're going to write a letter to whoever the CEO or top of the management is telling them you want to come back, because you didn't know any of that stuff was on your record, and you feel this was wrongful termination. They should have something implemented like a union to protect you."

"Yeah, they actually do, but since I wasn't a full-time employee I can't use it."

"Okay. I'm just giving you some ideas. Look it up and if you find something let me know."

For the rest of that day I was thinking of different ways to get my job back and then it hit me. I started looking through all of the paperwork we received when we first came to training with our rules and regulations. And it showed if an employee was terminated, they could appeal within 10 days from the time of termination. I forwarded all the documents to my aunt immediately.

I decided my aunt was correct and I should write the CEO and ask if I could get my job back. All AirStar employees could be reached via email, so I had access to the CEO, Mr. Sammy Watkins.

After a few hours I came up with the nice letter to send Sammy. I continued to review the rules and regulations, realizing all I had to do was call Billie Jean and tell her I wanted to appeal their decision. She was very helpful with the situation, giving me the number to call, and also who to email. This is the letter I sent.

Dear Mr. Edwards

Please forward this email as my letter of appeal of disqualifying me as a flight attendant during the In-Flight training.

I was told that I was disqualified because I did not disclose a misdemeanor on my record of 'Interfering with Police Investigation,' when I filled out my application. I reviewed the crimes that are FAA disqualifying for a flight attendant, and I was very glad to see the incident of me carrying a cup of cold Kool-Aid on a college campus is what led to a misdemeanor on my record. I had no idea something I thought was trivial would turn out to be so devastating in my life and my career.

I attended 21 out of 27 days of the In-Flight training and was probably the top in the class and very well-liked by the instructors and other students. My career as a flight attendant is very important to me, as my gravely ill grandmother insisted I attend the training and my attendance resulted in me missing her funeral service on March 12th.

When I completed the AirStar application months before I began the In-Flight training, and up to the training, was based on the fact that I did not have any disqualifying offenses according to an AirStar disqualification list.

Please accept my apologies for any and all miscommunicated information on my part. I am writing this letter of appeal because the information I submitted was based on me not having any disqualifying crimes. AirStar states they were going to do complete background checks prior to my invitation of training. On February 7, 2011, I also received an email from Billie Jean, that I have also attached, stating:

Very Important "If you have been convicted or are currently being charged with a criminal misdemeanor or felony that hsd happened since your interview you must inform us as soon as possible."

I had not had any charges since my interview. Therefore, my thoughts were confirmed that I had completed all forms accurately, as AirStar led me to believe that my background checks were made and approved prior to training. Reinstating me to complete my training will be sincerely appreciated on my part and AirStar will obtain the upmost committed flight attendant.

Thank you for your consideration.

After I gathered the information, thanks to my aunt, I sent that letter. For the first time since I'd had that fateful meeting, I was actually in a better mood and became more optimistic. Meanwhile, my brother OC had been calling me to come hang with him, so I decided to go over his house and see what he had to talk about.

As he opened the door, he greeted me, gave me a hug, and told me to follow him to the garage, because he had a surprise. I walked in the garage and saw some new things he'd done to the Benz.

He'd added black rims, new black paint, and black tinted windows. It was beautiful. I fell even more in love once I sat in the car and he showed me how I could press a button to make the hydraulics work to raise and lower it. After the male bonding ritual, he looked at me and said, "Man, how you doing?"

"I honestly have never been this sad in my life as I have been for the last few day. I'm a little bit better now. It is good to get out the house. I flew all the way to Utah, worked my ass off, made a lot of new friends, and got kicked out six days before graduation. Talking about being pissed. That's an understatement, but I will be okay. Aunt Chris and I are sending an appeal letter."

Tiff opened the garage door to tell us that Keke was on her way over. It was good I was actually able to finally talk to somebody about grandma's funeral.

He said, "It was impeccable. A lot of people showed up. It was so packed that people had to watch on the TV screen in the basement of the church. Aunt Chris had her mink coat with the matching hat, looking like Denzel in American Gangster. Keke did her thing and I had my $3000 Tom Ford glasses. The whole family showed up. Grandma went out in style. Everybody was kinda down because you could not be there, you know, it just didn't feel the same."

We walked into a room in his house and he pulled out a shoebox that had a lot of papers inside. And said, "These are some of the letters that grandma wrote me back when I was in jail."

OC, I'm here to tell you I love you. I helped raise you and know you have a good heart. I want you to become successful, but I think this is my last time writing you in here. I promise you I will not write you if you go back. So when you get out either get a real job or start your own business. Here is a little change for you. I hope it can help out.

We looked at each other and were thinking how much she always had our backs.

Keke knocked on the door and came in. "What's up? What's up? I see you were able to get Lando out of dad's basement," were her first words.

"Shut up," I said and gave her a hug.

OC looked at me and said, "Lando, she's been devastated over the last few days."

"Why?"

"Because she can't get free flights no more." He laughed. "She has been over here debating if she has to become a flight attendant so y'all get to fly for free."

We had a good night hanging out. There's nothing like family. I gave my hugs and left heading towards Inkster to visit mom. She'd been worried about me.

I woke up the next day and said to myself, *It's time to stop feeling sorry for yourself, Lando. It's time to get back in the game.*

The first thing I decided to do was start working on myself. Since I had more than enough time on my hands, it was time to start back learning my Spanish. I dedicated seven days a week at least about 3 hours a day to my studies. I went to the library, got a few books that would help me, and went to work.

Dad was happy to see me back to my regular self. I was so

focused, because I was ready to start back applying for jobs, so I could get another opportunity. I even decided from here on out to tell the truth. Whoever I applied to needed to know that I had a misdemeanor on my record, because I couldn't mentally take getting kicked out of another training.

On the hiring website I saw that Circle Airlines was accepting applications. Once I applied I received a response immediately. I decided to look up the airline and I was speechless. It wasn't a charter carrier. It wasn't mainline. It wasn't even a regional airline. It was Circle Airlines and one perk that sold me was I could receive commissions from the sales I made on the flights. The training was in Vegas, so that would be fun. The more I read up on the airline, the more I wanted an opportunity to work with them. Now the downfall was the open house was in Jokerville, Washington. *Where in the hell is that?*

I looked it up on the map and it was as far west as one could possibly go. Not to mention they didn't fly candidates to the interview. Once I saw that I didn't even bother to do any more research.

"Hey, son, you hear anything about any airlines?" dad asked as he walked into the living room with his black and gray silk robe on.

"No, not really."

"I see you been learning that Espanol again. Studying hard, huh?"

"Yup," I replied with a dry tone, trying to give him the hint to leave me the hell alone. He always seemed to come at the right time. Even the times I wanted to be in a bad mood and wasn't feeling sociable, he'd force a smile out of me. Once I realized I was being an asshole, I decided to talk to him.

"Actually, I see a cool airline I would be interested in. The name is Circle Airlines, and dad, they're so hyped they even let the flight attendants sell and make a commission on the flights."

"What you mean by that?" he responded confused.

"They have drinks and stuff on regular flights, but on this one, FAs can also sell vacation passes or something like an event to go see Michael Jackson in concert. A few people were saying that it adds up to decent money. I'm not sure exactly how everything works. I would have to go to the open house. The only thing is it's all the way in Washington and they aren't covering the cost. I'm not about to do that flight there. Probably costs way too much."

He stood up and started to walk to his room. "Just check the prices and see if you can find a cheap one."

I didn't respond, because as I thought about it, he really didn't want his son in a slump. So if he had to pay a few hundred dollars to make me happy then it would be worth it. Also, on the bright side, my ex-girlfriend Amanda wanted to see me. I knew she had a boyfriend, but I guess that was none of my business, because she sure said come over late night after she got out of class.

Some female company would be good, because leaving the house every night to let dad get some action had kinda gotten old, so I was definitely down to hang with her. I went to the liquor store to grab us some wine and I brought over a few bootleg movies I had laying around.

That was the first time I'd seen Amanda since we'd broken up. She lived in an apartment with one of her friends off campus. The drive was about an hour away, and to make matters worse, it was raining. When I finally got there she opened the door looking even sexier than I remembered. She was fair-skinned, about 5'2, black and Brazilian. The tight jeans she wore showed her perfect 117-pound coke bottle shaped body perfectly.

"Hey Lando. It's good to see you. How long has it been?"

"Man, I'm not even sure. It's been some years, but it's good to see you. What's been up? Oh yeah. I brought you some wine and a few good movies," I said handing them to her.

She gave me a tour of her little apartment and explained how she and a male cousin now shared a place. I was wondering why there was so much man stuff laying around.

"Mandy, you sure he is your cousin, because I don't want your boyfriend to walk in and get his ass beat."

"No stupid. Shut up. I don't have a boyfriend. Well, I'm kinda talking to somebody. So you might need to help me and give me some advice from the male perspective, but come on," she said.

As she guided me to her room, I noticed she had on my favorite perfume that she would always wore for me.

"So how is it to be a flight attendant? Tell me about it."

I cleared my throat. "Well...I haven't done a real flight yet. I just got out of training."

"Oh, okay. Where will you be stationed?"

"Texas."

"Oh yeah, I did see your post on Facebook about Austin. That's awesome. Good for you. I'm happy."

"Speaking of flying, I have to fly out to Washington in a few days to do some stuff. Can I use your laptop?"

"Yeah, you can." She pulled out the laptop that I'd brought her years ago.

"Oh, so somebody still has the computer I gave them, huh?"

She smiled. "Are you going to use it or not?"

I decided to book my flight to Washington while I was there, so she could think I was still in the industry. Dad had said do what I need to do to make it to the interview, just pay him back once I got the job.

"While you do that I'm going to get some glasses and get some wine, because I need it."

"So Mandy, tell me what's been up with you? How is life? How is school?"

"You know how I am with school. It's just been overwhelming. You know I take so many classes, then try to work and make some money, if I can."

"Where are you working now?"

"I help out at the school stores and do some mentoring to

help keep some money in my pockets. Here's your drink." She handed me a glass of wine.

"Um, ma'am who said I trusted you? Did you put some date rape drugs in there?"

"Lando, whatever! Everybody knows I don't need to put anything in that wine to get in your pants and see Pete." I laughed, because she was surely telling the truth.

"Hey now, I'm a wholesome young individual. Thank you." I made myself more comfortable on her bed and took a sip of the white wine. "So how's the love life been treating you?"

"It's complicated right now." She looked up at the ceiling as if she didn't know what to say. "I've been dating left and right. Whenever I had time, I would go on a date, then try again if that didn't work. You know I'm to myself, so my friends would always set me up with a nutcase that never works out."

I grabbed one of her pillows to lay on. "What type of guys you been going on dates with?"

"I would go on a date and the guy would expect me to pay for everything. I'm a woman and this is our first date. How do I look paying for you? I even tried to date a white guy from the school. He was very handsome, had swag, and I liked him, but come to find out the nigga was atheist." We both laughed. "Give me your opinion on this one. So the guy I been dating now we been talking for about a year and a half."

"Wait a minute..." I interrupted her. "Wait one damn minute. Did you say *dating* for a year and a half, Mandy?" I looked at her like she was crazy. "Are y'all together or just bang buddies?"

"No, no, we are kinda...that's what I need your advice with, if you would let me finish. So we been dating for a year and a half. I just don't know why he won't commit and just make it official."

"Okay, Amanda, now first I need more wine please and thank you before I say anymore words." I shoved my glass towards her and she smiled and filled my glass. "Have you met his parents?"

"No. His dad is locked up and he is not cool with his mom

like that."

"That's one flag. Have you been over to his place?"

"Yeah. He has a roommate, so he usually visits me more."

"Have you ever had that conversation with him about trying to make it official?"

"Yeah, whenever I do he avoids it and says 'you already know what we are.'" She imitated using her fake deep male voice.

"First thing is, you're too available for him. It's like what's the point of getting in a relationship if you get to have a bad chick, sex, and the other benefits he has. Also he can cheat without getting in too much trouble. Now I'm just wondering how the Amanda that didn't let me be in a relationship for at least one month without forcing me to change my Facebook status and this nigga get the pussy and all for a year in a half."

"Oh my god, Lando. Shut the hell up. You're just crazy. Man. What's wrong with you?"

"Aye, don't be mad at me, because I'm telling the truth. You hacked my Myspace account and was like who are those bitches on your page."

"No no no. That was your no good ass, because you was still trying to date Gina and me. I wasn't letting that crap happen. Now Lando." Then she calmed down and seemed ready to ask a serious question. "We've been broken up for some years and are friends now, so you can tell me the truth. Did you cheat on me when we were together?"

"Did you cheat on me?"

"No! What type of dumbass question is that?" she responded angrily.

"Amanda, I agree. What type of dumbass question is that?"

"Lando, stop playing. You know I didn't cheat on you."

"I don't know what the hell you were doing. Remember on Valentine's Day you were with some guy at your job all caked up? So I can't put nothing pass you."

"Whatever. So you will never answer that question, huh?"

"I answered it the same way you answered mine. What time do you have school tomorrow, lady?"

"7 a.m."

"You want me to get out of here so you could get some sleep?"

"No, you're okay. I thought you were spending the night. No need to drive all the way back."

Yes! Yes! Yes! Who da man! You Da Man! Who Da Man! You Da Man!

I'm happy because I don't have to do that long ass hour drive back home in the rain, especially after drinking. "Oh okay. I ppreciate it."

"Cool. Let me put on some pajamas." She got up with that perfect, small-sized booty and grabbed some pajamas and went on the bathroom.

I had been dating a chick named Gina and she moved to Cali. We decided to try a long distance relationship. I used to send her money, clothes, and held her down with whatever she needed. We had the same situation. We missed each other, but when I met Amanda through a friend, we exchanged numbers and started dating. Meanwhile in Cali, Gina met a guy from the east coast and started talking to him. We both knew what the situation was and agreed to part ways, because it was no point in cheating on each other, as long as she still gave me some of that good pussy whenever she came back home.

Amanda and I dated for a year and a half. That was my boo. I loved her, but we argued non-stop. We were both twenty when we got into a relationship. I acted as a twenty-year-old would act who had a condo, friends and some money. I partied my ass off. Every weekend my house was like a frat house, beer pong and all. She complained about my partying, but I still held her down.

Amanda would trick the hell out of the public eye. I mean everybody loved her. She was the biggest sweetheart in public, but behind closed doors the chick had serious anger issues. I mean she could go from 0-60 immediately. When she started it was as if all she saw was red. It was just so weird, because she was so little and cute, but had so much childhood anger built up in her. The other thing is I was an entrepreneur, I quit both of my jobs and went full time in Pre-Paid Legal. I was making crazy money and was a businessman and hustler. Most people that are in network marketing are basically brainwashed to be successful. That was my mindset: to become rich and successful. Her mind was straight education, go to school, get a good job, and work for forty years.

I had no problem with her going to school. I supported her, but felt like she wasn't there for me. Hell, I would bring relationship books home to work on, give her positive CDs to listen to while driving, but she just wasn't into it, so I feel we grew apart.

"Here's your wine." She passed me the glass. "Do you want to watch the Batman?"

"You always loved Batman, Mandy." She put the movie in and turned off the lights.

I already knew what the situation was. She'd gotten into it with her boyfriend, or whatever she wanted to call him, and was under the impression that he is cheating. It was her turn to do her dirt and that's what she was using me for.

Once we laid in the bed she pushed her little booty towards me, knowing I'm a big time cuddler. I grabbed her waist and pulled her a little bit towards me and...nothing. I couldn't do it. To this day I can't tell you exactly why. Probably because I figured she would have caught feelings and tried to get back together. I didn't want the drama. Hell, it might have been me. If I could go back to that day, I would have knocked that good ass pussy out of the ball park.

The next morning we overslept. I felt terrible that she missed school, but she insisted everything was okay and she would email the professor. She even cooked me a quick breakfast before we parted our ways.

"Hasta luego amor."

22

*E*verybody goes through adversity, my mentor Jim Rohn used to always say 'Life will happen to you. It's ahat you do about what happens to you that will determine your life's future.'

Lando, are you going to sit in the basement and cry because you got kicked out of a training? Are you the only person in history that's been kicked out of flight training? The answer was no and I doubted if I would be the last. It was time to get back on my feet and prove to the world I was destined to be great.

"Did you grab those cuff links?" dad asked as I was getting dressed in the bathroom for my interview.

"Oh, I forgot. Can I use yours, please?"

"So who you have picking you up?"

"Sean should be on his way now. They have me first flying to Houston, then to Seattle, and finally to that retarded city."

"How many people are on that forum talking about the interview?"

"I'm not sure. Most people are not talking about it. I only see about a handful of people coming to it." Sean beeped his horn. "Alright, dad, I'll be back in a few days."

"Okay, son, go out there and do your thing."

One thing I will never get tired of is looking at is all of the gorgeous women from all over the world. Boy, oh boy, I love Detroit Metro Airport. My first flight for that trip was on an American Airlines flight. Since it was my first time flying with them, I imagined all the flight attendants to be very old. Because they hadn't hired anybody since like 1985, the youngest flight attendant had to be like 62.

As I was walking through the airport, I saw a few friends and co-workers that still worked at the airport and they looked like they'd seen a ghost.

"Wow, Lando, you're actually a flight attendant now! I have been seeing you on Facebook traveling and stuff. That's what's up, man."

Once I walked on the plane, I sat at a window seat and in the middle was an Asian guy and in the aisle seat was his girlfriend, I assumed. The whole flight we never said a word to each other. I was excited because on the head rest of the seat in front of me had a TV and some good basketball games on. The flight attendants wouldn't stop talking. It seemed like every three seconds somebody was on the intercom talking. Every time they talked it cut off the sound of my TV, so I was pissed off the majority of the flight.

I heard them say we were descending and would be landing in twenty minutes. I decided to rest my eyes for a little bit.

I overslept and I could tell when I woke up that something just didn't feel right. Not one of those happy ass flight attendants that had been roaming around fucking with the passengers all flight were in sight.

The plane seemed to be flying very low, as if we were hovering. I looked at my watch and noticed we were thirty minutes pass our landing time. Then we heard the distinct sound signaling the captain was about to speak.

"Ladies and gentlemen, I know you're wondering why we

haven't landed yet. Our flaps are currently not working. We will be landing soon. When you see a lot of fire trucks and ambulances, don't be alarmed."

Immediately, my heart dropped and all I heard was Sean's voice in my head asking, "What happens if the plane crashes?"

Fuck me! My life passed before my eyes. I looked at the Asian guy and said, "Did this guy just say if we land and are surrounded by fire trucks and stuff, don't be alarmed?"

"I was just thinking the same thing."

"If we got to run out of this bitch be ready to go when I say so." I looked at his girlfriend and noticed she was passed out sleeping.

I told him, "I'm leaving her ass if she is not ready."

He woke her up speaking his native language, I assumed updating her on what was going on.

This was like the longest descent of my life. What were the fucking odds of that? Did I really want to be a flight attendant that much? As we approached, I saw about twenty different fire trucks and ambulances waiting for us.

Now correct me if I'm wrong, but when a pilot says no flaps, aren't flaps the things that slow a plane down in order to land?

We learned if we weren't able to stop, we would just crash into a building. So I guess that's what the fire trucks and ambulance there for, right?

That's when I made up in my mind. I said a prayer, got into the brace position I learned in flight training, and started to prepare myself for which exit I was going to take. I just knew I would not die in a plane crash. I'm a survivor.

Surprisingly, the landing went great, it was smooth and regular. It was just weird to be surrounded by fire trucks, but thank God I lived to fly another day.

As soon as I got off the plane, I called dad to tell him what happened, because my adrenaline was flowing.

"Dad, you won't believe what just happened to me!"

"What's up?"

"So we're on our way to Houston from Detroit, right. Why did the pilot come on the speaker and say don't be alarmed if you see fire trucks and ambulances as we land!"

"What was the problem?"

"He said the flaps stopped working."

"Aren't the flaps the things that stop the plane?"

"Yeah, that's what I thought. That's why I figured they had fire trucks everywhere when we landed. But everything went smooth and we landed good."

"Wow, thank God. Man, you have to be safe when you get in the air. I guess God tested you to see how much you want the job, you know."

"Yeah, I guess so."

"Are you going to hit up Kerry and Stacey while you out there?" he asked.

"I forgot that they even live in Houston."

"See, that's what I'm here for. Your memory's all messed up. It's ashame that you're that young and can't remember anything. You must get that from your momma's side."

"But I only got like a two-hour layover before my next flight, so I'm not even going to bother them."

"Okay, well hit me up later. Are you going to eat there?"

"No, not yet, because I have to fly to Washington next. I'll grab something there."

"Be safe. I forgot to tell you after you get that job I have some good news for you when you get back."

"I like good news. I'll keep you updated, pops."

I found my gate, pulled out my study guide book, and went to work until it was time to board. Yan called me and I told him how thick the women were in Houston.

"I can't lie, this process has been crazy. I actually started to write a book about it."

"Yo' lazy ass ain't gone write no book," he responded laughing, in true Yan style.

"You'll see."

"Well, if you do, I'm just gonna take credit for giving you the motivation." *This nigga!*

Changing the subject, I told him. "Man, I was ready to get married over ten times in two hours."

"The world better not let me become a flight attendant, because it's too many good-looking women out here."

I was ready to fly again and prayed that flight went safely. Once we landed in Washington, I was impressed by how nice and clean the airport was. I found a bar that sold food and had some TV screens. The best part, I was able to watch some basketball and also make some new friends. The bartender was very down to earth. We talked about everything from politics to the aviation industry. Even the guy sitting next to me joined in and started buying me drinks. By the time of my next flight I was ready to go.

The plane we flew in was hands down the smallest plane I have ever flown in. There were only about thirty passengers and the turbulence was in full effect all twenty-four minutes of the flight. We landed in Jokerville, Washington at the smallest airport I have ever seen in my life. I mean this was my first time getting off on the tarmac and all straight presidential style. I swear to you the airport couldn't have more than three gates. I called the number to the Best Western hotel I was staying at. The airline referred us to stay there, since we received a discounted rate and also it was the location for the open house. The person who came to pick me up was a white man around fifty years old named Roger. In addition to him being the shuttle driver, he was also the mechanic.

He started a conversation and we chatted about our origins and how we both came to be in Jokerville. From what he said, it seemed like a nice, sleepy town. It was a pleasant conversation. Roger seemed like a decent guy.

I walked into the hotel, greeted by a very nice woman at the reception desk. I felt like a boss. Soon as I walked up she was like, "Here is your key, Orlando."

"Girl, how you know it's me?"

In my mind I'm like *duh you're the first black man they have seen in years.*

It was only two floors. They had a nice sitting area and a waterfall type of thing over by the stairs. I guessed they'd disabled it since it was late though. My room was neat, but wasn't too big. I decided to change and take a little tour around the hotel to see if I could find some other people that were there for the interview.

I walked down the hall and saw a conference room, so I opened it. It was just what I needed to see. Assuming that was where we are doing the interview the next day, I stepped in, taking in the atmosphere. I could tell by the layout I was in the right place, so I figured it was the perfect time to practice. I walked up to the front of the room, which was very dark, since I had no idea where the light switch was.

"Thank you. Thank You, Ladies and Gentlemen. I'm Lando Success. Ha-ha Thanks for the applause. Please stop it. I'm serious. This bitch said I only got sixty seconds ha-ha. Well, it's a pleasure to be here today. I have taken in depth notes about the company and I know I will be a great asset to the team."

I paused and thought of what I was supposed to say next, but I was thinking out loud speaking to myself. "Lando, let's go, baby, you can do it. Nobody wants this like you want it. Nobody flew out here from Michigan. Nobody is prepared like you. Let's get it. Hello ladies and gentlemen the reason I'm perfectly qualified for the position is because of my customer service experience. I first started my career off in the cemetery business. *Lando, now break down how that has helped you,* I said mentally. Next, I got involved in the health care industry. *Break that down, Lando, and last talk about your most recent job.*

"Cool, let's get it." I walked out of the conference room pissed off and in the zone. I hadn't flown out there for no reason. Dad spent all that money for me to go out there, so I'd better be ready to get that job. I went back to the room and took some good notes on what I wanted to add to my speech. I decided to do a good workout in my room so I could calm my adrenaline down. That didn't work and I wanted to be in good spirits tomorrow, so I played some of Les Brown's speeches on YouTube before I fell asleep.

In the morning, I woke up happy with a big smile on my face, listening to Lupe Fiasco while getting dressed. Since I needed some luck to be on my side, I pulled out the pink I had worn for the AirStar interview. Gold cuff links, gold Rolex, pink tie with my navy blue suit. I looked in the mirror and said, "Damn, you look good, boy ha-ha."

The open house was scheduled to start at 8:00, so I decided to walk out around 7:30. There was already a long ass line in the hallway. I figured there were about forty-five people in front of me, so I walked to the back of the line. No lie everyone was staring at me. You know, like in the movies when you see the sexy woman and everything slows down. Yep, I was the sexy chick. I was scanning everybody, just leveling up my competition. I hadn't seen one black male or female, but that worked to my benefit, in my opinion. About thirty percent of the guys there had on a suit.

"Hey, how are you guys doing?" I spoke to the guy and girl in front of me.

They both turned towards me and respond, "Hey, I'm doing great. I'm Alex, by the way, and this is Nick."

"It's nice to meet you guys. I'm Lando. So where are from?"

"I'm from up the road about twenty minutes from here. Nick, where are you from?"

"Oh, I'm from Seattle and I just drove. It was only about a three-hour drive. I was going to come out last night and get a room, but didn't want to waste money, you know. What about you, Lando?" he said.

"I'm from Michigan."

"So you flew all the way from Michigan to the interview?"

"Yes, sir, it sure is not as easy as twenty minutes," I said, looking at Alex being sarcastic.

We all laughed and a lady I assumed was one of the recruiters said, "Ladies and Gentlemen, we are going to open the doors soon so you guys can get seated, but before you go in I want everybody to check in with Abby right over here. See you all soon."

The line started to move and I walked up to Abby, a white lady in her late thirties, looked in her eyes and said, "Hey Abby, it's a pleasure to meet you. I'm Orlando."

I walked into the room and looked to the left where they had a huge projection screen on the wall showing Circle Airlines' flight attendants having fun and working in various capacities. Chairs were lined up on two different sides. I went straight to the front row on the right side. My mentor always told me all the big money people sit in the front, no millionaires ever sat in back of the class. As everybody walked in, I grabbed my notepad, and scanned the competition. Can't remember exactly who I sat next to, but I was in the zone. The presenter greeted us with energy and excitement.

"Hello everyone! I'm Shelby Kream and I want to be the first person who welcomes you to our open house. Today, we want to give some information about our company, like how you get paid and things of that nature. If it's something you feel you're interested in then one by one everyone can come up and tell us a little about you and your background.

I completely love this company, since it was very different from the average airline. I've been here for six years and never looked back. Today, to help me is Rose over there and Mara will also be helping."

As the open house went on, I absolutely fell in love with the company. They were 100% the type of airline I was looking to work for. They showed a slide show and since their primary base was in Vegas, the job looked like a big ass party. Pictures with flight attendants dressing up as show girls, pictures with the Blue Man group, them on the plane in overhead bins and all. I could tell they were looking to add fun-spirited people to their crew.

Another thing that got me was that was the first airline I had ever heard of that paid commissions. Yep commissions, for selling stuff on the planes. That's who I am to the core of my being, a salesman and I love it. I'd have the opportunity to sell stuff on the planes. I think the whole crew split the commissions or whatever.

Circle was the airline that flew out of very little cities, like Jokerville, to major vacation places like Vegas or Orlando. Since everybody is going on vacation, nine times out of ten they're all happy and excited passengers. The only bad thing so far about the company was they had no overnights. Meaning the crew started and ended in Jokerville. That was not bad for someone who lived there, but for someone who wanted to commute back and forth it was nearly impossible.

For me, that meant I would have to move out there. At that moment, that was the last thing on my mind. I just needed to get hired somewhere.

After we came back from break about ten people had left. The recruiter said, "What we are going to do is have you come up to the front tell us about yourself. Pick one of these words which best fits you." The word was Circle Airlines and each letter had a different meaning.

Since I was sitting in the front I thought I was going to be one of the first ones up.

"We are going to do it differently today. Usually the people in the back don't want to go first, so we are starting in the back row and finishing in the front." *Fuck me!*

Now I'm pissed off because I wanted everybody to know me, so I could set the bar and get their attention early before the competition did. But I guess sometimes the best is saved for last. I took notes and kept tally marks of all the people that did great, and who I believed they would hire. On the forum they said they were looking for around twenty people, so I was trying to get a guess of good quality prospects. Also, I decided to change up my speech because I did fly over ten hours in total just to get to that damn interview and had an emergency landing, so I figured a way to include that in my speech. I watched people present themselves and I counted about eighteen people that did well enough to make it to the next step, in my opinion.

Then it hit me that my turn was coming soon. *Oh Lord. Come on, Lando, you better not forget what you're going to say. Now what are you going to start it off with?*

Hello, ladies and gentlemen. Damn hello sound too basic. Hey how is everybody doing? Okay that sounds better, right?

I scrambled through my notes and kept on reviewing my speech. *Okay Lando, you're gonna drive yourself crazy. Be calm, chill, relax and let's do it, baby. You flew ten hours for this shit. Ain't nobody on your level. Let's go!*

"Okay, who is next?" the recruiter asked in a monotone.

I stood up and yelled, "Yes! You gotta save the best for last, baby!"

Everyone laughed as I walked to the front.

"Hey everybody, I'm Orlando. First, I would like to thank the recruiters for taking time out of their schedules to be here. I had the pleasure of flying 8 hours and 32 minutes to be here today, starting from Detroit to Houston, Houston to Seattle and last flight to Jokerville, and I'm still excited.

The word I thought about, while patiently watching everybody before me go stealing my choice and answers over and over." They laughed. "I choose the letter A because I'm affable. I am very easygoing and very sociable. The reason I know I will be one of Circle's top employees is because of my previous customer service work experiences. I first started my career in the cemetery business as a family service counselor. In that job I learned how to deal with people's emotions during their times of need. Next, I became a certified nursing assistant, where I learned how to help families on a 24-hour basis with whatever needs they required around the house. My most recent employment is at Detroit Metro Airport as a manager of a few coffee shops and a bar. On a daily basis I deal with customers with all different backgrounds and managing staff on how to work together. With all of my experience I feel Circle is the perfect company that fits with my personality. Even though I have to travel 8 hours and 58 minutes to get back home, I will still be excited. I appreciate your time." I did a presidential wave and walked back to my seat to the applause of the attendees.

Fuck yeak boi! Lando, you nailed it! I'm the only person that they clapped for out of everybody who went. They can't stop you! I yelled internally to my alter ego.

Soon as I got back to my seat the guy next to me said, "Lando, you nail it. Good stuff."

I got a tap on the back from a chick. "Way to go. I wish I could have done mine like that," she said laughing.

"Oh you did great, Beth." She had the biggest smile on her face when I called her name.

"Okay everybody. Give us an hour and we will post a list on the door of all the people we would like to talk to. I don't want anyone to get discouraged, because this is a very competitive process. It took me three Circle interviews before I was hired, so don't give up. We will post the names of the people we want to talk to a little bit more."

I walked back to my room excited as hell and was going to call dad, but didn't want to jinx it. I'd just wait until I got the job. What I did was pulled out my book and reviewed some of the interview questions. I decided to go back into the waiting area to talk to my two friends and find out what they thought their chances were.

"Hey, Lando, you did excellent," Nick said.

"Thanks man, I was nervous as hell."

"You didn't show it," Alex said.

I looked at her hands. She had a McDonald's bag in her hand. She said quickly, "We were looking for you to see if you were hungry, but..."

I cut her off. "Oh naw, it's cool. I just went back to my room and relaxed."

"I can't believe you actually flew this far to come to this. If they don't hire you then they're crazy. Have you applied for any other airlines, Lando?"

"Yeah, I've been to open houses, but it's hard to get in."

"Tell me about it. I went to an AirStar interview a week ago and it was three times as many people than what's here now and was hard, but I think they only selected a few people."

Nick agreed, "I also interviewed with them and didn't get it."

"Lando, have you ever tried?"

I paused and a girl yelled, "They posted them!"

Whew! Saved by the bell, as everyone ran over towards the door. I had confidence walking over there and went to the door, already knowing I was on the list. Alex and Nick also made it to the next step. Next, were the two recruiters to one candidate interviews.

At that point, I wasn't nervous at all with this process. It really came down to just being myself. I would be okay.

"Hey Orlando, are you ready?" the recruiter asked as she walked into the lobby, where I was sitting, to greet me.

"As ready as I will ever be."

We walked into a room where one was on the computer behind a desk and had somebody next to her.

"We want to first congratulate you on making it this far. I'm Karen, one of the inflight recruiters with Circle, and I'm sure you already met Shelby. So tell us a little bit about yourself. It looks like you're from Michigan."

"Yes, I am. I looked into the company for a while and I liked what I saw, so I decided to come and check you guys out."

"What do you like most about the company?"

"Well, one thing that really stood out to me is that you can sell on the plane. That's my first time ever seeing an airline like this. I have a lot of sales experience, so it would be great to be able to make some commissions on top of the base pay."

"Tell us about the scariest flight you have ever been on."

"Wow, it's funny you'd ask me that, since it happened on my way here. My friend was dropping me off at the airport and before I got out of the car he told me he couldn't understand why would I want to be a flight attendant and put myself in danger of having a plane crash. So I told him the odds are so low if it happened, then it's my time. On my way here we had an emergency landing and oh my God I freaked out! I heard his voice over and over in my head..."

They laughed hysterically and asked, "Well, what happened?"

"The flaps stopped working and the captain came on the PA calmly telling us not to be alarmed when we land and are surrounded by fire trucks and ambulances. Thankfully, the landing went great and I made it here, so I just gotta hope the flight back is a lot better."

"That's a good thing you were so dedicated to be here. We are going to go over a few scenarios with you. Don't mind me when you see me writing notes down as we speak."

They went over about three different questions, and thanks to that book, I was well prepared, giving good answers to all of them. The last question was, "Tell me a time when you and a coworker did not get along, but you both had to find a median and work things out."

"I used to manage a coffee shop and the girl I closed with at nights was consistently very slow, and we would always leave past midnight. I recommended a way we could leave earlier by doing things my way, but she didn't want to. We had to work together the next few days, so I said let's do it your way tonight and my way tomorrow and let's see what time we leave. Once we did it my way and I got us out before midnight we never had any more problems."

"So do you have any questions for us, Lando?" Shelby asked.

I asked a few good ones, mainly wanting to know about the growth of the company and how long it took them to move up within the company. I shook both of their hands and left the room very confident that I would be hired. In the lobby we were all handed a form in the event we were hired. More than likely it had to do with obtaining the candidates background information and their drug tests.

Nick came over and asked, "How did it go?"

"Well, I think I did good. What about you?"

"Good. We were in there for a while and they asked a lot of questions, but you can never know."

"Hell yeah. You think you did perfect and they will mess around and not hire anybody."

"Man, I'm about sure you have nothing to worry about. You, by far, did the best, " Nick replied.

Once all three of us were done, we exchanged numbers and wished each other the best of luck, agreeing to stay in touch.

Finally, they were ready to show who got to stay for the drug test. Nick said he wanted to wait until everybody cleared out. I could tell he was nervous. On the other hand, I wanted to know as soon as possible.

You didn't fly out here to be scared, Lando. Just walk up there with confidence, look at your name, and smile.

Standing there looking, I didn't see my name. I didn't panic because the same thing happened to me at the AirStar interview. *Let me just look again.* Damn, still no Lando. Had they messed up? How was it possible my name wasn't on the list? I'd been amazing. On my third look it hit me at once. I didn't get hired. I started to walk back towards my room and Nick said, "You didn't get it?"

"Nope." I responded with my head down and tear-filled eyes.

"Hell, I know for a fact I didn't get it then. I shouldn't even walk over there."

I called dad once again and gave him the full update on what was going on and how everything turned out. Just by hearing his voice, I could tell he was equally as pissed as me. He knew that I gave it my all, but just couldn't get over the hump.

As I went back to the airport, I noticed how small it really was since it was pretty dark when I arrived the first time. The airport literally only had three different gates that they flew out of, and I could guess only a hand full of flights a day. From there I took a small regional airline back to Seattle then straight to Detroit.

Maybe it was a good thing I didn't get hired there. Hell, who wants to work for an airline that never has overnights anyway, and be stuck living there? In that case, I might as well have gotten a regular job.

Once we landed in Seattle, I walked over to my next gate and noticed a confused looking guy stumbling around as if he was drunk. The real problem was when he was boarding he was only speaking Spanish and I just had a feeling it wasn't gonna go well, especially since I didn't see him traveling with anyone.

The plane was big, but they had my seat all the way in the last row. I really didn't wanna be bothered, since I wasn't in a happy mood anyway. I kept wondering would I ever become a flight attendant or was it time to throw in the towel and try another career? I rarely get depressed, but at that point I'd given it my all.

I was seated next to a younger couple who were just happy to be out of the house, and were going on a vacation to Omaha or someplace that sounded boring.

Soon as we took off I fell asleep. After two hours of sleeping, I woke up and the plane was really quiet, dark, and most people were sleeping. I saw the same old Mexican guy stumbling towards the back. As soon as he reached my row, he passed out and fell right on me. The couple sitting next to me woke up and freaked out, pressing the call button. There had been so much aberration with this trip, I just shook my head and sat there thinking just my luck the drunk guy would pass out on me.

The flight attendant in the back yelled "Sir! Sir! Are you okay?"

They grabbed him and laid him on the ground and tried to communicate. I heard one crew member in the back say, "Aww hell, he don't even speak English."

A male flight attendant went to call the captain and find a Spanish speaker on the plane. While they were taking forever, a random guy walked up and started speaking Spanish to him, translating to the crew members that he was tired and felt very weak. Good thing we were close to our destination, because they would have made us divert for this and I damn sure wasn't trying to do another emergency landing.

Once we landed they made him lie on the ground until paramedics came on board to take him off. *Wow, what a trip.*

I finally got home and told dad about everything, expressing how I should have been chosen and how much I appreciated him helping me to pursue my dreams.

"Once I saw how serious you were and how hard you have been trying, I had your back. Remember the other day I told you I had some good news soon?"

"Yeah, what's up."

"What you think about Miami?"

"What you mean Miami?" I replied, confused.

"Me and RB found some of the best eye doctors in the country and they're at the University of Miami."

"What did Dr. Johnson say about it?"

"Man, I am not worried about what he is saying, Lake. He did his job," dad replied angrily.

"So is your eyesight getting any better?" I asked, kinda confused and concerned why he was so mad.

"Aw man, you just don't understand. *I can't see!*" he yelled. "It's different. He did good on the right eye, I feel the improvement. But the left eye feels like it done got worse, like if I cover my right eye..." he said as he placed his right hand over his right eye. "I can't see nothing out of this left eye. So Johnson did the best he could do, but now it's time to get another look by somebody else and you are pissing me off. I might need to call your sister and see if she is ready to hit *Miami, baby!*" He yelled out, back to his goofy, crazy ways.

Back when I was going to the library filling out applications, I applied for Toronto Air. Their bases were in Toronto and Denver. I received an email from them saying they would be calling me soon to do a phone interview.

"Hey dad!"

"Yeah, what's up?"

"Toronto Air just emailed me saying that I should be receiving a phone call soon to do a phone interview."

"So what's their spiel?" he asked.

I went to their site and started reading the breakdown. How much they pay, where their bases were located, and surprisingly, they did not hire smokers.

"What?" dad responded shocked.

"Yep. It says during your interview, they will do a hair sample and it will show if you have smoked within the last six months."

"Wow. See man, most people don't have any clue on how hard it is to get a job like this. If you think about it you really shouldn't be a smoker anyway doing this. You're in the air majority or the time, right? Now if you fly from Detroit to Denver and only sit there for a few minutes before your next flight, you think the captain is going to wait for you to get a quick puff in?"

"Wow, a guy posted right on the forum saying in bold, capital letters: *if you have smoked in the last 6 months don't go!*"

As I read on, he told a story about how he quit smoking for about a month, got invited to the open house, and they still found smoke in his system. On a positive note, being a nonsmoker would knock out half the competition.

"When did they say they should be calling?"

"They didn't say, but I assumed within the next few days." I thought about the weed I'd smoked recently.

As I was chilling at the house, Stacey called me saying there was a Commute open house in Detroit a few days away and if I was going.

"I didn't hear anything about it, but they have a Detroit base so I might as well try it."

She said she might fly out, but she would keep me updated.

"Hey, dad, we're out of food. Let's go to the grocery store and grab some stuff. I just got some money loaded to my account."

"That's cool. I have a few errands to run anyway and I wanted to get me, Kristian, Marcell and daddy an Easter suit for church, so we need to stop at Cannons or somewhere." Kristian and Marcell are my nephews.

In the grocery store, as we walked around, I told him that Stacey had called me about the open house.

"So are you going to go?"

"Yeah, I guess. It's right in my back yard and I don't have anything else better to do. But I have to get all of my stuff updated and summited today."

"Are you going to tell them about the misdemeanor?"

"Yeah, at this point, I can't afford to go all the way to training and get sent home. I just gotta tell everybody the truth and see where it gets me."

"I know that's right, son. See if any of that meat over there is on sale. I don't think we have any meat at home."

"Aye dad, these steaks are real cheap. You gotta show me how to cook one tonight."

"Okay, it's real easy. It all depends on how much oil you put in the pan really."

We stopped by Cannon's Menswear, a store owned by a good friend of dad's.

"Hey is that the cleanest man in Inkster right there?"

"Hey hey! What's going on, Greg?"

"Man, just in here slaving. Another day another dollar. You know how that is. So what brings you here, Ocie?"

"Well, I kinda already have what I need to wear for Easter, but I need something for my little grandsons and something for my daddy he might like." After he finished shopping, we went home.

I thawed out the steaks and dad told me to first watch how he cooked his and then do the same. He stabbed the meat to tenderize it, washed it off, and put a lot of different seasonings on it. Then he was showing off adding potatoes and mushrooms in there.

"Yeah, son, you can't be grown and trying to have a woman not knowing how to cook. See when me and your momma hooked up, she didn't know what she was doing, so she learned how to cook from me. What I'm trying to tell you is that if your chick don't know how to cook then..."

"I'm shit outta luck," I responded jokingly.

He laughed and said, "Yeah, if you don't learn how to cook these steaks."

I watched him and did the same thing, but as I cooked mine, I thought I needed a lot of oil, because it just made sense, right? Sike! As soon as I ate my steak I could tell by the way it tasted that I used too much oil.

"How does yours taste?"

"Um, it's okay. But I can tell I used too much oil."

"Yeah, you would think to use a lot, but if you watched how I did mine, I barely put a spoonful in there. Practice will make perfect, if you stick with it."

"Do you want to try some, dad? Mmm. Wow, this is so good. Come try some."

"Ha-ha, you can't fool me. I may be blind, but I'm sure not stupid."

I got up and decided to go over Alvin's place to update my resume for Commute. As soon as I got over there, his mom was so happy to see me. I played catch up with his family for a few minutes before heading to the back with Alvin.

"Oh yeah, come on back here I got just what you need."

As I logged in and started doing my work, Alvin walked in the room and pulled out his pistol.

"Man, I need to get my CCW asap, so I can carry my stuff. I heard Gibby's usually be having some real good trade shows up there."

"Yeah, I gotta check it out," I responded and I checked out his new toy.

"Just log out after you finish. I'm tired as hell."

After I finished submitting my resume and filling out some applications, I felt great. I felt like the old Lando, the one that would never give up no matter what the situation. Soon as I got home dad told me to get our flights booked for Miami. Just he and I were going since he didn't want to deal with anybody else. He wanted to take Keke or my cousin Cain. He was just more comfortable going with me, since I knew his routine and would take care of all the rightful business. I found us a hotel right off of Collins in South Beach Miami, right in the middle of all of the excitement. We had all our University of Miami appointments booked and the dates went together perfectly, because the plan was to come back on Monday and the open house with Commute was on Wednesday. I was about to enjoy that vacation.

23

We had Aunt Chris drop us off at the airport once we were ready to go. Dad had on his yellow crocodile hat with matching croc shoes and belt with gold jewelry. I was so excited to go to Miami before the open house, because I needed to get away from everything and everybody. As we arrived at the airport dad wanted wheelchair assistance. It worked out perfectly, so I didn't have to hold his hand walking all around the airport. We were able to cut through the security line and it was a cool young, black guy that was a little bit older than me strolling dad around. He told us when we came back just ask for Ryan and he would take care of us since dad was so cool and tipped him good.

By the time we got to our plane he told me to take down his number and when we land just text him. We flew American Airlines on a nonstop flight. I took a few pictures of dad on the plane, because it was the first time he had flown in years, when he'd gone to Vegas for a pool tournament. The flight attendants were cool, some older white ladies that were very friendly. Our plan was to get a rental car once we landed and I'd drive to the hotel.

After dealing with an issue with the rental car company, we were finally on our way. We were booked at the Nassau Hotel on Collins and 10th, so I knew that would be right in the prime area of everything.

Driving to the hotel, dad and I were in heaven, because of the beautiful palm trees, gorgeous women, and perfect area. Besides, we weren't stuck at home.

Victor, the guy at the front desk, a cool laidback Cuban kid, said he was going to upgrade us to a better room and from 7-8 p.m. we could get free drinks at the hotel across the street. When we walked into our room, we couldn't believe it.

There were two nice beds next to each other and a TV in front of both of the beds that was connected to this gadget to reposition the TV to be seen from any angle in the room. On the other side of the room was a table, a couch, a bar with two stools, and a full kitchen. Hell, it even had the pots in there already for us. Keke called dad while we were grabbing our stuff and he was telling her how live the room was.

"It's about 70 degrees, palm trees, and just nice out here. When we left Michigan they were saying it might snow," he said. "Now this is how a real boss is supposed to live. I can get use to this!"

I did my little tour around the hotel. They had a nice size workout area and a cool computer room. Dad was ready to get out and see what Miami was about, but the first thing we wanted to do was go grocery shopping. I knew that Washington Street had a few places that should sell some eggs and milk, so we hopped in the car and went up there. Since we'd been traveling all day we were kinda tired and knew we had to go to his appointment in the morning, with that in mind we decided to rest.

His appointment was scheduled for 8:30 at the University of Miami Medical Center. The facility was amazing. Dad had heard through Rob Green that it was one of the best places in the world to do eye surgery or retina stuff.

"So, dad, what's our overall goal here with this appointment?"

"If there is a will, there is a way, son. Dr. Johnson did the best he could do. He did his part, now I need another expert that can look at my eyes and see if they can come up with something different. We can't do surgery or nothing, because I'm not prepared to do anything like that."

"Well, let's do it," I said as we entered the building.

"Hello, how may we help you two gentlemen?" the lady at the front desk asked.

"Is this the eye department?"

"Yes, it is. Do you have an appointment?"

"Yes, we do," I responded with a smile.

"Okay, come over here and let me get you two guys taken care of. Now what's your name, sir?" After dad gave the requested information, she asked, "Is that your brother with you?" I looked at dad and started laughing.

"No, that's my son."

"Oh okay, I'm sorry you look young and you guys look alike."

"Okay. So that means I don't have to get the blood test," he responded to her as he looked at me.

"Ha-ha. You two are some funny guys and no you don't," she replied, laughing. "Go over there and grab the clipboard and help him fill out all the information on there so when the doctor calls you can have everything filled out."

After I filled everything out, I went on Facebook and saw everybody posting pictures of snow and how much they hate Michigan. It just made me smile inside that I was in Miami.

"Dad, everybody is pissed off how it's so much snow out there in Michigan."

"I heard. Chris told me about it. Man, this is how it's supposed to be. Like this don't even make sense. It's almost summer time here and it's snowing out there."

After about an hour went past, dad wanted me to find him something to eat. "I can't be going this long without some fruit or something. They should have a cafeteria or something around here."

I walked around and found a worker who agreed to escort me to it.

"So young man, what brings you to Miami?"

"I'm from Michigan, so anything to get away from that weather. Also my dad is legally blind, so he heard that they have some of the top doctors out here."

"Yes, sir. They have top quality specialists in almost every area." Arriving to our destination, he said, "Over here you have sandwiches, fruit and stuff."

"Thanks, I appreciate it. Are you from Florida?"

"Yep, from Fort Lauderdale originally, but moved around a few times here and there."

"That's cool. I have a few business partners out in this area."

"What business do you do?"

"Pre-Paid Legal."

"Oh, I heard about that through a friend before. You get those attorneys and stuff for cheap, right?"

"Yes, sir, I could give you a card, if you're interested in making some extra income on the side or need the service." I pulled out my card and gave it to him. "By the way, Greg, I'm Lando."

"It's a pleasure to meet you, brother."

"What's your number, Greg?" He gave it to me.

"Okay, I will contact you soon."

"Here you go, dad. I got you a turkey sandwich and orange juice. We can split a banana."

"Thanks. That's right on time."

The doctor came out and told us he was extra busy, and that it would be another twenty minutes before he could get to us.

"Have you heard from Keke's boy yet?" dad asked.

"Oh Valentino. Not yet. He said hit him up when we get here. I gotta text him. I know he will take us to a few good spots."

Finally, they were ready for us to go into an examination room. I handed the clipboard to the nurse.

"We need to first dilate his eyes," the nurse said, doing the regular routine.

"Okay, I need 20 percent. If not, they won't dilate," dad told her.

"Well, 10 percent usually does the job," she replied.

I just burst out laughing, as he started shaking his head. She looked at us as if she missed out on the inside joke, and said, "I don't think we have 20 percent, but I can check."

Soon as she walked out, dad said, "They just don't believe me. I don't know why they just won't put it in the chart."

"We do have 20 percent," she said, starting the procedure.

The doctor came into the room. He was very different than I was used to seeing. I couldn't pinpoint his nationality, but I liked the way he carried himself. Confident. I got the feeling that he thought dad was crazy for coming out that far just to get his eyes checked. But he analyzed dad a lot differently than Dr. Johnson. Once he looked at his eyes, he really got into it, like that was a true passion for him, as he jotted down a lot of notes. He even called somebody on the phone to look at dad's eyes.

Then he turned to us. "I want to thank you for flying out here. You came to the right place. Now I really haven't seen any eyes like yours, so that's why I called my colleague to also check you out. Our goal is to come up with some good notes and see what can be done, then send all the information back to your doctors in Michigan."

"Okay that's great, doctor, I greatly appreciate it," dad responded.

He sent us downstairs to another area, but there were nothing but old blind people, with the blind glasses on down there. I was happy I wore my black, red and green Gucci's with the shirt and wallet to match, because one sexy nurse was for sure checking me out from head to toe. Hell, I was in Miami. I might as well give her something to look at.

The second doctor read his chart. "What doctor did you have treating you out there?"

"I had a few different ones. But my primary one that did my surgery is Dr. Mark Johnson."

"Wow, you won't believe this. We went to school together back in Cincinnati, Ohio. Yeah, we roomed together and everything. He is a great guy."

"It's that small of a world," dad said.

The doctor was real laidback and cool as he did his review of dad's eyes and sent us on our way. Dad said his overall goal of this visit was for them to review his eyes and put everything in the notes so they could do the surgery out here or let one of Dr. Johnson's people take care of it.

On our way driving back to the room Valentino called me.

"Hey, what's the deal, my brother. Where you at, man? I got the hoes on the floor for you. We at Rolex tonight," Valentino said with an energetic tone.

Valentino was Keke's boy from Detroit that she went to high school with. He used to be one of the best men's barbers in Detroit, but for a better opportunity he moved to Atlanta and started doing women's hair, eventually moving to Miami where he obtained even more success. Eventually, he moved to Miami where he started doing female's makeup, hair, eyebrows and just about everything else. But the kicker was 90% of his clients were strippers, so whenever I came to Miami he'd kidnap me and have me stuck in strip clubs all day. *All day!* I tell y'all it was a gift and a curse.

After making plans, we all arrived at the hotel around the same time.

"Yo, what's some good spots to eat at? I'm hungry," dad asked Valentino.

"I know one of the best seafood spots in the area, if you're down for that." Soon as he said seafood dad was game, since that was one of his favorites.

We let Valentino drive our rental, so he wouldn't have to waste any of his gas. He was one of the best tour guides to have, because he was energetic, fun and knew where all the spots were. He told story after story, during our car ride, about how different Atlanta was compared to Detroit. It was considered the Black Hollywood when he first moved out there, but the area kinda got saturated by gays and Detroit people. So now Miami was the new spot for him to take it to the next level. The spot he took us to was literally off the water and was so beautiful.

"Anywhere specific you guys would like to sit?" the waitress asked.

"We would like sit by a window so my dad could see better."

We sat down. Dad told Valentino to get whatever he wanted, not to worry about anything. They both ordered some type of big ass lobster feast. I'm allergic to all that crap, so I ended up getting some chicken or something like that.

Our waitress was a gorgeous Cuban woman. During off-peak tourist season there was an abundance of regulars and gorgeous Spanish speaking woman. We told some funny stories and took some great pictures. Valentino told dad he had a little surprise for him. A little later on he would stop by, but he had to run some errands after he dropped us off.

Later on that day I decided to take dad on the beach walking around, so he could see the water and enjoy the Miami life. The weather was perfect, not too hot, not too cold, and we saw a few people in the water having fun. I looked at my phone and I saw a picture of this sexy dark-skinned chick sent from Valentino saying 'I got something for pops' as the caption. After taking a long walk with dad, it was time to rest.

I already had enough sleep. "I'm in Miami and it's time for me to hit up Wet Willies."

Wet Willies was like a 7-Eleven on steroids. Think of a place with about twenty different slurpees, but every single one has different liquor added to it. The strongest drink was called Call A Cab. On my first time coming there Valentine warned me. "If you want to get a chick fucked up and get laid, get her a Call A Cab. But don't get it for yourself."

That was the first drink I requested soon as I got there. And yes, I was faded. I walked up there, since all the hot spots were within walking distance on the south beach. The place wasn't jumping like it was Memorial Day weekend. It was a laidback atmosphere.

A host walked up and asked, "What can I get you?"

"I would like a sour apple mixed with a shock treatment, please." I decided to Tango Yan. He and JT were together.

"Man, what the hell are you doing at Wet Willies in the middle of damn April, fool?" JT yelled into the camera.

"Well, my friends, snow is not for a guy like me. But this 80 degree weather with gorgeous Cuban women is though."

"Okay, have fun, man. Drink one for a boy out there."

"Okay, I will. I'll hit y'all up later." As I was walking back to the hotel, I saw a few people sitting outside talking with Victor from the front desk. They introduced themselves and the next thing I know I was sitting along with them.

"My new amigo, Lando, have a beer with us," one said in Spanish.

For the rest of the night it went great. We even had a system going. They would speak Spanish and laugh, then Victor would translate for me.

The next morning Valentino came through at about 10 a.m. with the chick he had sent me a picture of.

"Hey Carmen, this is Ocie and Lando." I shook her hand and introduced myself. Now Carmen was not bad at all, she was dark-skinned and had that real clean shiny chocolate bunny skin. To make matters even better, she had a fat ass. He took her over to the bar and he brought in a big suitcase with nothing but hair products and make-up.

As he started doing her make-up, I was watching how he was doing it. The man was a pro. How she looked from the time she walked in to how she was when she left, was just about a different person. She already looked good, but with a little make-up and hair, he stepped her up to another level. Dad started small talk with her.

"Lando, ride with me to drop her off."

"Okay, I'm a game. Dad, I'll be back after a while. Let me know if you need some food or anything."

As we rode in the car, I chatted with her some more. She was a real cool chick, originally from Florida, who'd met Valentino through the clubs. Since he was one of the few real people who worked there, she brought a lot of business to him. Before we dropped her off, we had exchanged numbers, just in case she wanted to get out and hang with me and dad.

"Okay, Lando, real quick, let's stop over to my house, so I can change and we can grab some food, then stop at one of the clubs."

The first one we went to was called Rolex. I had on my fraternity hat. Come to find out the security guard was a frat brother. We kicked it and chatted for a while. He let me know that most of the clubs out there were run by my frat, so if I needed anything just hit him up. Rolex was more of an urban black only strip club. The prices weren't too bad and the dancers I had seen better, but I had also seen worse, so I couldn't complain.

The next one we went to was called the Office. Once we walked up, Valentino had his makeup bag and stuff on him, so security let him pass by, but soon as I walked up security said, "That will be ten dollars."

Valentino's dumb ass turned around and said, "He is with me and doing make-up today."

"We already have somebody to do make-up," the big bouncer said.

"Well, Lando Success is the new guy now," Valentino replied with confidence. They just let us walk right pass and since I was following Valentino, he took me straight to the dressing room. Oh my god! I was hyped as hell. The dressing room of a strip club is like a scene right out of the movie *Players Club*. Chicks walked around thick as hell, naked, some listened to music, some were drinking.

Valentino started talking to a few as he was setting up shop. A chick walked up to me and was like, "Success, I need my bangs done and a touch-up."

"Umm...I'm from out of town, so I got to grab all my stuff, but have no fear Valentino is here, my baby."

Man, I got out of that locker room so quick before they all caught on. The good thing about that club was the dances were cheap as hell. I was used to paying $20 for a dance in Detroit strip clubs. I think all the dances were like $5 or $10 here, so I was a happy camper. I learned my lesson that night. Valentino was there to make money. I had to make sure I didn't spend all of mine! We were hitting up several clubs that night.

I was getting a dance from this chick. She grabbed my hand and was like, "Are you a Mason?"

"Are you a star?" I replied.

"Naw, one of your brothers is the DJ. I'm going to introduce you to him. His name is Derrick."

Valentino saw me walking up to the DJ booth and had a 'what the hell is this nigga doing' look on his face. Once me and Derrick greeted each other, he said go to the bar and get a drink on him. We exchanged numbers and I told him if he ever came to Detroit to hit me up.

"Man, the whole city of Miami is showing me love." I told Valentino as we both sat at the bar having a drink.

"Yeah man, everybody out here is a traveler. That's how I

usually have so many connections with getting into the clubs."

The last club we went to was the one we dropped off his friend Carmen earlier. I couldn't wait to get a dance from her thick self. She had on this sexy outfit. The other dancers couldn't compare to her. She was on echelon all her own. It was obvious by how she respected and carried herself. She smelled so damn good as she grinded her body all over me. Surprisingly, she was a rough dancer and I didn't expect that. After being out with that nutcase all day, I was ready to go back and kick it with dad and watch some basketball or something.

Hours later, I finally convinced him to take me back and just told him if he needed a place to crash for the night then he was more than welcomed to stay with us. He was as ready to go to his home as I was to get back to the hotel room. As we pulled up to the hotel, I saw all of my Argentina amigos in the front again sitting and hanging out. I decided to sit down and kick it with them for a little bit. They were heading back home the next day. We had the debate going on as to who was the best current athletes. I was showing them YouTubes of how great Lebron was and they were showing me this one soccer player. I don't remember his name, but I couldn't lie, he was a man-child and was like the Jordan of soccer in their country. Before we parted, we all exchanged Facebook information and made plans for me to visit them once I became a flight attendant.

Dad and I decided we should stay for an extra day, because we were having so much fun and didn't want to go home. He'd even learned his way around the hotel by himself. I saw him in the workout room one day. I guess he and Victor also had their own personal system when I wasn't around. I'd forgotten all about my interview with Commute coming up.

"Oh yeah, I forgot all about that, son, but we can stay one more day and you could still make it back, right?"

"Looks like we gotta do what we gotta do, because we will be staying in South Beach, baby!"

24

 I was blessed that I was not born into wealth or spoiled. I feel I wouldn't be as well-rounded as I am right now. Being a black man in America is a tough situation. Especially being raised in the hood, because of the expectation to be hard to be accepted in the black community, yet smart enough to not be too tough. There was always a thin line between success and failure coming from Inkster.

 The first place I can remember staying at is on Douglas Court in Inkster. As I look back on it today, I'm glad I had a lot of siblings, because we would get into so much trouble. We stayed pissing each other off. When we stayed on Douglas Court I was about seven years old and even remember my first kiss was on that street.

 Our house back then seemed so big. Me, OC and Keke shared a room. Kelly was the oldest, so she had her own room. That's when I can remember Charles, my sister Mary's father, came into the mix. He was a truck driver and I would love when he would take me around in his semi to drive around with him. We didn't have a basement. Three bedrooms and one bathroom got the job done. As I look at the house now, I can't believe how big I thought that house was. I don't even know how we did it, but I guess if that's all you know then you have to just make it work.

Our next place was on the better side of Inkster and now on a bigger court with about fourteen houses. I don't know what fettish mom had with all these damn courts, but I loved our new home, because we had a big backyard, a basement, and hell, even two bathrooms. I just thank God for my mom knowing how to make ends meet and making do with the little we had. She kept us out of the streets as much as she could.

Aunt Chris *hated* where me and dad lived, because we stayed literally 'in da hood.' Since she picked dad up just about every day, she hated having to drive over there, so she was always pushing for dad to move and get a house or condo. I actually liked our place, because he only had to pay $500 a month. We'd decked out the inside with some of the best furniture, plus the perfect paint job. A basement and a little upstairs. It wasn't much, but for me and dad, we didn't complain. Hell, the hood was cool with us. Nobody ever broke into my car or nothing like that.

But thank God for my aunt helping us find a new spot. This time we would be on a golf course. *A fucking golf course!* It seemed crazy just saying it. Since I was always studying or something, it never really hit me that we were moving. I was thinking about how much crap we had to move over there and how much work I'd have to do. Really that was my only concern, with my lazy ass. But hell, 13th hole here we come!

I knew I was dreaming. I woke up and the basement was spic and span clean, bags everywhere, and appeared as if somebody came downstairs and robbed me and cleaned up on their way out.

"Get up, Lake. Get up," dad said as he came down the stairs.

"Um, dad what is going on?" I asked confusedly.

"Son, I can't play around with you. We closed on that house and have to get this cleaned up and get out of here," he said as he sipped his Red Bull.

"Wait, what? Dad, how long have you been up and why... Where are my clothes?"

"Aye man, I'm not playing any games with a lazy kid. Get up and get to cleaning or I'll throw everything away," he said as he took another sip.

"Dad! How many Red Bulls have you had?" I asked, laughing.

I wanted to be serious, but there was no way as I watched him moving around the house like Superman.

"I had two so far, and I have been up since six, so you see I'm hyped up. I gotta get as much done while I got the energy."

"Okay, man, I'll help you out."

After we were done Keke came over. "I heard you hung out with the Valentino's crazy butt while y'all was out there," she said to dad.

"Man, that's my boy right there. I might have to adopt him."

"Aw man, y'all did it like that?" she asked.

"He took us to this nice seafood restaurant. He and dad had a field day. They bought about $100 worth of lobster, eating bucket after bucket," I replied laughing. "Yeah, he went crazy. We were in 70 degree weather and we did it big. I'm going to start doing that trip once a year."

"What!" she responded, trying to hype dad up, as usual.

"Yeah, I even got my guy at the hotel helping me out. Victor is his name, we had a good time."

"So Lake, once you do your interview thing tomorrow I'm going to figure out how we are going to do the garage to the new house so we can start moving things in tomorrow."

"What are we going to tell Mrs. James?" I asked.

Honestly, dad didn't want to tell her, by the looks of it, but I'm not sure why. I guess he didn't want her to tell the whole world that Ocie was moving to a golf course. Since Sean had just gotten hired at his new job, I was thinking since it was only $500 to stay here. We both could have our own little spot for cheap, but it was just a thought.

∼

FOR THE INTERVIEW, I decided to go presidential with the outfit by wearing the red, white and blue, just something pretty basic. I woke up lethargic. I guess I just didn't want to go to the interview, because it was in cold Michigan, but I had to force myself. Once I arrived, outside I saw a few smokers with folders and notebooks, so I could tell that there was going to be a lot of people here. Since I arrived early, I had seen about thirty people just waiting around the conference area where the open house would be held and this good-looking short chick walked up to me saying, "Hey!"

I guess the expression on my face showed that I wasn't 100% sure who she was, so she followed up by saying, "This is Stacey, silly."

"What the heck are you doing here?" I responded, shocked as ever. "Why didn't you tell me you were coming?"

"I wanted to surprise you."

"Um, well you did. Where did you stay?"

"I stayed here at this hotel with my friend."

As she said that I noticed a very dark-skinned black guy behind her staring at me.

"Oh yeah, Lando, this is my friend Xavier."

"Hey, what's up, man." I said as we shook hands.

He was a little shorter than me and was very clean and firm, as if he was raised by a military family, but he was obviously gay.

"So just hit me up after you leave here and we can grab something to eat if y'all not busy," I said to her. I was confused that she didn't hit me up telling me she was in my town, but I would get to the bottom of that later. By the time we finished talking they'd already opened up the doors to start letting people into the conference area. There weren't too many seats open in the front, so I sat in the third row next to an attractive black chick. At this open house I noticed there were a lot of black woman there. Also there were about six guys and most of them were black. One of the recruiters walked to the front and did the basic overview of the airline.

The company actually had some decent benefits and it did sound kind of attractive to be based in Detroit. I was just thinking about how sweet it would be for Stacey to be based in Detroit with me. Oh yeah! By the way, she was looking sexy as hell, wearing a tight ass blue dress that was fitting her thick ass perfectly. She had her naturally long hair tied up looking like the perfect business woman. She had everything going for her except her make-up. There was too much red on her cheeks.

When it was my turn to do my speech, I honestly was not nervous as I walked up to the front with a smile, told a quick joke, and went into autopilot. I was at the point where everything flowed naturally with my speech, like clockwork. As I was doing my speech, I noticed Stacey looking at me with that 'damn this motherfucker is good' face. I did want to show off since she was there and would know that I was the real deal. One thing I did notice during my speech, in the back there was a table of about four recruiters watching. There was a white male in the back smiling, two white females that excitedly took notes of everything I was saying; so I definitely got a good vibe from them. Last there was this black chick. I swear on everything I could read exactly what she was thinking just by how she was looking at me with a look that said, 'Nigga you ain't shit.' Soon as I used my cemetery reference all the recruiters laughed and smiled, but she gave me an ugly frown. I prayed, *Lord, don't let me get interviewed by her.*

Once I sat down, the cute ghetto chick next to me gave me a nice compliment. "Wow, Lando, you're a natural. I'm not sure if anybody could beat that."

It was funny when Stacey went because she kinda choked up. She walked up there all short and cute and did her spiel, but in the middle she just went blank and was like "um dang, I forgot what I was about to say," but she brought it back and just kept on going. Her set up wasn't too bad, especially when she said she used to work at Trump Towers and everyone's eyes lit up and now she is a gate agent for Delta, but always wanted to become a flight attendant and this seemed like the perfect company for her.

Now when her guy friend went up, he actually did great, kinda what I would expect from him. He had his story ready and was very firm, so I could see him getting hired. A funny one was when this young black guy was called up. He walked up slowly and scared, when he made it to the front the brother completely froze up. I have never seen somebody choke this bad before. He was like, "Umm." He paused before continuing, "I worked at Footlocker... I'm Jason...Thank you," and sat down.

Everybody was in shock, like damn that was a real choke. One of the people I will always remember was this black chick. She was not attractive at all. but she was the type person that walks in the building and makes everybody smile with her great energy. She walked up to the front very fast and said, "Hello everybody! My name is Ashley and I bet you can guess that I'm not scared to speak in front of people!"

I mean this chick had a strong ass voice and we all completely loved her. Ugly or not, she was a top pick to get hired on my list, because she was that good. After everybody did their thing, I felt I should easily have a chance at getting hired, but I had seen it all, so I couldn't get too excited.

"We would like to thank everybody for taking time out of their day to be here. We said before, we have two different trainings set up within the next two months and what we are going to do is go over all the applications we have seen and then post a list of the names of the people we would like to see in the room next. If your name is not on the list you can try again in the next six months, thanks."

Soon as she said that I didn't even wait around for Stacey, because she obviously didn't want to hang out anyway. I went to the car and just chilled out for a second and grabbed some McDonald's. I wasn't too much in the mood to talk to anybody, feeling disgusted because I was kicked out of training and had to start back from ground zero. As I walked back into the building, I overheard a few people talking about how much they wanted the job and how nervous they were. Blah blah blah. I saw Stacey and her friend walk into the hotel with some food, so I guess they hitched a ride with somebody. The door opened up and one of the recruiters put the paper on the door. Everybody ran up and I rushed over. Yeah Boy! I also saw Stacey's name, so it was good that we'd both made it. There were about fourteen of us on the list. As we entered the room.

"Hey everybody! I'm glad that all you guys made it this far. What Derrick is handing out is paperwork, so we can do a background check and drug testing. Now the plan is to set up one-on-one interviews starting first thing in the morning. We are making a list starting from 7 a.m. to 3 p.m., so decide on what the time that's best for you."

I didn't want to be last nor first, but I still wanted to get in early so I choose 8:30. Stacey was complaining about her flight or that she only booked her hotel for one day and asked could she do hers today. Honestly, I really didn't care what the hell she had going on, because if she had played her cards right, she could have stayed the night with me.

I went home and told dad what went on. "What! Stacey was there?" he repeated in excitement.

"Yeah, she was there with some black gay guy."

"How you know he is gay?"

"Believe me, I know..."

"Man, that probably was her man. I bet money on it, he is probably knocking her off."

"Oh Lord, here you go again," I said laughing, since dad always thought somebody was giving up sex.

"Okay, okay hear me out. Now did you meet the guy?"

"Yeah, I did."

"And how did he act towards you?"

"He kinda had an attitude or something."

"Okay, okay now. Did she tell you in advance if she was coming?"

"No, she said she wanted to surprise me."

Dad's crazy ass looked at me like I was retarded and said, "And last, but not least, where did they stay at last night?"

"Well, they stayed in the same room."

"I told you that's why she probably got kicked out of her training, doing too much partying," dad stated referring to her getting released from the training class she'd attended a while back.

As the words were coming out my mouth, I realize that I was just helping out this crazy old man's story.

"Umm, hello!" he yelled out sarcastically.

All I could do was laugh and shake my head at him.

"So what time will you have to go back up there tomorrow?" he asked.

"At 8:30."

"Oh yeah, we want to get everything moved to the new house by Friday and by then everything should be up to code with the state. See if you can get one of your boys to start helping you move stuff."

"Okay, it shouldn't be too much, because if you think about it all we have is a few big items like beds and furniture. That's more than half of the battle."

Somebody knocked on the door. "Who is it?" I yelled.

"It's Alvin, baby!"

"What's the deal, Alvin?" I said as we greeted.

He looked around and said, "Y'all aren't playing over here. You're ready to move."

"Yeah man, we got to get out of the hood someday. It's good you're over here, you can help Lake take some of this stuff to the new house. Have you been over there yet?"

"Nope, not yet."

"Well, Lake will take you through there."

While riding in the car to the new house, Alvin said he was thinking about ending his relationship with his girl.

"Dad said it's going to be hard to raise another man's baby at such a young age and you got your parents all involved. You know how they can be sometimes."

"Yeah, my mom pissed me off the other day. That's what I had called you to talk about. So I didn't want to see Sheri and haven't responded to any of her texts all day. So why when I get home do I see her and the baby?"

"Oh man, Alvin, no they didn't do you like that, bro," I responded laughing.

"Hell yeah, I was pissed off, so we got into it about the situation. I was trying to tell her that's not cool."

"You told that to your mom or to Sheri?" I asked.

"My mom."

"So how far did that get you, sir?"

"She basically said fuck me and the horse I rode on," he said as we both laughed and made our way to the new house.

The next day at the interview I arrived early. There were only two of us in the lobby waiting. The other person was a white male in his thirties and he looked straight. Once we greeted each other, I got his story. This guy was a mechanic that got laid off and was now trying to be flight attendant.

First, they called him to come back and the lady asked my name, then told me I would be next up. I started to think optimistically, hoping that I got somebody that was cool to interview me. Once it was my turn I was ready to get it over with, since I had to get up and dressed all early. I walked into a room and saw my interviewer was an older white male. Gave him a firm handshake and got it started.

He asked the basic interview questions and I answered them well with confidence. He seemed as if he liked me, so I asked, "If I were to get hired when would training start?"

"Actually, we have one in like three weeks so that's why we're trying to hire like crazy right now. If you're picked, then you should know right away. Orlando, I have to ask you," he said as he grabbed a piece of paper from his desk and looked over it. "I see you have a misdemeanor on your record. What's that about?"

I appreciated that he asked me man to man straight up. To be honest, I didn't expect him to ask that, so I thought quickly.

Come on, Lando, don't freeze up. Just take a deep breath and start talking.

"Yeah, I received one about a year ago. I was at a friend's party and got into a disagreement with an officer and they took me to jail for interfering with a police investigation."

"Okay, Orlando, I have to tell you how much I appreciate you for being honest with me, because most people won't. It's just sad to see how bad the justice system is for some people. Well, do you have any other questions that you can think of?"

"No, sir, you answered just about everything I needed to know."

I left feeling positive. It was time to play the waiting game. As days went by, I felt my timeframe started to get shorter and shorter. When I was in training and everybody on Facebook would see *Lando from Inkster, Michigan is a flight attendant traveling the world and he made it.*

But in reality I was sitting at home in Inkster hiding from everybody. I felt that I'd let everybody down, but I still had to make it somehow. Inkster has produced some of the top athletes and smartest kids in the state, but most never made it out of the hood. I had a friend, Damon Cannon, that was one of the most talented football players I'd ever seen. He was a straight play maker with God given talent. I just knew he was going to make it big one day. But that hood mentality of hanging out, smoking weed, fornication, and other distractions brought him down.

Dad told me the story about his boy AB he used to coach back in the day. He was the best basketball player in the state of Michigan. He even went to a basketball camp with Chauncey

Billups and Kevin Garnet. At the camp, he outplayed future Hall of Famers and everybody knew how good they were. It was easy to see him as a superstar in the making. But the hood and drugs got him. He had a big time camp or something he was supposed to attend, but since he was already a big deal he was out partying and everything the night before. KG and Billups showed out at the camp, but JB was on the sideline trying his best not to throw up from all the partying he did the night before. The 'hood nigga' mentality can really mess up a person's life.

ONCE WE OFFICIALLY GOT MOVED INTO the house, our first project was to get the garage hooked up. Dad offered to pay me as long as I got the garage painted and done within a respectable amount of time, and if not, he would pay someone else to do it. I agreed since my money was running low. Percy owed me a favor for helping him paint his whole damn house when he moved, so he was the first person I called to help. Also I figured I could get Mary and my nephew Marcell to help me, and I would pay them a few dollars to do the kiddie stuff I would need them to do. Now the condo we moved into was right onthe corner. It actually had been a model house, with the garage previously being the sales office. The walls were white and the floor just was regular cement. Dad bought a mixture of paint with metallic flakes to paint the garage floor, giving the concrete a cleaner look. I convinced my team to come over and help. Yan called me while I was in the garage working.

"What's up, boy?"

"Man, at the new crib. I just recruited Mary and Marcell to help me paint this garage."

"Um, do you know how to paint?" he asked.

"We about to find out, aren't we."

"Well, my turtle friend, speaking of recruiting, did you hear about Michigan football team's newest recruit?"

"Naw, lay it on me."

"Okay, so Inkster High, you know how all of a sudden they just became a big time high school overnight and started going to the championships, right? Well, this is not an accident. Their quarterback is a guy name Devin Gardner and guess who recruited him?"

"What the hell? The University of Michigan recruited a nigga from Inkster?" I responded surprised.

"Yup, well he is originally from Detroit, but moved to Inkster to play for the school."

"Dad is not going to believe this. So you know what we need to do right?"

"Aye, I'm already on it, chief," he responded since we talked sports so much we were usually on the same page.

"Inkster will see us at a football game for the first time in history, huh?" I replied in excitement. "Carlton's younger brother just left Romulus High School to go over there. Yan, would you ever think growing up that kids would want to go to Inkster High School? Wow, this is too funny."

Mary looked over at me and shook her head, saying

"Why do y'all speak a whole different language? Nobody understands that crazy stuff."

"Whatever, my little friend, you will be okay. This is the deal. I need y'all to help me tape off the corners."

Once we were finished taping, I called Percy and Alvin came along with him.

Percy and I are like brothers, since we have been through a lot, all we do is talk trash about each other. We call it 'blazing.' I mean for hours we would go back and forth.

"What's up y'all? P, how's everything, bro?"

"Man, everything is everything. Just got hired to work for the City of Inkster."

"Doing what?" I asked.

"Driving around and cleaning shit up. You know the guys that have on the lime green vest driving around?"

"Yeah."

"That's going to be me."

"That's what's up. Mom is going to be calling your ass every day trying to get y'all to chop down trees and shit."

"No, she's is going to be calling me, but not for any trees. Ha-ha."

"Okay man."

"My bad, I'll stop. Show me the crib, this garage is big as hell."

I gave them a tour and the plan was to paint the garage blue, because the floor stuff dad got was gray with blue flakes and would match.

As we were painting, I yelled, "P, put on some instrumentals. I know you been rapping and writing lately, let me see what you got."

"I haven't really been on it like that, but James came over the other day, we went over his parents' house, and dropped a track."

We spent hours listening to music and capping on each other as we worked. Sometimes it's good to have some fun and not be so serious all the time. We'd all been on our grown man shit trying to handle business. It was just what we all needed.

I really hadn't been out in a while and decided to go out on a date. I really just wanted some type of female company, so I decided to call up Melissa. Now she was always available for me, I just had to be ready to spend some money. One thing I loved about her is whenever we were about to go out somewhere special, she'd let me dress her.

First, she would call to ask me where we were going, then ask what I wanted her to wear before sending me the pictures of options she had available for me to have my pick. But this time I told her to throw on a dress and just look cute. I only wanted to go grab some food and get some drinks.

Once I picked her up, she was looking good, as usual. We got updated on each other's lives. She was ready to go back to Atlanta, since that was one of her favorite cities and she loved the strip clubs out there. Melissa loved to travel as much as she could. One of the main reasons we never worked out in a serious relationship, is because we're 100% the same people. She liked strip clubs. I liked strip clubs. We both liked to party and drink. She is just a little bit younger and probably more immature. We went to Fridays restaurant and the Orlando Magic was playing Oklahoma City Thunder. Since Melissa is kind of a tom boy at heart, she also likes sports.

Once she started cheering for the Oklahoma City Thunder, I warned her, "The Magic's just too good, so it's no need to root for them."

"Whoever loses has to buy shots."

"Oh hell yeah! That's like taking candy from a baby, my love, let's do it."

That was the type of relationship we had. Overall, we had a fun night and I started to think how everything would be if we were in a relationship, because we are so compatible with each other. Then I realized what I said earlier. She would be cheating, I'd be cheating, we just both wouldn't be shit ha-ha.

"How is your dad and do you like the new house?"

"Well, once we leave here I can show you the new crib way better than I can tell you," I responded in a flirtatious way, letting her know she would get fucked if she brought that sexy ass over to the house. "It's not finished or anything yet, but I can show you."

Melissa had a perfect, petite body about 125 pounds. Nice light brown skin with just enough ass.

"You might as well come over, since I did move outta the hood." I smiled, knowing I had all bad intentions to get her alone, and was praying that she wasn't on her period.

We made it to the house and I was happy dad decided to stay at our old place that night to finish packing some things.

"This is beautiful I love it here. Show me around," she stated as she walked into the condo. As I gave her the tour, all I could do was think about how long and hard the journey was to finally have sex with her. It took well over a year. Thank god we were finally pass the waiting game.

25

"Have you heard back from Commute yet?" dad asked.

"No, I haven't. I don't like my chances, because they basically said if they're going to hire you, then they would have called by now, since they have a training coming up."

"Well no news is good news sometimes, Lake."

"Dad, I guess you're right about that. On another note, I just saw on the forums that Samer Airlines is hosting another open house in Detroit," I said to keep the conversation flowing.

"Son, I don't know how many signs you want God to throw at you. Ever since you started looking to become an attendant they have been trying to hire you. So I would at least give them a try. I know on that forum stuff you read people are always trying to bash that company, but they're all still working there, I'm trying to tell you."

"Yeah, you're right. The way I look at it, if you don't like a job, then move on and stop complaining. Go do something you love," I said as dad started to motivate me.

Later on that day my phone gave me a new email notification. I received the good ole 'Thanks, but no thanks' from Commute.

Damn. For some reason after I saw that email, I felt that my flight attendant journey was done. I really never got too discouraged, but damn that was like my 100th rejection. I felt like I was wasting dad's money and my damn time. To be honest, I didn't think I had much fight left in me, because it took a lot to keep applying and getting rejected over and over again and still trying to stay positive. I didn't want to tell dad about it yet, so I kept it to myself, since he was such in good spirits today.

I decided to read Samer forums once again for the 100th time and saw two ladies were talking about meeting up with each other and driving to the open house from Chicago. If these two ladies were willing to do a five-hour drive to come here, hell I guess I could go up the street. Fuck it! Samer, here I come.

Now the crazy part is that I get to the interview and there were only four of us in attendance, including the recruiter. There was the white gay guy in his mid-thirties who was hosting, the two ladies from Chicago, and myself. He asked if we minded if he went out for a smoke.

"I guess I'm coming too," one of the ladies said as they both left to head outside. By the time he came back it was only three of us here. Myself and two older ladies. *Lando, why did you let dad convince you to come to this interview?* I said to myself, because I didn't want to sit through a full interview process. This airline is so bad nobody even wanted to come to an interview. What the hell?

"Hello everybody! My name is Adam Bell. I have been with Samer for a total of six years. I left after my 2nd year and went to US Airways, but realized I liked it more at Samer so decided to come back."

"So you left Samer for World?" I asked him surprised. World was a major airline.

"Yes sir, I did and would do it again. This company is just for more me, personally. And I was able to find my boyfriend here, so everything worked out," he said with a smile.

"So I got involved with union work and then became the BRB

Union President and resigned after two years. Then came back to become Union President for the next election. I just recently decided to become a recruiter, because I guess by now y'all can see I like to keep myself busy and that keeps me out of trouble. So I did have this fantastic presentation ready for you guys, but since it's only four of us I figure we can say to heck with the projector and just talk one on one. Is that okay with everybody?"

"Yeah, we are down with that," I replied as I looked at the ladies.

"So starting with the ladies, where are you guys from and what brought you to this interview?" One of the ladies was foreign, she looked as if she could be Bolivarian.

"I'm Lavina, Sharon and I drove here together from Chicago, and I am not working right now and saw a job posting, so decided to apply for the job."

Jean was your average white lady, slim body, nice gold hair with a raspy smoker's voice, but just by looking at her I could tell she was drop dead gorgeous when she was younger.

"Hello, I'm Sharon and also from Illinois. I have one son that is sixteen years old. Been married for thirty years now and I always wanted to be a flight attendant. Recently, I got tired of having a desk job and figured why not give it a shot. I met Lavina on the forum where everybody talks about the airlines and we saw that both of us were planning on driving here, so it was no point to do the drive separately, so here we are."

"Hello, I'm Orlando, and I've also been married for over thirty years," I said with a smirk on my face.

"Whatever Orlando and I was Santa Claus," Adam said, laughing.

"I'm from Detroit and live down the street, so decided to come out. Unfortunately, I wasn't able to do that five-hour drive like you ladies," I said in a humorous fashion. "I recently worked at the Detroit Metro Airport, managing some coffee shops and a bar and that's about it."

"Okay, now let's get started, shall we," said Adam.

He went over the basics, saying their bases were Chicago, Washington Dulles, Phoenix and Charlotte. They also had some random bases in Hawaii. He said it was impossible to get to Phoenix or Charlotte within the first few years of employment and we would probably end up in Chicago or Dulles. Also every blue moon somebody from the training class got Hawaii.

"You guys have never seen real tears until you have seen a little daddy's girl get called for Hawaii," Adam stated was a smirk on his face. "Is it bad that I find it funny?" he replied laughing.

"Look, we're not here to judge anybody," Sharon said joking.

The session was going perfectly until I saw the starting off pay. When I say low, this is probably the lowest I have seen and I have been to just about all the airlines open houses. The starting pay was like $15 an hour to $1 per diem. The graph showed us making like $1200 a month.

"Um, how can anybody live off of that, Adam?"

"Now you are getting a raise after six months and another after one year and so on, but this is the base of our guarantee. Basically, the minimum you would make."

"Oh okay, I get it," I said. "So that's the worst case scenario."

Even though we only had three people show up, this was one of the coolest interviews I had ever been to. Adam was very down to earth and just an easygoing type of person. After the overview he needed to take a smoke and right after he would do one-on-one interviews.

When Adam called me, he held the one-on-ones in the same room as our open house. The only thing is he moved a desk around so we could face each other and talk as he took down notes.

"Okay, Lando, first I gotta say I like you. But on your record you have that misdemeanor. Do you want to explain that?"

So I explain it calmly and with confidence, thanks to that guy at Commute asking me the same question, so I was more prepared, but I was still kinda surprised. Throughout the process, he asked tough questions straight off the back. As we continued with the one-on-one, I noticed out of all the interviews I had been to, Samer Airlines actually had the hardest questions. Now they weren't so hard where I couldn't answer, I just had to seriously think about it a little bit more. As we shook hands, he told me that I should hear something within the next three weeks. I was walking out and saw Sharon in the lobby. She wanted to exchange numbers, so we could see who got the job and to just keep in touch.

When I was in the car driving home, Percy called. "Yo, where you at, bro?"

"On Merriman driving. What's good?"

"Aye, meet me at Coney. I'm about to grab something to eat."

"Okay, I'm on my way." I already knew which Coney Island he was talking about, because we used to meet there and eat all the time back in the day.

"What's up, P?" I said as we greeted each other.

"Man, what yo black ass coming from a funeral?" he blurted out. "I'm just playing with you, bro," he stated quickly, so we wouldn't have a confrontation.

"You better be before I talk about how your fat ass invited me to an all-you-can-eat date. What's good, man?"

"I need some advice. Well, basically just your input on this. So you know me and Keesha is back living together. I just said fuck it, she got my son and been holding me down for years, so I might as well just stick it out. Now she already did her CNA classes, so I'm thinking of just getting her in the LPN classes, so she can be a nurse. If she goes straight through, within two years she could be certified making bank! Then I can go back to school and get all the certs I need."

"That's funny you want to be a nurse. But fuck it, do your thing and get that money," I replied encouraging him.

"How's your book coming?" he asked, since I'd told him due

to how much adversity I'd been having with this industry, I might as well write a book to tell people the journey.

"It's going. I was writing a lot, but kinda slowed down when I got fired from the other airline, you know."

"Yeah, I feel you. But have you been going to any other interviews?"

I give him a dumb look as he glanced at the suit I had on and started laughing. "Oh okay, never mind, man. My bad."

Percy was excited and hyped. He really didn't want any advice. He already had a solid plan, he just wanted to share his thoughts and his future plans with me.

On my drive home, I did think about my book and how I had so much faith throughout this process. I literally started writing a book about the process and didn't have an ending. At first, I started writing with anger at being denied so much. Thinking I highly doubted if anybody else had to go though being kicked out of training, having false information on their background, and just going to so many interviews. I just wanted the world to hear my story, I would imagine myself on Oprah.

"Lando, how did you do it? You have been denied time after time, interview after interview, and you even missed your grandmother's funeral... Tell the people what was your motivation."

"Well, Oprah, first I would like to thank you for giving me the opportunity to be on your show. This is a dream come true. When I first started writing this book, I didn't even have a job as a flight attendant. I was just writing off of faith, knowing that I was going to get the job."

After talking to Percy, I realized I hadn't written anything since I left training. Probably because I had started to lose faith.

"Dad, I can't lie to you. The Samer interview was nice."

"See I'm trying to tell you. Wait till you look up their stock prices. Samer already went bankrupt, so once you do that all you can do is go up from there."

As he said that I kinda laughed at our process and how he was so supportive and involved with my career path.

A few weeks went by, and honestly I checked the forums a few times, but kinda gave up on Samer. I didn't think too much about it until one day dad asked had I heard from them.

"Naw, they said it would take about three weeks."

"How long has it been?"

"Um, let me see, probably right around three weeks."

"Hello! You better call them and see what's going on. The squeaky wheel gets all the oil. Y'all kids nowadays are just lazy, man, and scared to get some money. I just talked to Keke and she still hasn't gotten her paperwork in to her attorney to get y'all some money. Well, I'm doing good over here. Y'all can live y'all stupid lives," he said walking towards his room. "Oh yeah, and we're about to get new carpet and new tiles in the kitchen soon. I'm just giving you a heads up."

I honestly can't even remember how I got the number to call Samer, but I decided to give them a call. Jewel Boron was over recruiting and when I received an email from there her name was always on it.

"Hello Mrs. Boron, I had an interview on the 4th with Adam Bell and I just wanted to check up on the status, since I never heard anything."

"Oh, okay give me one second, Orlando."

She paused for a second, as I assumed she went to look up my file.

"Lando, are you there?" she asked in her southern voice. I could just tell over the phone she was old and sexy.

"Yes, I'm still here."

"Okay, I was just about to call you. I'm sorry we took so long, but one of our recruiters will call you sometime today and give you a final phone interview."

"Okay, thanks Mrs. Boron. I appreciate it."

I was shocked and just a little excited all at the same time, but there was no point telling dad anything yet until I got the job. My phone rang and it was from an unfamiliar number so I answered, "Orlando speaking." It was my good friend Trevor. "Man, I'm over here thinking it's a fucking job calling me and it's your sad ass. Anyway, what's good, player?"

"Since you all big time now, you don't mess with us little people no more, huh?"

"Whatever, negro, you change your number every time you get a new woman, so I'm not tryna hear that."

"Ha-ha, you might be right, but me and a few of my niggas 'bout to hit up the court on Inkster Road. You trying to roll?"

"Hell yeah, come pick me up. I'll send you the address to our new spot."

"Cool, I'll be ready in thirty minutes."

Trevor was originally my best friend since we were in the first grade. He lived a few blocks away and we had always been close until high school. His people moved, so we stayed friends, but didn't talk as much. He was that one friend that it didn't matter how long I didn't hear from him, if he needed anything I had his back, and vice versa.

He came to pick me up. One of his boys I'd never met was with him. We headed down the street to the court. Not to sound cocky, but I had great sports acumen. It was just one of my gifts. I was good at pretty much any sport I tried.

"Aye, yo' little short ass is going to shoot the ball and start 21," Trev demanded as he passed me the basketball.

"Don't rush an ass whooping, boy," I responded as I shot the ball and it went in.

We all were just happy to be able to play basketball outside with some decent weather, just like old times, because that was all we did in the summers when we were younger. I'm not the most talented in basketball, but if there was a shit talking competition, then I would win every time. I was playing decent, but Trevor's tall ass was balling. He was always more of a street baller type of player. For some reason, I decided to take a quick break and go check my phone and soon as I grabbed it, I noticed a random number calling me. My heart stopped, because I had a feeling it was Samer.

"Hello Orlando speaking!"

"Hey, what's going on, Lando? This is Adam Bell from Samer."

"Oh hey, what's up, Adam? How you been, man?" I responded, sounding out of breath.

"Busy as ever. I'm so sorry we hadn't gotten back to you. But I wanted to call you and do a quick phone interview with you."

"Okay, that's cool."

"Are you available now?"

I looked around and saw cars driving, people playing basketball, yelling and all.

"Um, yeah, I'm open. I was just outside going for a quick run."

"So if we hired you, are you willing to relocate?"

"Yes, sir," I responded as I was tried to catch my breath.

"Okay great. And if you're on a plane and you have a passenger complaining about her connecting flight and you have a mother with a crying baby asking you to bring them some milk, who do you service first?"

"Who do I service first? Umm. First, can I ask you a question?"

"Yes, you can."

"Who is paying more for their seats?"

"Wow, awesome! That's the answer I actually wanted you to say. If you have a premier member versus somebody in coach, that baby better wait, because that frequent flyer is going to bring us more revenue. Okay, Lando, we want to hire you and this is our only road block. Now with you having a misdemeanor on your record, when you fly to Canada there could be some restrictions, since they have different rules over there. Now yours doesn't sound like anything too important."

I cut him off. "Yeah, I did some research on the issue and if I didn't commit certain crimes, then I should be okay," I replied quickly.

"Okay, well double check for me. And would you be able to attend training on July 26?"

"Yes, I can," I said happily as Trevor yelled for me to come over and play.

"I'm going to email you everything else you need to be ready. And we will send you your training packet. Your job is to study that before your training."

Once he said that I was ecstatic. In a very high pitched voice I said, "Adam, I really, really appreciate you, brother. You won't regret it. All I needed was a chance."

I hung up and went crazy "Yes! Thank you, Lord!"

I told Trevor the good news and couldn't wait to tell dad what had just happened, so I rushed home.

Once I got home dad wasn't even there, so I went on Facebook to update a status and to give God his praise.

"Thank the Man above for not letting me give up. Hard work always pays off."

"Lake, go grab those bags outside," dad said as he walked into the house.

I gave Aunt Chris a hug and asked how grandpa was doing. She told me to check on him, since it was her bowling day. I agreed.

"How was your basketball game, son?"

"Man, it was good at first, but turned out to be great once I got a *phone call!*"

"A phone call from whom?"

"You didn't hear me, man! A phone call from *Samer Airlines!*"

"What!" He was so excited.

"What they say?"

"Nothing too much, just asked me if I would be ready for training the 26th of July."

"Oh man, Lake, you can't be lying to me like that. What really happened?" he joked.

I laughed and said, "He called and gave me a phone interview and offered me the job, but said I might have problems going to Canada, just double check that I can go over and I'm good."

"Wow, God is good. We have to go to church on Sunday. Ever since momma passed, our family has been getting a lot of blessings."

"Okay, I'm down."

"See now we have to hurry up and get this house together, because they're going to call you way before that date."

"How you figure?"

"I just know, so clean up that nasty downstairs and get ready for training, because it's go time."

"Okay, I hear you." There was doubt in my voice.

"Man, you think I'm playing. I can't be messing around with you and be stuck here by myself to do this work when they call."

"How are they are going to change it, if they just gave me a date?"

"Okay, you will see," he said as he shook his head as he walked away.

So the next few weeks dad was serious as hell. I mean that dude was on a mission to clean up the whole house and get everything ready to go. We were almost was fully moved into the new house, but still had to clean up the old one and grab some last minute things so we were back and forth until the last day.

I hated moving. And I hated having to convince friends to help me out or spending money to hire people. Got couches that never fit properly in the door. It was just usually too much extra work that I never really wanted to do. Before leaving, I decided to say my goodbye to Miss James.

"Hey Miss James, this is Lando," I stated as I walked up to her screen door, knowing she was watching her General Hospital or whatever TV show she watched religiously at 4 p.m. each day.

"Hey babe, how are you doing? Y'all about to leave me, huh?"

"Yeah, we're moving out of the hood."

"Isn't that right. You have to write down your number, so I can stay in touch with you and make sure everything is going well with your father. You better take care of that handsome man now."

I agreed, laughing.

"Lando, you know if you need a place to stay, come back next door, okay? Because you and your father don't cause any trouble, you hear me?"

"Yes, ma'am."

We had officially moved into the new place and I decided to have my room in the basement, so I could have my privacy. Entering the condo there was a little room to the left, that would make a nice computer room. The three-piece guest bathroom was next to it. And across from the bathroom were stairs leading straight towards the basement. The basement area was huge, way more than enough space, but it wasn't finished. In the future it would need a lot of work. The living room was spacious, big kitchen and my favorite thing was our deck in the backyard. We lived literally off the 13th hole. We could even see the tee off spot where golfers started at. I could see myself sitting back watching the golfers come and go, as we all enjoyed the weather.

I had fully painted the whole garage blue and it really came out nice. The last thing I had to do was put down this paint stuff for the floor. The directions said first fully sweep and mop multiple times also using some sort of solution that was included. It took a while to get it fully done, because I had to sweep, then mop, and once that was done, painting the whole floor gray. Finally, I could spread the sprinkles on the floor. I decided to put myself and dad's name on the floor, since we were starting new beginnings and this was our new place to call home. Everything was starting to look a lot better around the house slowly, but surely.

During the first month the place looked like a construction site. Every day we had somebody over working on the countertops, next day ripping up the floor. We didn't have real furniture for about a month, because dad wanted to wait to get a certain wood floor put in. When I tell you dad put money into that place, he wasn't playing no games. Marble kitchen counters, all new wood cabinets with new knobs on them, so he could easily open them. New sinks in the bathrooms and all. The new place was starting to grow on me. One day I was on the patio watching the golfers and I heard dad yell, "Lake!"

I thought something was wrong, so I ran into the house. "Hey man, what's up? You okay?"

"Man, I have been calling you. Listen to this." He handed me his phone and I played the voice message.

"Hey Lando, this is Jewel Boron from Samer Airlines and we actually have an opening of an earlier training spot, but I need you to call me as soon as possible."

"What?!" I was shocked. "Oh man! Why did they call you?" I asked him kinda confused.

"I don't know. I saw them calling, but I didn't know the number, so I didn't answer. But when I heard this message I had to let you know. I told you Samer isn't going to be playing around. I knew they were going to call you early, that's why we moved here as quickly as I could. Man, you better hurry up and see what's up before somebody gets your spot."

I heard him loud and clear, then wasted no time calling her back.

"Oh hey, Lando, this is the situation. We have a training starting on Monday. I know this is last minute. Have you studied the packet we sent you?"

"Oh yeah, I did already," I responded quickly.

"Would you be interested in starting training on June 2nd?"

"Oh, you want me to go to the training that's in three days?"

"Yeah, only if you can, because we only have two spots, since somebody canceled."

"Um, yeah, I'll do it. I'm down."

"Okay perfect. I'm about to send you the information."

Everything she said from there was just a blur, I just wanted to get on my knees and thank God.

Dad looked at me and said, "Wow, man, I didn't even know you studied already."

I look at him and smiled. "I didn't."

FINAL THOUGHTS FROM THE AUTHOR...

I encourage everyone to travel the United States and at least a few countries. It's important to get outside of the comfort zone. People spend their whole lives in the hood where they grew up. Traveling the world expands one's thinking that there is more to life than what is seen on a regular basis. It's truly liberating.

www.ingramcontent.com/pod-product-compliance
Lightning Source LLC
Chambersburg PA
CBHW052012070526
44584CB00016B/1719